HOW TO WRITE ABOUT THEATRE

HOW TO WRITE ABOUT THEATRE

MARK FISHER

Foreword by Chris Jones

methuen | drama

LONDON • NEW YORK • OXFORD • NEW DELHI • SYDNEY

METHUEN DRAMA
Bloomsbury Publishing Plc
50 Bedford Square, London, WC1B 3DP, UK
1385 Broadway, New York, NY 10018, USA

BLOOMSBURY, METHUEN DRAMA and the Methuen Drama
logo are trademarks of Bloomsbury Publishing Plc

First published in Great Britain 2015
Reprinted by Bloomsbury Methuen Drama 2015, 2016 (twice), 2019

A catalogue record for this book is available from the British Library.

A catalog record for this book is available from the Library of Congress.

ISBN: HB: 978-1-4742-4629-3
PB: 978-1-4725-2054-8
ePDF: 978-1-4725-2056-2
eBook: 978-1-4725-2055-5

Typeset by RefineCatch Limited, Bungay, Suffolk
Printed and bound in Great Britain

To find out more about our authors and books visit
www.bloomsbury.com and sign up for our newsletters.

To **Robin Hodge**, for giving me the chance to learn on the job

CONTENTS

ACKNOWLEDGEMENTS

Thanks to Sarah-Jane Fisher and Caroline Johnston for their language skills; to Neil Cooper, Robert Cushman, Karen Fricker, Joyce McMillan, Amy Taylor, Lisa Warrington and Tonnvane Wiswell for their critical wisdom; to Simon Beaufoy, Rob Drummond, Rupert Goold, Zinnie Harris and Kelly McAndrew for insights into their work; to Anna Brewer for her patience as an editor; to my anonymous reviewer, who offered some extremely insightful comments; and to Jane, Lotte and Archie for putting up with me.

Mark Fisher

FOREWORD

You've picked up a book, an excellent, thoughtful, insight-laden book by Mark Fisher, on how to write about the theatre. Most introductions laud what you are about to read. Behold the opposite approach.

They asked a professional theatre critic, didn't they? Mr Fisher is supposed to be discussing criticism, isn't he? So how about an introduction that criticizes the book?

Alas, there is little or nothing in the pages that follow that can help you with the very thing that I find hardest of all about writing about the theatre, even though I do it pretty much every day of my life and have done for years. Today, in fact, is a very typical weekend autumnal day for me: two shows to see, two reviews to write. And, sigh, a due (or is that overdue?) introduction to a book designed to serve young critics. Only there is one way it cannot serve them – heck, a way in which it might well get in their way. Your way, dear reader.

How to Write About Theatre can do an awful lot for you. This is what it cannot do for you.

To write about theatre, you actually have to write.

Sure, critics criticize. That's what the general public thinks we do the most – we're assumed to sit there in the dark, ready to destroy careers on a whim, or make summary judgements, or just *label* things, ad nauseam. Thumbs up, thumbs down. Good play. Lousy performance. Two-and-a-half stars. I was moved. I was bored stiff. The earth moved. No it didn't. Whatever. A few years of merely that on a daily basis, and an existential crisis results. Trust me.

Actors avoid us in the foyer. We're used as cold-hearted antagonists in movies like *Birdman* or *Chef* or *Ratatouille*. These films can't end without our judgements, for there is no other way to document struggles overcome. Our quotes are taken out of context and emblazoned on marquees (why did the spell check just make that *embalmed*?) in Times Square or Leicester Square. (Most of us love that, even though we have to pretend total indifference.) We're employed to gussy up collections of amateur performances: who'd have watched *Britain's Got Talent* without the thrill of public critical judgement? Nobody, that's who. Our vocabulary is copied, but not our journalistic ethics, millions of times a day, on Yelp and TripAdvisor. Our motives are impugned. Not just our prejudices but our personalities, or the lack thereof, are dissected by those we've never met.

But really, all of that is noise. You want to be a critic? You must write. Every day, ideally. Now, ideally.

That means you have to commit fingers to keys, summon up inspiration from the dark recesses of your soul, take a stand on something, put yourself out there, risk it all, create. You have to stop reading, thinking, messing around, avoiding the task at hand. In a short while you'll have to put down this very fine book. You won't be able to cling to its advice; it won't write your review for you, and I'll bet your deadline is fast approaching. So why are you wasting time reading this introduction anyway?

Most writers are procrastinators (did I mention I was supposed to write this last week?). And most writers are insecure. This includes critics – well, any critic worth reading.

Look back at the start of this introduction. It is, in some small way, a conceptual approach to the writing task at hand. You might even call it risky, although it is never wise to start thinking that anything in the bourgeois world of writing about the arts has a life-or-death importance, even though some of those you are writing about may claim so. Do not be taken in. In the theatre, there is always another night. Artists change. Forgiveness is possible. Most of them get better with age.

Still, everything that has followed that first paragraph has flowed from my initial risk. And so here I am, in paragraph 10 (Damn! Now I can't go back and revise, and, damn it again, what if the editor changes the number of paragraphs? Too late) committed to an idea. Yet I don't know if Mr Fisher will like it, nor his editor. I can't worry about that, really, otherwise I will disappear down the rabbit hole of the expectations of others. I just have to write the truth as I see it, as I feel it in this moment, for arts criticism is a time-bound activity and what feels profound on a Sunday morning can feel like stale bread by Thursday.

Write about the truth of the moment. That's all a critic can do, really. Whatever she is writing, and for whomever.

This book – and it really is a fine book – will give you lots of different ways to organize your thoughts, think about the job at hand. It offers things to try and always include, traps to avoid, help with understanding the history of those who have tried to make a living doing what you are doing.

I'll just add a couple of thoughts. To write about the theatre is to write about life. To write about life is to write about death – especially the way we all exit our tawdry existence at a time and place not of our own choosing. Think about the plays you love the most; dollars to doughnuts they are about this very thing. As a critic, you are constantly searching for truth, and to do so is to look for better ways to understand the end that befalls us all.

'What?', you protest. 'This fool is saying my review of *Cats* has to be about death? My review of the sequel to the sequel of some heavy-metal jukebox musical that was lousy to begin with has to make some profound assertion about existential truth?'

Yes, that *is* what this fool is saying. And some humour would help. It's a tough life. And you are writing about showbiz.

I've worked hard today on avoiding writing this introduction. That included taking time to read my email – always my favourite way to not write.

I happened to write a column in my newspaper today defending critics from the constant charge that what we do costs us nothing, even though the artist puts their very soul on the line. I argued that it costs us critics plenty to write a negative review, because we actually *do* know how much the artist has risked, how much they care, what our verdict might mean in terms of money or future opportunity, how much the artist has sacrificed.

For very, very few people do theatre for the money. They always deserve respect (so keep that in mind).

I also argued that it costs us even more to write a positive review, for then we hang out there with the artist, maybe even farther out than the artist, given that artists are expected to believe in themselves. When we love something, we take the biggest risks of all, hoping our readers will go and then still trust us the next time, praying that we will be on the right side of the historical verdict that is still years away from being rendered. If a critic tells a reader they love something, and then the reader does not, the reader feels superior to the critic. This is dangerous. But it must be done. A critic must risk something on the back of her passions. Why bother, otherwise?

Alas, critical risk is rarely appreciated. My email was filled with reactions to this column. One was scathing: 'Your profession is a good case in point of everything that is wrong, false, misleading, contradictory and disastrous in this society', a correspondent wrote. 'The people who actually make the effort, actually try to do something, actually take the risks are subjected to examination and judgement by those who can do nothing, do do nothing, have no intention of doing anything practical and who, in the height of injustice, get to keep their jobs no matter what stupidities they say or write.'

Ouch. Zing. You still want to write about the theatre after reading that?

Of course you do. You must. There is no theatre without those who write about it. And to write about theatre is just an excuse to write about life, and there is no better way to spend your life.

Deadlines are a blessing. Without one, I'd never have written this. I would have created nothing.

So read this book and then go write, well. Care. Risk it all. And do it today. Your email can wait.

Chris Jones, chief theatre critic, *Chicago Tribune*
December 2014

1
INTRODUCTION

The job of the theatre critic

Writing about theatre is an act of translation. It turns the language of performance into the language of words. More precisely, it turns the languages, *plural*, of performance into the language of words. Every show speaks in many tongues and, whether you are writing a tweet, a Facebook update, an over-night review, a critical essay, a blog, a radio broadcast or a YouTube review, you will find yourself moving from the rich Babel-like conversation of live performance to plain, two-dimensional prose. Things will get lost in translation.

You start with a performance. It begins at a fixed time and has a predetermined length, yet, moment to moment, it is fluid and organic, already resistant to ordinary words. It may have a literary component and perhaps that will give the writer some security, yet it is also sculptural, visual and dynamic. Its meaning may be communicated through words, gesture, music, lighting, costumes, choreography, design or, more likely, some juxtaposition of all these elements. For the literary drama critic, who studies only the words of a published script, this need not be a concern. But for the journalistic theatre critic, who considers drama in performance, it is fundamental. Richard Steele, one of the first journalistic theatre critics, understood this. He was also a playwright and in the 1733 preface to his play *The Conscious Lovers*, he praised the role of the actor in giving three-dimensional life to a script:

It must be remember'd, a Play is to be seen, and is made to be Represented with the Advantage of Action, nor can appear but with half the Spirit, without it; for the greatest Effect of a Play in reading is to excite the Reader to go see it; and when he does so, it is then a Play has the Effect of Example and Precept.[1]

The effect Steele refers to is complex. Samuel Taylor Coleridge said for an audience to accept a play required a 'temporary half-faith'[2] similar to the act of dreaming. Just as we neither believe nor disbelieve a dream, so we experience theatre in a state midway between credulity and reason. Thinking along similar lines, David Mamet said we 'respond to drama to that extent to which it corresponds to our dream life'.[3] Like a dream, theatre plays on your conscious mind as well as your subconscious mind, it toys with your intellect and your emotions, it makes you think and it makes you feel. What you end up with, at the other end of the critic's process, is a set of words that attempt to encapsulate this experience, to translate the subconscious into the conscious and to pin down this elusive dream with its many languages, impressions and multiple meanings. Those words will be approximate, a rough draft, an impression, always an imperfect translation. Have you ever given a satisfactory account of what one of your dreams was like? The impossible quest for perfection is what makes writing about theatre so rewarding; it is nearly attainable and forever just beyond your grasp.

Writing abut theatre comes in many forms, from learned treatise to Facebook post. In this book, we'll focus primarily on the craft of the review, both as it has traditionally been practised in newspapers and as it now predominantly appears online. For ease of expression, I will talk about writers and readers, but the book pertains equally to podcasters and listeners, vloggers and viewers. Neither is this to discount other ways of writing about theatre, be it a school essay or a celebrity interview; it is just that reviewing requires such a dynamic response to live performance that its lessons are applicable almost universally. If you can describe a gorgeous set design or a heart-stopping performance or a provocative idea in an over-night review, you can describe it anywhere.

My own experience as a theatre critic began at some point in the late 1980s when I was working at *The List* magazine, an arts and events guide for central Scotland. By that time, I had graduated with a degree in drama from the University of Kent at Canterbury, where I remember being the only one in my class who, when given the option, wrote a series of reviews rather than a conventional essay. It was an early example of my twin interest in writing and theatre, although it wasn't immediately apparent that that would become my chosen career. Officially, I was employed at *The List* as a production assistant, but Sarah Hemming, the theatre editor, kept seeing me at the theatre and encouraged me to write. By the time she left, I was in pole position to take over her job. Still only in my mid-twenties, I was given a tremendous opportunity to review everything from student shows to major international productions, as well as to interview all manner of actors, directors and playwrights. I went on to launch and edit a quarterly magazine called *Theatre Scotland*, which lasted four years before the money ran out, and worked as a freelance theatre critic and feature writer for *The Herald* in Glasgow and subsequently *The Guardian*. As a lot of this book talks about the critic's bias, prejudice and cultural assumptions, I should give an indication of my own perspective: I write as someone who is white, male, heterosexual, middle class, middle-aged, able-bodied, left-leaning, liberal-minded, English and living in Scotland. The bulk of my theatre writing has been for traditional magazines and newspapers, and I have a longstanding presence on the internet through my website www.theatrescotland. com, plus sundry blogs and social media activity. You'll find more about this book at www.howtowriteabouttheatre.com and on Twitter @writeabouttheat

The twenty-first century critic

So what precisely is the job we are talking about? The cliché of the day says everyone is a critic – and if that were the case, it would suggest there's not much to it. As with most clichés, the idea has a kernel of truth. A UK survey by Ticketmaster in 2013[4] reported that one in five theatregoers had written 'reviews' of shows they had seen. Many of these people had done so regularly and most were using social media. Should that lead us to believe that 20 per cent of audience members are critics? That seems unlikely, especially as the survey did not give a definition of what constituted a review, but even so there is no doubt the internet has been a liberating democratic force, providing a voice to anyone who wants to be heard. Add to this the decline of newspaper sales and the consequent laying-off of journalists (arts writers often being the first to go) and, early in the twenty-first century, it feels as though a shift in cultural power has taken place. Out has gone the top-down school of criticism, with definitive judgements made by the few; in has come a more egalitarian system. Now the opinions of a self-selecting group of 'dead white men',[5] to use the phrase of Nicholas Hytner in 2007 when he was artistic director of National Theatre of Great Britain, counts for no more than any other group.

Does this make everyone a critic? I'm not so sure. For as long as theatre has existed, every member of the audience has had an opinion about it. Often the opinion is simply expressed ('I loved it' . . . 'It was OK' . . . 'I was bored'), but it is an opinion nonetheless. When it comes to opinions, critics have never held the monopoly. Much of the noise you hear in the bar after the show is the sound of people telling each other what they thought. And much of the social-media traffic generated by a show amounts to the same thing. This is all good, but most of the time, a 140-character tweet has more in common with casual post-show chatter than with criticism (which isn't to say post-show chatter cannot be insightful).

Here are some comments seen on Twitter about the 2014 West End production of *Let the Right One In*:

Great time @RightOneIn #ApolloTheatre Highly recommend. Fantastic staging & cast. Never seen a play like it.

If you haven't seen @RightOneIn yet, go see it. It's the most beautiful play. Choreography is stunning, especially the shadow knife scene.

#LTROI was amazing! Loved every minute off it, set was beautiful and acting was unreal! Must see! :p

The people who wrote these messages would be very surprised to be told they were performing the same task as the lead critic of *The New York Times*. They'd be more surprised still to find themselves held up as examples in a book about theatre criticism. They were just saying what they thought. Perhaps they were no different to the unfortunate fifteen factory workers who were made to sign up as people's theatre critics in the former East Germany. In an attempt to do away with the ideologically unsound bourgeois journalists of old, the communist authorities gave writer Erich Loest the task of training a group of workers in the skills of the job. According to Anne Applebaum's *Iron Curtain: The Crushing of Eastern Europe 1944–56*, the scheme fell flat. Loest told her:

> We went to the theatre together and afterwards or the next day we met. And I told them, tried to tell them, what a theatre review is about. And then we wrote a review together. I was twenty-five by then and I had liked going to the theatre . . . It was horrible. We were all unhappy. I was unhappy, they were even more unhappy . . . They were supposed to write a theatre review, they could not do that and they did not learn it with me. After half a year the whole thing collapsed.[6]

Technology has allowed everyone's opinions to be widely disseminated – and that's culturally exciting – but there's more to being a critic than having your opinions heard. Opinions are commonplace; it is analysis that makes a critic. What counts is the reasoning behind your opinions and not everyone is interested in providing that. All the same, in today's world, the distinction is not clear cut. You'll find many professional theatre reviews that convey little more than the tweets above – and you'll also find tweets that push the possibilities of the medium to the maximum. Using the Twitter name @Snap140, Snap Reviews promised 'theatre reviews in 140 characters or less'. Here are three examples from December 2013:

> ** not great. The numbers are not good and feel tacked on. Bells and whistles but no drama or structure.

> **** first half drags. 2nd more than makes up for it. Blinding. @ RebJBenson gives stunning perf. Go.

> ** sad that a piece celebrating the imagination has so little itself. Blame the direction. Cast do their best.

Given the narrow parameters, these instant judgements covered a surprising amount of ground. They pointed out strengths as well as weaknesses ('Bells and whistles but no drama or structure') and apportioned credit and blame ('Blame the direction. Cast do their best.') In just eleven words ('sad that a piece celebrating the imagination has so little itself'), the writer managed to pack in both an analysis of what the show was trying to do and a verdict on how well it did it. Reinforced by the star ratings, these tweets gave an unambiguous consumer guide.

EXERCISE

Review a show in the form of a 140-character tweet. Aim to convey as much critical information, including description, analysis and evaluation, as you can. How well did you do?

Reviewer or critic?

In a very short period of time, the critical landscape has changed. One way to make sense of what's going on is to distinguish between a reviewer and a critic. As the traditional definition has it, a reviewer is the voice of the theatregoer, someone who writes with immediacy, often over night, painting a picture of what has taken place and offering thumbs-up/thumbs-down consumer advice. Nearly everyone who supplies social-media updates would fit into this category. A critic, by

n o t e s

- Review
  ↳ Paint a
    Pic of
    What takes
    Place

er, someone who presents reflections that roader context, less concerned with its than what it means in the greater scheme , philosophy, aesthetics, politics, sociology inates the work. You may find this type of , but almost certainly not in a 140-character same person).

good starting point for discussing what and there is a strong case for adhering to confusion. This is primarily because few ake the distinction themselves. Professional n Theatre Critics Association, the Canadian

Theatre Critics Association, the Critics' Awards for Theatre in Scotland, the Critics' Circle (in the UK), the International Association of Theatre Critics and the New York Drama Critics' Circle almost always use the word 'critic'. This is the case even though, by the laws of probability, some of their members must sometimes turn out writing that better fits the description of a review. In a study of the profession, Lehman Engel wrote that he would *'not* be writing about *critics*' because 'what we read daily are pieces by journalist-reviewers', yet he said this in a book he called *The Critics*.[7] What's more, in practice, the distinction is fuzzy. A reviewer working to a tight deadline with a limited amount of space is still capable of an insight we may call criticism. A critic, taking time and space to be discursive, may also make review-like observations as they go. Definitions that are precise in theory are blurred in real life. For these reasons, in this book, I have stuck with the word 'critic'. Better to sidestep the idea that you're either a critic or a reviewer (because, of course, you can be both) and explore the multitude of tasks writers take on between the extremes of snap judgement and analytical essay. As far as this book is concerned, anyone who steps beyond the purely experiential ('I liked it') to the quizzical ('Why did I like it?') is a critic.

In the chapters ahead, we will look at the different forms critical writing takes, consider the various reasons people read it and analyse the many competing pressures on the critic. These range from the need to write entertainingly to the willingness to expose personal feelings; from the ability to put forward a convincing argument to the awareness of bias; from the skill of giving permanence to an ephemeral art to the capacity to set that art in its cultural context. We will also look in detail at the many skills that come together in the theatre, be that the art of the actor, playwright, director, composer, choreographer or technical crew. By the end, we'll have not so much a rule book as a palate of possibilities.

On the way, we'll try out some exercises to test out some of the ideas: theatre criticism is a practical art and the best way to learn about it is to do it. First, though, we'll take a look at the story so far with a quick trot through the history of criticism, particularly as it applies to the newspapers and periodicals of the last four centuries. Times and attitudes have changed, but understanding the development of criticism, culminating with the three critical questions formulated by Alessandro Manzoni at the start of the nineteenth century, is the best way of making sense of writing about theatre in the age of the internet.

EXERCISE

Write about the same show twice for different publications. In the first, you are a reviewer, producing a 200-word write-up for a local events guide that gives advice on what to see. In the second, you are a critic, writing anything up to 1,000 words for an international theatre magazine read by foreigners interested in the place of theatre in society.

Notes

1   Steele, Richard (1761), *The Dramatic Works of Sir Richard Steele, Knt*, J. and R. Tonson, S. Crowder, T. Caslon, T. Lownds, H. Woodgate and S. Brookes.

2   Coleridge, Samuel Taylor (1907), *Coleridge's Lectures on Shakespeare and Other Poets and Dramatists*, J. M. Dent & Sons.

3   Mamet, David (1994), 'A National Dream Life', in *A Whore's Profession*, Faber and Faber.

4   Ticketmaster (2013), *State of Play: Theatre UK*, http://blog.ticketmaster \ (co.uk/news/theatre-uk-evolving-engaging-2013–2209).

5   Hoyle, Ben (14 May 2007), 'Dead white men in the critic's chair scorning work of women directors', in *The Times*.

6   Applebaum, Anne (2013), *Iron Curtain: The Crushing of Eastern Europe 1944–56*, Penguin Books.

7   Engel, Lehman (1976), *The Critics*, Macmillan.

2
HOW TO LEARN FROM CRITICS OF THE PAST

The story so far

Criticism is everywhere you look. It's in the hyped-up opinions of *X Factor* judges; it's in the instant reactions of first-night tweets; it's in the lengthy essays of the *London Review of Books*; and in the short sharp commentaries of the daily newspapers. With criticism being fired at us from all directions, it's easy to forget it wasn't always like this. The approach we take today is not inevitable but the product of a long history of evolving critical thought. It has been shaped by great thinkers and influenced by ever-changing social values. Many of the ideas go back more than two millennia to the time of the ancient Greeks. Other ideas, especially where it comes to journalistic reviewing, are much more recent – just two or three centuries old. Getting to grips with how this history played out gives us a better understanding of the functions of criticism and a shrewder sense of what it is today's critics are actually doing, whether they are the TV pundit or the free-ranging blogger.

In the modern era, the story begins in the Renaissance when a set of beliefs developed in Europe about the characteristics of good theatre. The intellectual crucible was Italy, where cultural commentators had long taken inspiration from Horace's *Ars Poetica* (*The Art of Poetry*), published around 18BC. Things shifted up a gear with the rediscovery of Aristotle, whose *Poetics* was published in Italy in a series of translations between 1498 and 1548. Horace had formulated his ideas in response to Roman drama, while Aristotle had been conditioned by the Greek drama of his day, especially the tragedies of Sophocles. They were offering a description of what they found rather than an immutable rule book. The Renaissance critics, by contrast, showed no interest in theories based on the theatre of their own time and preferred instead to take lessons from the classical era.

From this emerged a set of rules to which they believed playwrights should adhere even though they took little account of contemporary theatre practice. Foremost among these were the unities of time, place and action, meaning a play should happen in real time or within 'one revolution of the sun' and in one location and should be about one main story. The rules didn't stop there. An almost religious set of beliefs known as the 'neo-classical ideals' grew up. It was felt that comedy should concern itself with the lower orders and tragedy with the high-born, and that the two should never mix in the same play. The narrative structure should not deviate from the norm: comedy should go from chaos to happiness; tragedy from happiness to sadness. Characters should speak as they were expected to speak – kings as kings, servants as servants – and wrongdoers should be duly punished. The action had to take place in real life, good was expected to triumph over evil and the play had to teach a moral lesson.

These rules may strike us as pedantic, but the neo-classical revival was also an expression of a broader sociological shift. As the cultural critic Terry Eagleton put it, the rules were based on reason and argument and, in this way, turned 'their back on the insolence of aristocratic authority'.[1] They were part of a movement towards rational thought that would characterize the Age of Enlightenment in the seventeenth and eighteenth centuries. A social tier was emerging in Europe, a liberal middle class that depended on its own resourcefulness and not the inherited privilege of a hierarchical elite. Within a century of the birth of the newspaper in the early 1600s, this new bourgeoisie was able to claim a place for itself in civic society in a 'public sphere' made up of clubs, coffee houses and print publications where 'polite, informed public opinion' could hold its own against the 'arbitrary diktats of authority'. Even though the rules themselves were absolute, they emerged from a redistribution of power and were actually part of a peaceful revolution.

EXERCISE

Ask a friend to devise a set of spurious rules that theatre should adhere to. They can be as surreal and as unreasonable as they like. Your task is to write a 250-word review of a show on the basis of how much it adheres to these rules. How much can you express your own opinion before the rules get in the way?

Where once the gentry and aristocracy had been the sole arbiters of taste and behaviour, now a wider circle of people could get in on the act. Through its debates in the developing public sphere, this new social class could define itself. Criticism, whether of literature, art, theatre or politics, was a way of establishing parameters of decency and taste. Its purpose was about much more than the thing being criticized. It was to do with society at large. It is why morality played such a prominent role in this early criticism: it was about a society mapping out an ethical terrain for itself. The new values needed new moral justifications.

This was especially the case in an era when the church was so quick to condemn the theatre. 'The cause of plagues is sinne, if you look to it well; and the cause of sinne are playes: therefore, the cause of plagues are playes',[2] the Reverend T. Wilcocke told the congregation in the grounds of Old St Paul's Cathedral in 1577. In the face of this kind of attack, theatre's supporters were cornered into emphasizing the moral values that plays could instil – and to criticize those plays they deemed less wholesome. If they could demonstrate a play's high-minded purpose, they had a chance of silencing those puritans who believed theatre to be inherently wicked.

Meanwhile, the job of the critic was to judge plays on the basis of the preordained criteria. Before a play could be enjoyed, it had to be weighed up against its classical precedents. There was some room for manoeuvre; rather like the follower of a religion, a critic could value some tenets more highly than others. What was not called into question was the basic idea of a right and a wrong way to write plays. You would decide on your critical principles then put them into practice. Art, of course, doesn't react kindly to rules and, even as the neo-classical theories were being developed, the playwrights were following their own instincts. Critical thinking had some influence on the stage, but theatremakers listened primarily to their audiences, who had no care for rules, only for entertainment.

By the eighteenth century, critics who had based their viewpoint on classical values were faced with the inconvenient truth of both Elizabethan drama and restoration comedy, which had prospered despite disregarding the rules. If the critics could just about make a case against the minor playwrights, they faced a particular dilemma with Shakespeare whose genius was hard to deny and impossible to square with their system. Only two of his plays – *The Tempest* and *The Comedy of Errors* – adhere to the three unities and even then you can imagine the purists bristling at the mixture of high sentiment and low comedy. The best they could say was that Shakespeare's deviations were the product of a less civilized era, which allowed them to admire his achievements in spite of his aberrations.

The advent of the journalist critic

Most of the story so far took place before the arrival of journalistic theatre criticism as we know it today. In his rigorously researched *Theatrical Criticism in London to 1795*,[3] Charles Harold Gray made a case for the earliest tentative examples having appeared in *The Gentleman's Journal* in the early 1690s, seventy years after the first British newspaper. He argued it wasn't until the 1730s that it was common for performances to be discussed in print and only in the 1770s that periodicals began reviewing theatre with any regularity and consistency. In the early part of the eighteenth century, there had been notable (if isolated) contributions by Richard Steele and Joseph Addison, but England's first proper journal devoted to the theatre arrived in the form of *The Prompter*[4] which was not launched until November 1734. Written by Aaron Hill and William Popple – arguably the first professional theatre critics – it came out twice a week and ran articles about theatre managements, government legislation, the standard of acting, the behaviour of audiences, theatrical characters and what constituted a proper subject for the stage.

A lot of early criticism was partisan and unduly influenced by theatre managers, but the idea of an independent voice describing and commenting on a performance was taking shape. Although those voices may have been independent, they were not free of the values of their time. Prescriptive neo-classical rules held sway, as is clear from this preamble to a review of Edward Moore's *The Gamester* by a critic using the name of Oxymel Busby in *The Scourge* in 1753:

> The first thing to be considered in a dramatic piece is the moral. This our author hath well adhered to, every action conducing to inculcate an abhorrence of gaming, therefore no defect can be found here.
>
> The next consideration is the manner how the poet's design is to be executed, and those, who judge best, say the unities of action, time, and place are essential. That the characters are to be contrasted, distinguished and uniform. That the diction should be decent, apt, and strong. That nothing puerile or foreign to the purpose should be introduced, and that action and narration should be intermixed with judgement, since it would be highly absurd either to see all or hear all.
>
> Now let us consider this Tragedy by the help of these rules and see how it squares with them.[5]

By the 1770s, the producers of a new London play could expect a write-up of some kind in at least half-a-dozen daily or twice-weekly publications as well as in other monthly periodicals. The theatre profession itself was only too aware of this development. Catching the mood of the times in 1779, Richard Brinsley Sheridan wrote *The Critic*, a satire of the whole theatre industry that remains popular to this day. In his prologue, the playwright complained that the vogue for morality and decorum had produced a lot of dull theatre in which 'insipidity succeeds bombast'[6] and went on to have much fun sending up those who tied themselves in knots trying to reconcile their instinctive love of entertainment with the belief that art should be instructive. The cracks in the neo-classical system were beginning to show.

Sheridan's central critic Mr Dangle says he is an avid reader of the 'theatrical intelligence' in *The Morning Chronicle*. First published in 1769, this paper would go on to give William Hazlitt his first break as a parliamentary reporter in 1812 and then as a critic – indeed, the foremost critic of his age.

Similar developments were happening elsewhere in the world. In the US, *The Pennsylvania Gazette* carried reviews of plays from as early as 1757. Taking their lead from Europe, the early American critics were under the hold of those same neo-classical ideas – and like their European counterparts, they were pulled in two directions by theory and practice. Reviewing *The Contrast* by Royall Tyler in 1790, the critic of *The Universal Asylum and Columbian Magazine* had to recognize the play's failure to live up to the Aristotelian model: 'We cannot by any means pronounce this a perfect comedy. Little or no adherence has been paid to rules.'[7] Awkwardly, however, this was the first professionally produced comedy written by an American citizen, so the critic could not overlook its landmark status: 'But as it is the first American attempt at this species of composition, and as it may induce others to follow and improve upon it, we think it worthy of the public attention, and cheerfully add our tribute of applause.'

The arrival of the railways in the mid-nineteenth century opened up new audiences for touring theatre companies in North America as well as a new national readership for theatre criticism in sundry periodicals. A commercial market for theatre criticism was now in place.

In Dublin, Paul Hiffernan was writing criticism of the Theatre Royal as early as 1748 in his journal *The Tickler*. The first publication of its kind in Scotland was the *Edinburgh Theatrical Censor*, which came and went in twelve issues during 1803, its aim being to act as a 'valuable repository of living opinions' that 'would serve as a vehicle for the communication and diffusion of those refinements, which tend eminently to the well-being of a civilized community'.[8] This sense of a society defining itself by its taste and morality would persist for some time.

In Canada, where theatrical performances had been puffed in newspapers since the 1770s, it took a little longer for independently minded criticism to take a hold. William Lyon Mackenzie in the *York Colonial Advocate* and Joseph Howe in the *Novascotian* led the field in the 1820s, followed with greater consistency from the 1850s as city populations increased in size. Down in Chicago, the *Tribune* published its first theatre review in 1853 ('the selection of pieces, both for interest and moral, has been very judicious'[9]), kicking off a 150-year history anthologized by critic Chris Jones in *Bigger, Brighter, Louder. The Australian* carried theatre reviews from at least as early as 1834 when the Sydney Theatre showed 'due sense' by staging *Othello*[10] and the critic explained that 'candid and just criticism is an encouragement to exertion, and by no means detracts from the real merits of the actors'. The *New Zealand Gazette and Wellington Spectator* carried news of the opening of a theatre in 1843, its report morphing into a review of *The Rover of the Seas*, a melodrama by Edward Geoghegan 'which, with a little more practice, and some curtailing, will be likely to prove a favourite representation'.[11] Similar stories were played out elsewhere in the world in response to the development of the theatre industry itself.

Back in London, by the time Leigh Hunt started reviewing for *The News* in 1805 and Hazlitt for *The Morning Chronicle* in 1813, theatre criticism was an established profession. These writers are sometimes identified as the originators of journalistic criticism, but it is fairer to say they built on a young but thriving tradition, introducing new levels of precision and erudition. Hunt's innovation was to show his reasoning as well as his judgement, opening up the possibility that the reader may come to a different opinion. Hazlitt praised him for giving the 'true *pine-apple* flavour to theatrical criticism, making it a pleasant mixture of sharp and sweet'.[12] In his turn, Hazlitt was noted for the degree of precision he brought to his writing and it is thanks to him that we have such a vivid idea of the acting technique of Edmund Kean with his 'convulsed motions of the hands, and the involuntary swellings of the veins of the forehead'.[13] With writing as vivid as this and with readers ready to be enlightened, the age of the journalistic critic had arrived.

Manzoni's three questions

There had always been those who took issue with at least some of the neo-classical rules, and with the Romantic movement came the backlash. Influenced by the thinking of Jean-Jacques Rousseau, who favoured the rights of the individual over the authority of the government, a new generation of poets, novelists, critics and playwrights started to react against the neo-classical certainties and to celebrate the beauty of nature and the creativity of the individual. For critics, it meant a new framework. Instead of beginning with a set of more-or-less fixed rules and applying them to any given artwork, they took their cue from the artwork itself. Now what mattered was something more subjective: not an external checklist or some universal truth, but the impression the artwork made on them.

Among those at the forefront of the Romantic movement was the German poet and philosopher Karl Friedrich von Schlegel whose theories about artworks being organic creations influenced Alessandro Manzoni, an Italian novelist and playwright. Manzoni came to the conclusion that every work of art had its own reason to exist and should therefore be judged on its own terms. He put Romantic theory into practice in his tragedy *Il conte di Carmagnola* (*The Count of Carmagnola*), published in 1819. This was a play that paid no heed to the three unities, imposed no restrictions on the number of characters and broke free of traditional rhetoric. What matters to us, however, is Manzoni's preface in which he wrote:

> Besides which, any work of art contains within it the elements necessary to enable anyone wishing to do so to form an opinion on it. In my view they are the following: What did the author set out to do? Was this a reasonable ambition in the first place? Has the author achieved what they set out to do?
>
> Failing to look at a work of art from this angle and insisting at all costs on judging every piece according to a set of rules (the certainty and universality of which is open to question) is to risk taking a wholly wrong approach to a piece of work. Though it must be said that this is one of the lesser evils which might befall us in this world.[14]

Here we see the first iteration of a philosophy that has characterized theatre criticism to this day, whether you are talking about William Archer, Max Beerbohm and George Bernard Shaw in Victorian London, early twentieth-century Americans such as George Jean Nathan, Dorothy Parker and Alexander Woollcott, or their successors including Katharine Brisbane in Australia, Harold Clurman in the USA, Kenneth Tynan in the UK and Herbert Whittaker in Canada.

The formulation reached us by a circuitous route. In 1820, the British journal *Quarterly Review* gave an unfavourable review to *The Count of Carmagnola*. It was then that Manzoni found a champion in Johann Wolfgang von Goethe. The German writer edited his own journal, *Über Kunst und Alterthum*, and here in 1821, he defended the play and picked up on Manzoni's idea. Once again, he was dismissive of dogmatic rules-based criticism and in favour of a more fluid, artist-centred approach:

> There is both destructive and productive criticism. The former is very easy. You need only establish in your mind some benchmark,

some exemplary model, however narrow-minded it may be, so that you can then be boldly certain: this work of art does not match the benchmark and is therefore not much good. The matter is then brushed aside and, without a second thought, you can declare your requirement has not been satisfied. Productive criticism is a good deal more difficult. You would ask: 'What did the author intend? Is this intention reasonable and prudent? And to what extent has it been successfully carried out?'[15]

Goethe usually gets the credit for these three questions, but they properly belong to Manzoni. For our purposes, they may be better considered in a different order and expressed as:

1   What were the theatremakers trying to do?

2   How well did they do it?

3   Was it worth it?

These questions are at the heart of this book and we will return to them repeatedly. Let's consider each in a little more detail.

What were the theatremakers trying to do?

To ask this question is to assess a piece of theatre on its own terms. It ensures that your first consideration is what the show is, not what you would like it to be. Imagine, for example, that you preferred pantomime to tragedy. You'd be entitled to your opinion, but that wouldn't make it reasonable to criticize a tragedy for not casting a man in a dress. Just as you wouldn't fault a pole vaulter for lack of swimming skills, so it would be unreasonable to damn a theatre production for something it wasn't intending to do in the first place. If you focus on what the theatremakers were attempting, however, your review should end up with some relationship to the world as it is and not to your own personal fantasy. It's a question of assuming everything you see on stage is deliberate, that it is there for a reason, and to work from there.

On the surface, that sounds straightforward, but how failsafe an approach is it? Among those who argue it doesn't work are proponents of the intentional fallacy. This is the theory put forward by W.K. Wimsatt and Monroe C. Beardsley in *The Verbal Icon: Studies in the Meaning of Poetry*, where they argue that it is neither possible nor relevant to know an author's intentions. The theory rests on three objections. First is that it would be impossible to get inside an artist's head to find out what they were thinking and, even if they had explained their intentions in public, you couldn't be certain they were telling the truth. Second is that if you chose instead to deduce the intention from the artwork rather than from the artist, you would be guilty of circular thinking: you'd be judging in terms that the artwork itself had given you. And third is that, even if it were possible to identify them, the author's intentions should have no bearing on critical evaluation. A review should be about achievement, not intent. As Wimsatt and Beardsley put it:

> The design or intention of the author is neither available nor desirable as a standard for judging the success of a work of literary art [. . .] One must ask how a critic expects to get an answer to the question about intention. How is he to find out what the poet tried to do? If the poet succeeded in doing it, then the poem itself shows what he was trying to do. And if the poet did not succeed, then the poem is not adequate evidence, and the critic must go outside the poem for evidence of an intention that did not become effective in the poem.[16]

Roland Barthes took a similar line in his 1967 essay 'The Death of the Author', in which he argued that interpreting a work through the lens of the artist's biography inevitably limits its meaning, a post-structuralist idea taken up by Michel Foucault in his 1969 lecture 'What Is an Author?'. If you hold with this thinking, then you'd say your job would become even harder when you had to imagine the intentions of playwrights from distant cultures and ancient periods in history. How could the critic possibly know? Even with biographies and research material, you could hope for no more than an educated guess. Further, it's not hard to argue that artists themselves don't know the true intention of their work. Asking a theatremaker what they were aiming for may produce an answer that is eccentric or downright untrue. On other occasions, the intention may not be apparent in the execution. A playwright friend told me of his surprise at the audience's laughter during a rehearsed reading of a work in progress. It hadn't been his intention to make them laugh, although his play was no worse for it. It's impossible for artists to be in control of how their work is received; there are too many external factors at play. Had I been reviewing my friend's rehearsed reading, would it have been reasonable to assume he was trying to be funny? With the audience laughing all around me, how would I have known he wasn't? At the very least, there must be a margin of error.

All this may be true, but in the day-to-day job of being a critic, figuring out theatremakers' intentions is rarely a problem. Perhaps it would be different in a more individualistic artform such as poetry, but in the arena of theatre, created collectively, performed live, the clues are generally easy to read. Theatremakers are skilled in making their intentions clear; that's how they connect with audiences. There are many things we can say with confidence. My friend may not have expected laughter, but no audience would have supposed his intention had been to write an opera, create a sculpture or choreograph a piece of flamenco. In general terms, they knew what he was aiming at; they followed the story and recognized the genre, stylistic conventions, topical references and political perspective. There was room for interpretation, but they knew enough to make a pretty good stab at what he was trying to do. In the majority of cases, a critic would be right to assume the effect the theatremakers achieved was the effect they wanted. Even when theatremakers are unsuccessful, it's not hard to tell what they're being unsuccessful at: the rhythm of a joke suggests comedy; intense expressions suggest melodrama; a live band suggests a musical. These are all pretty good clues about what was intended, whether or not they have succeeded in making you laugh, cry or sing along.

As well as this intuitive understanding, we have lots of external evidence from publicity material, geographical location, choice of play, tone of delivery and a whole load of other contextual clues. For the purposes of writing a theatre review, all this evidence should be enough to keep the intentional fallacy at bay. Yes, we have to take care to read the intentions correctly and, yes, we'll sometimes come to the wrong conclusions, but our hit rate is pretty high. Even if we can't answer Manzoni's first question with absolute precision and certainty, we can answer it precisely and certainly enough to deal with the next two questions – the first of which ensures that we judge the execution rather than the intention.

EXERCISE

Write a 250-word review of a show you disliked that focuses exclusively on the intentions of the theatremakers. Does it make things easier or harder to see things from their perspective?

How well did they do it?

With this question, we are still in the territory of the theatremakers, but we are introducing our own powers of discrimination. If, after the first question, we have determined their intention was to stage a trouser-dropping farce, we would now judge their work in terms of trouser-dropping farces. When the doors jam, the jokes fall flat and the trousers do not drop, we may reasonably say the production has failed in its own terms. When the whole thing runs like clockwork and the audience's laughter levels leave them gasping for breath, we can say the company has achieved what it set out to do.

At this stage of the thought process, the critic's personal like or dislike of trouser-dropping farces is not relevant. Nor is the observation that you'd rather have been watching some other theatrical genre. Theatremakers get justifiably frustrated when a critic faults them for failing to do something they never intended to do. You can still give praise or find fault, but it has to have some bearing on the thing being attempted. If it doesn't, then you are little different to the neo-classical critics who would mark down anything that didn't have a wholesome moral even if wholesome morals were not the intention. This approach is good for your readers too. From their point of view, the more clearly and dispassionately you can set out what was attempted and what was achieved, the better they can imagine their own reaction. If the reader is a fan of trouser-dropping farces, they'll find it more valuable to know whether this is a good example of a trouser-dropping farce than whether the critic happens to like the genre or not.

Even at this level, the critic has tremendous room for expression. No two critics will make the same assessment of a production's multitude of strengths and weaknesses. How well the theatremakers did it is open to wide interpretation and the answer will depend on the critic's experience, discrimination, taste, standards and interpretative powers. Even so, in the absence of a wider critical perspective, if you

EXERCISE

Write a 250-word review that deliberately misunderstands the theatremakers' intentions. If it's a musical, treat it as a tragedy; if it's a farce, treat it as performance art; if it is aimed at teenagers, treat it like a show for retired holidaymakers; if it's a thriller, treat it as a comedy. How distorted an impression can you create?

do not go beyond Manzoni's first two questions, every review is in danger of ending up with the gloriously circular observation that if you like this kind of thing, this is the kind of thing you will like. So let's move on to question three.

Was it worth it?

Manzoni asked whether the artist's intentions were 'reasonable' ('ragionevole'). Goethe wanted them to be 'reasonable and prudent' ('vernünftig und verständig'). Even if those are not the exact words we would choose today, we can recognize the impulse. Perhaps we'd ask whether the artist's aims had been bold or provocative, or whether the artist had attempted to move audiences in a way that seemed fresh and original. Any such adjective reflects the values of the time and will change from critic to critic and generation to generation. But whether we're looking for the reasonable and prudent, or the bold and original, when we ask whether the artist's efforts were worth it, we open the door to rich critical discussion.

This is the part of the formulation that is most fully about the critic's perspective. The first two questions consider the theatremakers' achievement in their own terms. This third question is about the terms themselves. It's not about whether the theatremakers think their attempt was worth the effort (it would be odd if they thought otherwise), but whether, in the opinion of the critic, it was worth it. Consider the case of a show that sets out with mediocre ambitions and achieves them. With only the first two of Manzoni's questions, the critic would have to give the highest praise. 'What were the theatremakers trying to do? Something mediocre. How well did they do it? Perfectly.' With the third question, the critic can call the mediocrity to account: 'Yes, you have done what you set out to do, but what you set out to do was beneath your talents.'

For the word 'mediocre', you can substitute any adjective. However well it succeeds in its own terms, a show with left-wing ambitions is unlikely to satisfy a right-wing critic; a show with evangelical ambitions couldn't expect to get the approval of an atheist critic; and a show with misogynist ambitions would be challenged by a feminist critic. The terms needn't be negative: 'What were the theatremakers trying to do? Change the world. How will did they do it? With limited success. Was it worth it? Yes, trying to change the world is always worth it.' A critic who strongly approved of what the theatremakers were trying to do may choose to underplay any weaknesses in their level of accomplishment. An ambitious show that fails can seem more worthwhile than an unambitious show that succeeds.

To use the distinction we discussed in the last chapter, Manzoni's third question is the one that turns a reviewer into a critic. It takes us away from box-office appeal and shallow like/dislike judgements, and towards deeper questions about value and meaning. Put less stridently, it could be worded, 'What was its worth?' or 'What was interesting about it?' The idea has been expressed in different ways. The critic A.B. Walkley borrowed from Matthew Arnold to say that where the regular theatregoer asks merely whether they are pleased, the critic asks: 'Am I right to be pleased?'[17] There are many ambitions a production may have and the ability to please is only one them. If the pleasure is at the expense of truth, justice, morality, innovation, radical politics or any other quality the critic holds dear, then maybe it is not right to be pleased.

Think of a long-running West End or Broadway musical that has been slammed by the critics yet loved by audiences. It needn't be a contradiction that what Arnold called the 'practical man'[18] enjoys it for the straight-forward pleasure it offers, yet the critic complains about its weaknesses in other respects. You often hear producers and fans insisting the critics were wrong to dismiss a show that went on to be a commercial hit. They will give as evidence *We Will Rock You*, which enjoyed a twelve-year run at London's Dominion Theatre in spite of the derogatory comments of its first-night critics. Their thinking is the same as that of the backer of a 1966 production of *Sweet Charity* who sent a weekly copy of the box-office receipts to Stanley Kauffmann after his negative review in *The New York Times*. That backer would have agreed with Mrs Dangle in Sheridan's *The Critic* who chastises her husband's critical pretensions on the basis that for managers and authors 'the public is their critic – without whose fair approbation they know no play can rest on the stage'.[19]

Mr Dangle is a justifiable figure of fun and managers are quite right to focus primarily on the box office, but this analysis is a misunderstanding of the critic's job – and of Manzoni's third question. Brian Logan, who described *We Will Rock You* as 'ruthlessly manufactured'[20] in his two-star review, was not employed by *The Guardian* to offer an assessment of the show's commercial potential. It was to give his personal evaluation of the production on that night. It's the job of the market to show what's popular; the job of the critic is to say what's valuable. It does not follow that a popular show is never valuable nor that a valuable show is never popular, but neither is the connection automatic.

Answering all three of Manzoni's questions at the same time pushes you towards the most complete form of review. It is one that pays due respect to the theatremakers' achievement as well as recognizing the individual insight of the critic who, in the course of making an argument, will situate the production in its social, historical and aesthetic context. The three questions give you a way to think about a production before you start writing and need have no bearing on how you structure your review. They should, however, keep you away from the two extremes of indulging the theatremakers and indulging your ego. In the next chapter, we'll take a look at where different critics situate themselves on the line between these two extremes according to the demands of their readers and their personal predilections.

EXERCISE

Select a review that has been professionally published. Read through it line by line identifying which of Manzoni's three questions the critic is dealing with at any one time.

Notes

1 Eagleton, Terry (1984), *The Function of Criticism*, Verso.

2 Littlewood, S.R. (1939), *Dramatic Criticism*, Pitman.

3 Gray, Charles Harold (1931), *Theatrical Criticism in London to 1795*, Columbia University Press.

4 Appleton, William W. and Burnim, Kalman A., eds (1966), *The Prompter: A Theatrical Paper (1734–1736)*, Benjamin Blom.

5 Gray, Charles Harold (1931), *Theatrical Criticism in London to 1795*, Columbia University Press.

6 Sheridan, Richard Brinsley (1779), *The Critic*.

7 Wolter, Jürgen C. (1993), *The Dawning of American Drama: American Dramatic Criticism, 1746–1915*, Greenwood Press.

8 Stratman, Carl J. (1963), 'Scotland's first dramatic periodical: *The Edinburgh Theatrical Censor*', in *Theatre Notebook*, Vol. XVII, No. 3.

9 Jones, Chris (2013), *Bigger, Brighter, Louder*, University of Chicago Press.

10 Anonymous (19 July 1834), 'Theatricals', in *The Australian*.

11 Anonymous (16 September 1843), 'The rapo act', in the *New Zealand Gazette and Wellington Spectator*, Vol. IV, Issue 281.

12 Prescott, Paul (2013), *Reviewing Shakespeare: Journalism and Performance from the Eighteenth Century to the Present*, Cambridge University Press.

13 Ibid.

14 Manzoni, Alessandro (1819), *Il conte di Carmagnola*.

15 Goethe, Johann Wolfgang von (1821), *Über Kunst und Alterthum, Vol. III*.

16 Wimsatt, W.K. and Beardsley, Monroe C. (1954), *The Verbal Icon: Studies in the Meaning of Poetry*, University Press of Kentucky.

17 Walkley, A.B. (1903), *Dramatic Criticism*, John Murray.

18 Collini, Stefan, ed. (1993), 'The Function of Criticism at the Present Time', in *Arnold: Culture and Anarchy and Other Writings*, Cambridge University Press.

19 Sheridan, Richard Brinsley (1779), *The Critic*.

20 Logan, Brian (15 May 2002), 'We Will Rock You', in *The Guardian*.

3

HOW TO TAKE ON DIFFERENT CRITICAL STYLES

What do you think you are doing?

The three questions we take from Alessandro Manzoni – what were the theatremakers trying to do, how well did they do it and was it worth it? – should ensure a respectful, creative and fruitful relationship between critic and theatremaker. But they are only the start of the story. There are many ways to deal with the questions. Should you answer all three? If you do, how much emphasis should you give to each? And should you follow the same pattern in every review?

It just depends.

A critic recommending a show in an events guide may skim over the first question ('What were the theatremakers trying to do?'), prioritize the second ('How well did they do it?') and ignore the third ('Was it worth it?'). A critic who is in love with the theatre may get no further than the first question because they care only about what the theatremaker is trying to do. A more philosophical critic concerned with theatre's place in the culture may focus almost exclusively on the third: 'What was the worth of the event in the greater scheme of things?' Straight away, this gives us a variety of critical approaches. Add the many ways the questions can be answered, and take into account the different readerships a critic may be writing for, and you end up with a near infinite range. Most critics will use several approaches at the same time. See how often you recognize yourself in the descriptions that make up this chapter.

The critic as reporter

When you read a crime report in your local newspaper, you expect to be told the facts of the case and not what the journalist thinks about them. The reporter's job is to communicate clearly, accurately and neutrally, with neither opinion nor bias. Their personality should not affect the information being conveyed. The critic as reporter takes the same approach by sticking with our first question – 'What were the theatremakers trying to do?' – and going no further. It is perfectly possible to do this. You just keep to the facts, from the names of the actors to the details of the plot, and describe what happened. You can comment on how the audience reacted, but should stop short of mentioning your own emotional or intellectual reaction: that would be too subjective. Like a report of a news event or a sports fixture, everything must boil down to verifiable facts.

If the critic adheres strictly to these rules, their personality will be absent from the review. Think of a local newspaper journalist who, assigned to cover the latest youth-theatre performance, will file the kind of upbeat factual review that gets all the names right, offends no one and keeps the mums and dads happy. It is not necessary, however, for the critic as reporter to be quite so retiring. The instinct to record underscores the work of many great critics, writers who have combined factual description with personal flair and critical insight. The earliest precedent is none other than Aristotle himself. As a descriptive critic, the Greek thinker based his theories on what he observed on stage not what he thought he ought to have seen. We think of Kenneth Tynan as the most flamboyant of critics, yet he was responding to a similar impulse when he said the purpose of criticism was 'to give permanence to something impermanent'. The descriptive critic pins down the ephemeral art of theatre for future generations, recognizing that such people are more likely to care about what an event was like than what an individual critic thought of it. Posterity hungers for description, not opinion. Taking on the role of critic as reporter means sharpening your powers of observation and cultivating your descriptive skills. You are all that stands between the theatre and forgetting.

EXERCISE

Put yourself in the role of critic as reporter and write a 200-word review that contains no judgement and no direct evidence of your own presence. See how much you can say about the success of a show using only your powers of description and reference to external factors such as the behaviour of the audience.

The critic as judge

Some people are uncomfortable about casting judgement. They think it reeks of self-importance. 'Who are you to say that?' they ask. Isn't it undemocratic for one person to make their opinion heard above everyone else's? When that opinion is couched in forthright journalistic language, free of doubt and hesitation, it seems arrogant. It's why in popular culture, you commonly come across portrayals of critics as elitist and aloof. They are pompous, friendless and often malicious and go about the job of belittling everything they see, off stage as well as on. You don't need to pander to this stereotype to recognize that judgement is a core part of the job. Perhaps you'd prefer the word 'evaluation'. It sounds less aggressive. But it means the same thing. The critic asks 'How well did they do it?' and then, 'Was it worth it?', questions it would be impossible to answer without the ability to discriminate.

For many critics, expressing strident opinions is what they're paid to do. Certainly, from the reader's point of view, critical writing is often at its most compelling when its judgements are unequivocal. People quote Tynan not when he was being ambivalent but when he was at his most absolute: 'I doubt if I could love anyone who did not wish to see *Look Back in Anger*. It is the best young play of its decade.'[1] The more certain the opinions, the more readable – and the more notorious – the critic as judge is likely to be. In the past, the tendency to judge has often put the critic in the role of cultural gatekeeper, not simply expressing an opinion but setting out an agenda for what is acceptable and what is not. Even today, you come across critics writing in the tone of severe school teachers handing down grades to their unworthy pupils. This is an idea we'll return to below when we consider the critic as arbiter of taste.

EXERCISE

Draw up a table with three columns. In the first column list all the elements that make up a production: acting, design, plot, direction, ideas, music and so on. You could also include some qualitative phrases such as 'value for money' and 'level of entertainment'. Give the second column the heading 'excellent' and the third column the heading 'terrible'. After seeing a show, go through your checklist and, for each entry, place a tick in the 'excellent' or 'terrible' column. How difficult is it to make such an extreme judgement?

The critic as consumer guide

Whenever we go online to buy holidays, hi-fis or home insurance, we are routinely subjected to a barrage of professional reviews and consumer opinions. These help us make choices based on the amount of money we're willing to spend and what we want to use the product for. With so much to choose from, we're grateful for anything that makes our decision easier. For many people, buying a ticket to the theatre is no different. At the point of purchase, they are not concerned with deeper meanings, sociological resonances or historical context. They just want to see something good. Maybe it's their only night out all year. Most likely they'll be taking friends or family whom they don't want to let down. Why would they choose to blow a load of money on something second rate? They don't regard themselves as specialists; they can't tell one show from another, especially when faced with the enormity of a theatre festival, the West End or Broadway. What they need is an expert to guide, advise and reassure them about the perfect show for them.

It's a job the critic as consumer guide steps forward to do, although straight away it feels like a different sort of consumer advice. If I want to buy a television, I need to tell the technology reviewer only the size of screen I'd like and the amount of money I'm willing to spend. But if I want to buy a night at the theatre, my parameters are much harder to pin down. Even if I declared an interest in musicals, how would the critic know whether I'd prefer a show about the French revolution or a ghost who haunts a theatre? That's a question I couldn't answer myself – never mind whether I'd prefer the mainstream melodies of a Lloyd Webber or the less obvious variations of a Sondheim. And if value for money were an issue, as it would be for any other consumer product, by what standard could the critic decide if I'd think £10 was an expensive ticket or £200 cheap? With most consumer products there is a direct relationship between price and quality, but there's little reason to suppose a person who spends £200 to go to the theatre will enjoy themselves twenty times more than the person who spends £10 – frequently, the reverse is true. A critic who attempted to cater to readers in this way with any degree of accuracy would almost certainly fail. A strategy more likely to succeed for the critic as consumer guide is to write for a defined market whose tastes broadly coincide with their own. That way they can write honestly without having to imagine what someone else may or may not like.

One such critic is Tonnvane Wiswell of the 'Life in the Cheap Seats' blog. 'I want my readers to take chances with new theater – supporting it is very important to me', she told me in an email. Writing on a website subtitled 'London Theater reviews by an American expat – on a budget', she said she was aiming at theatregoers trying to decide what to see. For her, theatregoing was a hobby rather than a profession and she said she had neither the academic background nor the time to do the kind of research that might qualify her as a 'proper reviewer':

> I write about my experience, and I expect people who want that other stuff to look at programs and proper reviewers' work and to get it there. And, if they don't have time to research a show before or after, I hope they spend two minutes looking at my review and rather quickly decide yay or nay – not necessarily the same as me, but that their sense of my opinions lets them know how they would receive something I saw.

To be effective, the critic as consumer guide needs to earn the respect of their readers either through the immediate clarity of their opinions, as Wiswell suggested, or through proving reliable in the long term. The more instinctively tuned in to tastes of their readers, the more useful a service they will provide.

EXERCISE

Think of the last five shows you have seen. For each one, complete the sentence 'If you like [. . .], you will like this show', where the missing words could be the name of another production, a film, a book, a song or some other cultural reference. Ask yourself how similar the two things really are.

The critic as theatrical analyst

Even without its relationship with the wider society, the stage is a pretty interesting place. A critic who focuses purely on the technical craft and artistry that make it work will never be short of things to say. Our second question – 'How well did they do it?' – sends the critic off on an endless investigation. What does a great actor do to achieve a great performance? How does a playwright structure a successful farce? What spatial awareness does it take for a director to turn the stage into a dynamic place of the imagination? How does the interplay of sound, light and set design create the atmosphere? The questions go on. To a greater or lesser extent, every critic will end up wrestling with them.

EXERCISE

Write a 250-word review that focuses entirely on the craft of the various theatremakers, from the costume designer to the movement director to the vocal coach and so on. How easy is to identify and describe their contribution?

The critic as champion

By championing Bertolt Brecht and John Osborne, Tynan was setting himself against what he saw as the blandness of the West End theatre of his day and, by implication, all that was dull and conservative about British society in general. When he rallied behind *Look Back in Anger*,[2] he was doing more than telling his readers about a pleasant night at the theatre. He was attaching his name to what felt at the time like a revolutionary cultural movement. It was with similar zeal that a group of bohemian critics in mid-nineteenth-century New York promoted French plays to their readers. Likewise, William Archer championed the plays of Henrik Ibsen, George Jean Nathan flew the flag for Eugene O'Neill, Stark Young introduced his readers to the theatre of Japan and Harold Hobson championed Samuel Beckett.

These critics took our third question – 'Was it worth it?' – and made it proactive. Being dissatisfied with the prevalent theatre of their day, they took it upon themselves to argue for something better. It's an attitude that requires the critic to take a stand. Instead of reacting to each new production as it comes along, taking each on its own merits, the critic as champion sees the bigger picture and tries to educate readers on what may be new, unfamiliar and unsettling. Such an attitude has led to much of the most fiery, articulate and persuasive criticism. The chief risk is of the critic championing a writer or a theatrical movement so vehemently that they become too partial. When the culture moves on or when the playwright runs out of steam, the critic must try not to let old affiliations cloud their judgement.

EXERCISE

The next time you are excited by a show – or a particular contribution to a show – write a 400-word review arguing that the artist or artists are the future of theatre. For the purpose of the exercise, you are allowed to exaggerate. Do you find your writing has a different quality?

The critic as educator

Theatre critics are specialists. The very act of frequent theatregoing sees to that. With only a small amount of study of theatre history or research into a particular production, the critic is quickly ahead of the pack. Consequently, a key part of the critic's job is to explain what's going on, giving the reader insights that can inform their understanding and enrich their theatregoing pleasure. The deeper and truer the insight, the more rewarding the review for the reader.

There is a lot of explaining to be done. In *On Criticism*,[3] Nöel Carroll identified the component parts of a review. He argued that the one essential element of criticism was evaluation (the work of the critic as judge) which he said was performed in conjunction with up to six further tasks: 'description, classification, contextualization, elucidation, interpretation and analysis'. All of these are forms of explanation and all educate the reader about the event. Carroll said that what turns critics into experts is not their verdicts (everyone has them) but their being 'adept at backing those verdicts up with reasons'. Those reasons are the tools of the critic as educator.

With so many thousand years of theatre history behind us, even the simple act of classification can require a bank of knowledge. Are we talking about Greek tragedy, Victorian melodrama, Brechtian cabaret or site-specific verbatim comedy? Could it be deliberately working in opposition to one of those genres? And what do the genres entail? Each one carries with it a set of conventions and expectations that the critic must understand and convey.

Coupled with description, this classification is the first step on the road to elucidation. This is about the critic responding to our first question: 'What were the theatremakers trying to do?' To answer that question sounds simple enough, but in practice, it requires considerable knowledge and sensitivity. The critic's educative role continues through interpretation (what was it trying to say on a deeper level?), analysis (how did it make its meanings apparent?) and contextualization (where did it fit in the greater scheme of things?). If the critic points the reader in the right direction, it can significantly enrich their appreciation of the

EXERCISE

Write a 300-word review aimed at someone who has never been to the theatre before. Explain everything you know about the production's genre, the theatre's history, the play's origins, the theatremakers' credentials and other background details that make the show what it is. How much do you know without even realizing it?

show. The spectator who understands the reasons for what's
happening on stage has a very different experience to the one who
does not.

The critic as arbiter of taste

In 1922, James Agate complained that in his time, the role of the critic
had changed: 'in place of the old obligation to lead public taste the
modern urgency is to pursue it'.[4] Unlike most critics of today, he
missed the once deferential attitude shown to the profession:

> When formerly a great actor arose the polite world held its breath
> until a Hazlitt, a Lewes, or even a Clement Scott had pronounced
> judgment. But the acting of the actor is no longer supposed to be
> the reader's concern. He is offered, in place of criticism, irrelevant
> gossip after the manner of the servants' hall.

The critic as arbiter of taste believes criticism exists to keep up high
artistic standards. 'To direct our taste, and conduct the poet up to
perfection has ever been the true critic's province,'[5] said Oliver
Goldsmith in 1757, creating the impression of the critic as a superior
being, condescendingly applying a refined judgement on an imperfect
world. Such critics are like gatekeepers, allowing through that which
meets with their approval and turning back anything that doesn't. The
greater their influence, the more they can determine the shows that
prosper.

It's an idea with its roots in a patrician society, one more inclined
than our own to defer to the wealthy and privileged. It stems also from
the prescriptive criticism of the neo-classical era when the rules gave
the critic a seemingly failsafe set of standards to which art should
aspire. A critic with this knowledge could decree whether a play met
the expected level of morality, whether it was of sufficient value to
humanity and whether it met the aesthetic standards handed down

from Aristotle. Fall foul of the rules and you fell foul of the critic. As well as fixed standards of morality, this critic writes with lofty and unyielding artistic principles.

Today, the critic as arbiter of taste is not so prevalent, but has not disappeared altogether. Think of those newspaper review round-ups called things like 'What to Say About . . .' – as in 'What to Say About *Hamlet* with Michael Sheen'.[6] The implication is that readers use opinions as a kind of cultural currency, something to trade and exchange at a dinner party to make them seem tuned in and up to speed. Seeing Michael Sheen in *Hamlet* for themselves is less important than being able to say the right thing about it. The degree to which that is true means there is still a role for the critic as arbiter of taste.

EXERCISE

Pretend your views about taste, behaviour and decency are either extremely conservative or extremely liberal. Write a 300-word review that lectures your readers about why the production is very bad for them. How comfortable do you feel playing this game of make-believe?

The critic as reformer

Some critics enter the profession with a missionary zeal. They love theatre, but want to make it better. Having caught sight of the best – or perhaps just imagined something superior – they take it upon themselves to campaign for higher standards. In this frame of mind, with every negative review, a critic challenges the theatre to up its game.

Theatre is always changing and that's because the world around it is always changing. What strikes a chord one year may be passé the next, but theatre programmers and audiences frequently suffer from a cultural lag. They tend to fall into a pattern of the familiar, the comforting and the orthodox. In such instances, it takes a reforming critic to question their complacency. Popularity alone is not a measure of a play's worth. The critic as reformer is the diametric opposite of the critic as consumer guide. The concern here is not whether the audience will be entertained or feel the evening was money well spent. This is a critic who takes the lead from our third question – 'Was it worth it?' – and insists on treating theatre as art, holding it up to account in terms of its greater achievement.

In the commercial theatre, where the financial stakes are high, such a critic is unpopular. In 1966, a delegation of Broadway producers lobbied *The New York Times* to protest against the reviews of Stanley Kauffmann because, as the critic believed, his standards had been too high for them.[7] He liked theatre too much to accept the second rate. An independently minded critic can swim against the tide of lazy opinion while drawing attention to innovations elsewhere that may otherwise go overlooked. Such critics have lobbied for and against censorship, advocated state funding and made the case against theatrical conventions that have fallen into cliché. The intention of the critic as reformer is to make theatre better.

EXERCISE

Write a 400-word review of a show you have enjoyed, arguing that it could have been so much better if it had been created under better conditions and if the theatremakers had been more ambitious. How do you feel about being negative about a show you liked?

The critic as cultural commentator

In addition to writing about individual productions, the critic will also be called upon to write about the broader artistic scene. Like the critic as reformer and the critic as champion, the critic as cultural commentator needs to consider the social structures that allow theatre to take place. This is the world of arts councils, government subsidy, board-level decisions and artistic management. In among the theatre reviews anthologized in Katharine Brisbane's *Not Wrong Just Different: Observations on the Rise of Contemporary Australian Theatre*[8] were polemics about the board structure of the Australian Elizabethan Theatre Trust, the funding policies of the New South Wales state government and a 'make it Australian' campaign by Actors' Equity. Whether she was writing as Brisbane the critic, or Brisbane the columnist, she wanted theatre to thrive. That meant a desire to see the highest artistic standards on stage and the most conducive political set-up behind the scenes.

A respected critic can be at their most influential when they take up the cudgels in this way. Exploiting their familiarity with the theatre scene and canvassing the opinions of insiders, they can lead a civic debate in a manner that is informed, passionate and a good deal more stylish than a routine news report. The danger in certain cases is that when the critic returns to regular reviewing, they could be accused of having a vendetta against the people they have been commenting on. The challenge for the critic as cultural commentator, as well as being well informed, is to be transparent and not bear grudges.

EXERCISE

Research your local arts scene. Find out how theatres are funded and what relationship the theatremakers have with their individual donors, corporate sponsors, public subsidizers and ticket buyers. Are there any tensions or contradictions in the way the money is raised? What other issues are being debated in the arts community?

The critic as social commentator

In this role, the critic goes beyond the first two questions about whether a show is good or bad on its own terms to ask what it means in the context of the world outside the theatre. What does it say about the times we live in? How does it relate to the community in which it takes place? What need does it satisfy by existing at all? For this critic, theatre is a social event that has implications for everyone.

Such implications are always there, but sometimes they are more apparent. In Chicago, for example, a number of theatres have staged plays on the subject of gun-related crime in the city. In the *Chicago Tribune* in 2014, Chris Jones wrote that 'these theaters have been fulfilling a moral obligation to the community they serve and have had an impact'.[9] It was a point he emphasized as he signed off his review of *The Gospel of Lovingkindness* by Marcus Gardley at the Victory Gardens Theater: 'Outside the doors of the theater the leaders of the city and the kids who walk some of its streets, are still struggling with that very same question.' Taking on the role of critic as social commentator, Jones refused to view the production as an isolated artefact, like an exotic object on display in a museum, but as something that directly related to that particular city at that particular time.

As an artform that depends on the presence of an audience and operates on an essentially local level, theatre always has a relationship to society. That was the animating idea behind Michael Billington's *State of the Nation: British Theatre Since 1945*[10] which treated theatre as a cultural barometer, reflecting, anticipating and sometimes shaping the political agenda. The critic drew connections between J.B. Priestley's *An Inspector Calls* and the arrival of the National Health Service; John Osborne's *The Entertainer* and the Suez crisis; and the popularity of Andrew Lloyd Webber and Margaret Thatcher's defeat of the miners.

In the words of Philadelphia critic Wendy Rosenfield, writing for the *Broad Street Review*,[11] the job is to analyse a work in its larger socio-political context and to ask: 'Why this play? Why here? Why now?'

She felt strongly that it was her role to call a company to account for what she saw as exclusionary practices in, for example, the representation of minority races or the employment of female writers. Not to do so, she argued, would be an injustice in itself and an abnegation of the critic's role: 'to see exclusionary practices and not comment on them is to perpetuate them, but also, to pretend a show exists in a cultural vacuum does a disservice to the role of art'.

EXERCISE

Write a 400-word review that makes the connection between the production and society at large. This could be a response to a theme in the play or a comment on some aspect of the production, such as casting, or of company policy. What do you feel about setting the work in its wider context?

The critic as insider

In the introduction to *Light Fantastic: Adventures in Theatre,*[12] the *New Yorker* critic John Lahr identified himself as a 'theatrical' – that is, a person of the theatre – and allied himself not with the audience or his readers, as many critics would, but primarily with the theatremakers themselves. His father was Bert Lahr, best known as the Cowardly Lion in *The Wizard of Oz*, and his mother was a chorus girl. This was a 'raffish pedigree' he was proud of. The proximity had influenced his approach to writing articles, which he regarded not as independent, disinterested commentaries but as 'collaborations with the makers'. The artists' job was to make a metaphor, his was to 'interpret it and make connections to the world we bustle in'. He wanted to lay down a historical record of the life of the theatre. That meant telling the reader more about the event than his mere opinion. The director and author Todd London said Lahr was 'less of a critic than a benevolent, long distance dramaturg'.[13] That puts him in good company: the history of dramaturgy begins with Gotthold Ephraim Lessing who was hired as an in-house critic by the Hamburg National Theatre in 1767, making him the first critic as insider.

In *The Empty Space*, Peter Brook argued that 'the more the critic becomes an insider, the better'.[14] He acknowledged the 'tiny social problem' of critics mixing with theatremakers whom they had damned in print, but said that was of minor concern compared with the advantages of cultivating a vital connection to the artform. What he wanted to see was journalistic criticism that was as 'absolutely precise' as the criticism made by theatremakers themselves, something he felt required an intimate theatrical understanding. Brook's sometime collaborator Charles Marowitz went one step further and made the case for what he called an 'in-house critic'.[15] Writing in 1986, he argued there was 'no such thing as a work of art' that was not 'fertilized by a critical spirit' and proposed that a theatre company should hire an in-house critic who would write reviews of the first run-through, the first dress rehearsal and the first preview. Not designed for public consumption, those reviews would be circulated to the artistic team for their consideration.

Like Lahr's idea of 'collaborations with the makers', Marowitz's proposal resurfaced at the start of the twenty-first century when the interactivity of the internet opened up criticism to two-way traffic. Where once a review may have been regarded as the end of a discussion, now it could be seen as the start – and, if both parties were willing, it could herald a conversation between critic and theatremaker.

But how cordial can this conversation be? When Andrew Haydon had the opportunity to follow the Actors Touring Company to Kurdistan in 2012, he and his friends joked about him being an 'embedded critic'.[16] As a journalist in Iraq closely attached to a company, he was the theatre world's equivalent of the embedded journalists who had travelled alongside coalition forces during their 2003 invasion of that same country. The idea that a theatre critic has anything in common with a war reporter is, of course, ludicrous, but from this joke, the phrase 'embedded criticism' stuck. Like the practice of embedded journalism, it is problematic. During the Iraq war, reporters were accused of being complicit in army propaganda; there was a widespread feeling that in return for unprecedented access to frontline operations, they had sacrificed their independence. Likewise, a journalist who is privy to a theatre company's daily activities, whether sitting in on rehearsals or travelling together on the road, is likely to have plenty of interesting things to say but will find it hard to maintain the cool-headed independence that defined an older school of criticism.

The problem, however, is with the terminology rather than the practice. Everyone agrees 'embedded criticism' is a neat phrase, but few seem comfortable using it. The criticism students at Ontario's Brock University have called themselves 'behind-the-scenes reporters'. Another term could be 'digital dramaturg'. That's what Andy Horwitz called himself when, working at PS122 in New York in 2003, he tried to redefine the three-way relationship between artist, critic and audience. He wanted the opportunity on the one hand to contribute intellectually to the creative process, and on the other to help communicate the artists' ideas to the wider public. Thanks to digital technology, it was now possible to engage audiences at points in that process other than just the first night. 'This is writing intended for the Internet, criticism from a networked perspective',[17] Horwitz wrote on his Culturebot website. He used the phrase 'critical horizontalism'[18] to describe a process in which 'the writer exists in subjective relation to the work of the artist' rather than the traditional top-down approach in which 'the critic "objectively" judges the merits of a given performance'. Under this model, the artist initiates a conversation, the critic continues it and, by publishing on the internet, opens up a 'horizontal field of discourse' in which everyone can investigate the ideas further.

In a similar spirit in 2011, British theatremaker Chris Goode set up Chris Goode and Company and invited critic Maddy Costa to take a central role. He wanted someone who could document the company's work, communicate its story to audiences and take away some of the mystique of the creative process. Perhaps they could also be some kind of dramaturg. After much deliberation, the name they gave to this role was critic in residence. Being at one remove from the creative process allowed Costa a perspective that could help the artists. At a later stage, she could also act as the company's memory, reflecting on its work not in the moment – as is the way with the conventional review – but weeks, months or even years after the event.

The nature of these relationships are still being negotiated. Horwitz's critical horizontalism assumes people will join the discussion and, for that to happen, there must be something interesting going on in the rehearsal room and a critic who is able to write interestingly about it. If those conditions are met and if the theatremakers are willing, then the critic as insider can take on the role of critic as educator, enhancing the audience's appreciation of the theatrical event through their privileged insight into its creation. Critics operating in this way can be mediators between art and audience, not denying their own critical perspectives but not claiming them as definitive either. In that sense, they are the opposite of our next critic.

EXERCISE

Get in touch with a local producing theatre or touring company and ask if you could sit in on a rehearsal. Explain that it is for your critical training and in the interests of understanding how theatre gets made, so as to write more responsible and informed criticism. Some directors prefer not to have outsiders in the rehearsal room so may turn you down, but if they are willing, write an extended response to what you observe. Does it feel like writing a review or is it something different?

The critic as ego

William Kendrick was an eighteenth-century critic who, according to Charles Gray, had an 'utter indifference to the consequences of his remarks or to their truth, as long as he created a sensation'.[19] If this was true, Kendrick was the forefather of today's celebrity critics whose fame and facility with language counts for more than whatever they are writing about. If you care about theatre, it's easy to get annoyed by this. It trivializes the artform and it trivializes criticism. But it's also true to say that any act of criticism involves a degree of egotism. To write a review presupposes someone will be interested in what you have to say and your opinion is worth hearing. You have to be egotistical to want to make your voice heard, yet the more egotistical you are, the less justice you will do to the performance.

Our first question is a valuable corrective to this. When you take on board what the theatremakers are trying to do, you can't be entirely narcissistic. It's as you get deeper into the second and third questions that your own personality comes into play and questions of ego come to the fore. At this point, it may be more honest to say that reviews are as much about the writer as they are about the performance. The nineteenth-century French poet and novelist Anatole France wrote that 'the good critic is he who relates the adventures of his soul among masterpieces'.[20] In the same essay, he went on to write: 'The critic ought to say: "Gentlemen, I am going to talk about myself on the subject of Shakespeare, or Racine, or Pascal, or Goethe – subjects that offer me a beautiful opportunity." '

On the assumption that all critics will be egotistical to some extent, the question is how far down the road to self-involvement you allow yourself to go. The more the critic foregrounds their reactions, as opposed to their reasoning, the less likely the reader is to understand their criteria for judgement. For a gifted stylist such as Dorothy Parker, this can be part of their charm, but at the most extreme, the critic as egotist, sitting at the centre of their own universe, caring only for their gut response, is at best philistine and at worst damaging to the art of theatre. If a show puzzles them or makes them feel uncomfortable, they will declare it to be bad without any attempt to investigate whether that was the effect the theatremakers had intended. It will not cross their mind that they may have misinterpreted the work or that their own reaction may not be universal. None of us can escape our egos, but the more self-aware we are and the more rigorously we answer our first question, the better we should be at avoiding the charge of narcissism.

EXERCISE

Review the same show you wrote about in the guise as critic as reporter, but this time in egotistical style, talking about it only in terms of its relationship to you and your life. Aim for 300 words, but continue for as long as your ego allows. How different does this review feel to the first one?

The critic as visionary

Tynan said a good drama critic is 'one who perceives what is happening in the theatre of his time', while a great drama critic 'also perceives what is not happening'.[21] Edgar Allan Poe, a critic as well as the writer of horror stories, said something similar: 'A man who has never seen the sun cannot be blamed for thinking that no glory can exceed that of the moon. It is the business of the critic so to soar that he shall see the sun.'[22] In *The Empty Space*, Brook warned against the 'deadly critic'[23] who either did not love theatre or did not express that love with critical clarity. The opposite was the 'vital critic' who 'has clearly formulated for himself what the theatre could be – and who is bold enough to throw this formula into jeopardy each time he participates in a theatrical event'.

All are examples of the critic as visionary, a writer who does not merely react to the immediate piece of theatre under review, but who sees the possibilities beyond it. An example is Tynan's 1954 piece *West End Apathy*,[24] in which he railed against the lack of intelligent drama on the London stage of his day. There was no shortage of playwrights, he said, the problem was 'they are all writing the same play'. What he wanted were stories about 'cabmen and demi-gods . . . warriors, politicians and grocers'. This was a critic identifying the space which, two years later, John Osborne would fill in *Look Back in Anger*, a play about 'post-war youth as it really is', unromantic, spiky and drawn from a social class common everywhere but the stage. Unsurprisingly, Tynan embraced it with a passion; it was almost as if he had willed it into life.

As with all things, you must be careful what you wish for. Reviewing the Sydney Ensemble Theatre in John Herbert's *Fortune and Men's Eyes*, Katharine Brisbane said she felt 'hoist by her own petard'.[25] It was, she said, 'the kind of committed drama I keep demanding to put some virility back into the theatre – yet I can't say I like it'.

So much for your approach as a critic; let's put a little more thought into who your readers are and why they may be reading you. In the next chapter we'll consider everyone from the keen theatregoer to the accidental browser and ask how their various levels of interest will affect the way you write.

EXERCISE

Before going to your next show, think of something you believe is lacking in contemporary theatre. It could be genuine or made up for the purpose of this exercise. Write a 500-word review that considers the show in relation to that lack, using it as a jumping off point to make a broader point about your theatrical vision. What do you think the theatremakers would think if they saw this review?

Notes

1 Tynan, Kenneth (1975), *A View of the English Stage*, Davis-Poynter.

2 Ibid.

3 Carroll, Nöel (2009), *On Criticism*, Routledge.

4 Agate, James (1922), 'The Decay of Criticism', in *Alarums and Excursions*, George H. Doran Company.

5 Goldsmith, Oliver (1757), '*Douglas: A Tragedy*', in *The Monthly Review*, Vol. 16.

6 Benedictus, Leo (10 November 2011), 'What to say about . . . *Hamlet* with Michael Sheen', in *The Guardian*.

7 Cardullo, Bert (1 October 2004), 'The Once and Future Theater Critic: An Interview with Stanley Kauffmann', in *Midwest Quarterly*.

8 Brisbane, Katharine (2005), *Not Wrong Just Different: Observations on the Rise of Contemporary Australian Theatre*, Currency.

9 Jones, Chris (10 March 2014), '*Gospel* preaches from the heart about Chicago gun violence', in the *Chicago Tribune*.

10 Billington, Michael (2007), *State of the Nation: British Theatre Since 1945*, Faber and Faber.

11 Rosenfield, Wendy (19 February 2014), 'The role of the theater critic – Diversity onstage: a critical issue', in the *Broad Street Review*.

12 Lahr, John (1996), *Light Fantastic: Adventures in Theatre*, Bloomsbury.

13 London, Todd (2013), *The Importance of Staying Earnest*, NoPassport Press.

14 Brook, Peter (1968), *The Empty Space*, McGibbon & Kee.

15 Marowitz, Charles (1986), *Prospero's Staff*, Marion Boyars.

16 Haydon, Andrew (16 April 2012), 'Embedded', on Postcards from the Gods (http://postcardsgods.blogspot.co.uk/2012/04/embedded.html).

17 Horwitz, Andy (31 March 2012), 'Culturebot and the new criticism', on Culturebot (http://www.culturebot.org/2012/03/12883/culturebot-and-the-new-criticism).

18 Ibid.

19 Gray, Charles Harold (1931), *Theatrical Criticism in London to 1795*, Columbia University Press.

20 Lewisohn, Ludwig (1919), 'The Adventures of the Soul', in *A Modern Book of Criticism*, Boni & Liveright.

21 Tynan, Kenneth (1967), *Right and Left*, Longman.

22 Meister, Charles W. (1985), *Dramatic Criticism: A History*, McFarland & Co.

23 Brook, Peter (1968), *The Empty Space*, McGibbon & Kee.

24 Tynan, Kenneth (31 October 1954), 'West End Apathy', *The Observer*.

25 Brisbane, Katharine (2005), *Not Wrong Just Different: Observations on the Rise of Contemporary Australian Theatre*, Currency.

4
HOW TO WRITE FOR YOUR READERS

Consumers or connoisseurs?

If you're the kind of person who reads only one-star and five-star reviews, you are not alone. Many people do the same. The reason for reading a five-star review is easy to guess: we want to find out about something exceptional and, quite possibly, we'd like to experience it for ourselves. But why would anyone read a one-star review? The answer is much the same: we want to find out about something exceptional, only in this case, it would be exceptionally bad. We would hope to draw pleasure from the critic's barbed comments and perhaps take delight in the failure of others, what the Germans call *Schadenfreude*. Straight away, this tells us something about the readers of theatre reviews and that is, unlike the readers of hotel reviews on Trip Advisor, they are not necessarily looking for consumer advice. If that was all they wanted, how would we explain the publication of review anthologies, ranging from *Our Theatre in the Nineties*, the three volumes of criticism by George Bernard Shaw published in 1932, to *Field of Dreams*, the collected reviews of the *Scotsman*'s Joyce McMillan published in 2015? Any reader turning to those books to find out what to see tonight would be quickly frustrated. There must be other reasons for reading. Let's run though some of the possibilities, bearing in mind that the way you write your reviews will be influenced by what your readers are looking for.

The would-be audience member

If your review appears before the end of a run, and especially if you are writing for an events guide, a local newspaper or a what's-on style website, then it is reasonable to assume some of your readers will want your help in deciding what to see. What information do they need to make that decision? It's tempting to imagine the five stars you put at the top of your rave review would be reason enough to convince someone to go, but that isn't the case. Many well reviewed shows have performed poorly at the box office, just as many badly reviewed shows have done well. That's partly because audiences are influenced by many other factors, such as advertising, ticket price and, crucially, word of mouth, but it's also because they need something more than just a thumbs up or a thumbs down from the critics. Think how many times you've read a review imploring you to 'go see it', 'don't miss' or 'rush out and buy it today', and how infrequently you have acted on that advice (the instruction to 'avoid like the plague' is easier to follow). Only with a very trusted reviewer would enthusiasm alone be enough to drive you straight to the box office.

Otherwise, readers need facts. They need the name of the show, where and when it's on, an indication of genre and an impression of what it's about. This should be obvious, but in their haste to talk about their reaction, critics sometimes omit to say what they are reacting to. The reader may delight in the verbal fireworks but be none the wiser about the event. On this factual level, your review is performing a similar function to a press release. It is why you should take the same care over accuracy as you would with any news story. Unless you double-check places, dates, facts and spellings, you will be doing your readers a disservice. Likewise, the more vividly you can describe what the experience is like, the better you will enable the reader to decide whether to have the same experience themselves.

The difficulty for the critic is the impossibility of knowing what will attract or repulse any given reader. Publications make assumptions about their readers – the girl who reads *Cosmopolitan*, the young trend-setter who reads fanzines, the mainstream home owner who reads a mass-circulation tabloid – but these are at best generalizations and at worst wishful thinking by the advertising department. To base a recommendation of a production on the basis not of what you think but of what an imagined reader might think can only be guess work and will inevitably lead to misjudgements. Publications avoid this by employing critics whose worldview most closely matches that of the perceived readership. Such critics develop a relationship with their readers who will base their ticket-buying decisions on a broader understanding of the critic's tastes, prejudices and enthusiasms. It leaves the critic free to follow their own instincts without having to speak for anyone else.

The audience that has already seen it

Many theatres display their favourable reviews in the foyer. After a show, you'll see the audience reading them. Clearly these readers need none of the factual information we talked about above. They know where the show took place, who created it and what it was like. They also know what they thought of it or, at least, what they think they thought of it – straight after a show, opinions have not always settled. Yet something compels them to read reviews that offer them information and opinion, two things they already have. Why should this be?

The phenomenon lends support to the idea that a review is the start of a conversation. The critic says, 'This is what I found, this is how I interpreted it, this is what I thought . . . What did you think?' In this sense, a review is a more considered equivalent of the chat you have in the bar with your friends at the end of the night. At its best, it may provide elucidation, bringing clarification to aspects that may have been obscure or hard to fathom, and contextualization, framing the work in terms of its social, historical and artistic place. With a clearly reasoned argument, the critic may also make the reader think differently about a work or, if they disagree, challenge them to justify their own reasoning.

When critics say that giving opinions is the least interesting aspect of their job, what they mean, I think, is all these other aspects are more interesting. Writing for the would-be audience member and giving a thumbs up/thumbs down recommendation is a mundane task compared with initiating a discussion with those who have already seen it. What these readers want varies from confirmation to provocation, a kindred spirit or an alternative voice. They want to extend their experience, think more deeply about it, give words to nebulous feelings or enjoy the pleasure of a moment shared.

The culturally aware

Whether you write for a newspaper that covers the whole of a country or on the internet, which is accessible to the whole world, there is every chance people will read one of your reviews with neither the intention nor the capability of seeing the show. Perhaps they live too far away or perhaps they have other things to do. Perhaps they don't particularly like going to the theatre. Such readers are not interested in being persuaded to see or avoid the performance and do not have an experience to compare with yours, but they do like to keep up with what's going on. Some of them will have a professional interest, others like to be able to hold their own at dinner-party conversations, others still simply have a curiosity about contemporary culture. For these readers, the critic is a cultural reporter. More than most, they will rely on the critic's ability to describe what the event was like so they may experience it at one remove. Additionally, they will want to know what distinguishes this theatrical event in this particular time and place from any other.

The reader of the future

Like the culturally aware reader, the reader of the future will never experience the things you write about for themselves. Because they live in the future, we have even less certainty about their reasons for reading. We do know, though, that theatre is an ephemeral art and frequently the only trace it leaves behind is what has been written about it. To have any sense of what it was like to see Edmund Kean as Richard III, Henry Irving as Macbeth or Mrs Patrick Campbell as Juliet, we must turn to William Hazlitt, Clement Scott and George Bernard Shaw. James Agate called critics 'monumental masons whose works are headstones'[1] – without them, he implied, actors would lie in the equivalent of an unmarked grave. The advent of film and video has added an extra layer of evidence, but it takes the critics to tell us what a performance felt like and what it meant.

This is an important part of understanding our past. Academics, journalists and researchers routinely delve into the written evidence left by critics. As well as discovering what theatre was like, we can learn much about social attitudes and cultural values. Whether it is Scott Palmer considering the history of lighting design in *Light*[2] or Nicholas de Jongh looking back at theatre censorship in the twentieth century in *Politics, Prudery and Perversions: The Censoring of the English Stage, 1901–1968,*[3] old theatre reviews provide both documentary evidence and the ammunition for debate.

You can see why John Simon ('You write both for the present and for posterity, if it will have you'[4]) and Kenneth Tynan ('the impulse to be an eyewitness for posterity'[5]) claimed to write with the future in mind. On a practical level, however, this raises a problem, because how can you know what the future wants? The critics quoted by Palmer and De Jongh could not have known their reviews would prove useful in the study of lighting design and censorship – and if they had, they would have written them differently. The critic can aim to give as full an account of an event as possible, something the future reader is likely to appreciate, but they can only be true to their own time. The idea of writing for posterity, aside from being a grandiose ambition, is surely not as practical as writing for the readers you know you have today.

The artist

Those of us who have been brought up in the tradition of newspaper reviewing are used to saying we do not write for theatremakers. Our potential readership is drawn from the thousands of people who buy the newspaper or the millions who could stumble across the review online. If those people are not informed and entertained by what we write, we are not doing our job. What the artists think is none of our concern.

There is a big advantage in this approach: when you write for the everyday reader, you give your honest opinion without fear of hurting anyone's feelings or the temptation to flatter. But there is also a contradiction. As we've seen, it's impossible to know exactly who your readers are. Far more certain is the one group of people you are supposedly not writing for: the theatremakers. At the very least, there will be a publicist ready to filter your review for attractive quotes and a social-media manager ready to tweet about it. Many actors say they don't read their reviews during a run (or perhaps ever), but it's hard to imagine the same level of restraint from the playwright, the director, the artistic director and the rest of the production team, let alone friends and family who will surely let slip what the critics have been saying.

It means that however determined you are to write for the general newspaper reader, you have to make a special effort not to imagine a glowing review being pinned up backstage or a pan turning your name to mud in the green room. If you are truly not writing for the theatremakers – and there's a strong case to say you shouldn't – it takes guts to be honest.

The alternative is to accept that the artists are among your potential readership. In Europe, this is not unusual. Here, there is a strong tradition of critics addressing their thoughts primarily to directors, actors and designers, and secondly to audiences. In English-speaking countries, there is little equivalent of this, but as the old hierarchies break down and the democratizing influence of the internet takes hold, the idea of the critic as a kind of freelance dramaturg talking to the company is gaining currency. In 2014, Glasgow critic Gareth K. Vile wrestled with the question directly in an audio review of Philip Ridley's *The Pitchfork Disney*, the debut production of Heroes Theatre. In a piece called *Vile Three Way,*[6] he provided three reviews in succession, the first aimed at the company, the second at potential audiences and the third 'at posterity'. Addressing the company, he took on the guise of a benign workshop leader pinpointing what he felt were the strengths and weaknesses. 'These are all exciting questions that I hope that you are going to be answering in the next few years', he said in a spirit of creative collaboration. Moving on to the audience, he was concerned with what the experience was like and why he thought people should see it. Then addressing posterity, he put the production into the context of recent Scottish and English theatre and the traditions of language-based and physical performance.

In an article for the Theatre Bristol website, critic and performer Christopher X. Atack said the experience of writing about other people's work had made him a better artist – had, in fact, made him want to become a theatremaker himself. Perhaps his background made him more than typically sympathetic towards critics, but he made the case that criticism is an invaluable part of an artist's 'conversation' with their audiences: 'If people don't feel the desire to interrogate your work, negatively, positively, whatever – it's dead to the world.'[7]

So who exactly are you writing for?

These broad categories identify just some of the people who may be reading what you write. The list is far from definitive. Even if you narrow down the likely readers, you can never say for sure what will draw someone's attention. That's what Michael Billington discovered in 2014 after writing about a London revival of *Do I Hear a Waltz?* by Stephen Sondheim and Richard Rodgers. There was nothing out of the ordinary about his three-star review (he gave it modest praise for exuding a 'a pleasant, watery charm'[8]), so *The Guardian* critic was surprised to find the online stats rocketing. The reason turned out to be a comment by reader Oliver Beatson who entered into a conversation with someone known only as 100Objects about whether it had been worth staying for the second half. Beatson enquired whether 100Objects, who had left at the interval, had been with a young man 'with whom I shared a few brief looks, and regrettably no words'. It prompted Billington to tweet: 'Never realised before that a review could trigger a dating proposal.' More than 360 readers recommended Beatson's comment and over 1,000 shared the review on Facebook.

Billington may have supposed his readers would be in any of the categories listed above, but he could not have anticipated the readers who were sucked into that social-media hurricane. Yet still, if he was doing his job as a journalist, he had to write in a way that would be comprehensible to them. It illustrates what a complex job the critic is doing. In most cases, their reviews have to satisfy a mind-bogglingly broad range of readers. If you emailed a close friend about a play you'd seen, you could make all sorts of allowances for them. You'd know if they were familiar with the theatre and the theatremakers, you'd know what their tastes and interests were and you'd know if they were planning to see it, had already seen it or had no intention of seeing it. As soon as you step into the public domain, you can make no such allowances. You can't even be sure they're not reading just to pass the time. As a consequence, unless you are writing for a publication with a precisely defined readership, you have to negotiate a path that suits everyone: neither too basic for the expert nor too erudite for the newcomer; neither too revealing for the would-be audience member nor too circumspect for the reader who'll never see it; neither too philosophical for the ordinary theatregoer nor too mundane for the cultural theorist. In the next chapter, we'll consider how you can prepare yourself to be ready for any eventuality.

EXERCISE

Follow the example of critic Gareth K. Vile and write three 200-word reviews of the same show: one aimed at the company, one at potential audiences and one 'at posterity'. Observe how your perspective changes.

Notes

1   Agate, James (1922), *Alarums and Excursions*, George H. Doran Company.

2   Palmer, Scott (2013), *Light*, Palgrave Macmillan.

3   De Jongh, Nicholas (2000), *Politics, Prudery and Perversions: The Censoring of the English Stage, 1901–1968*, Methuen.

4   Napoleon, Davi (Spring 1997), 'John Simon, The Art of Criticism No. 4', in *The Paris Review*, No. 142.

5   Novick, Julius (21 April 1959), 'Eyewitness for Posterity', in *The Harvard Crimson*.

6   Vile, Gareth K. (April 2014), 'Vile Three Way: *The Pitchfork Disney*', on Mixcloud (www.mixcloud.com/garethkvile/vile-three-way-the-pitchfork-disney).

7   Atack, Christopher X. (2014), 'Bad news everyone', on Theatre Bristol (http://theatrebristolwriters.net/BAD-NEWS-EVERYONE).

8   Billington, Michael (7 March 2014), 'Do I Hear a Waltz?', in *The Guardian*.

5
HOW TO DO YOUR RESEARCH

A qualified opinion

In any discussion about what distinguishes professional critics from casual bloggers, someone always points to the bank of knowledge the professionals have accumulated. J.C. Trewin's *Five and Eighty Hamlets*[1] referred to the number of productions of Shakespeare's play he had seen in the sixty years since 1922. Trewin was not alone. *The Daily Mail*'s Michael Coveney calculated the 2009 *Hamlet* starring Jude Law was his forty-ninth. You turn to such critics expecting experience and expertise. Their long years in the job seeing five shows a week has given them a wisdom that allows them to contextualize the work with greater accuracy, to discriminate between the excellent and the merely good, and to keep their cool when others have been carried away by the excitement of the moment.

Although there's a general truth in this, the argument is not watertight. Even if we leave aside the increasing probability of an independent blogger having just as much experience as a professional, the logic of the argument goes only so far. There is no evidence that those with the longest experience are automatically the best critics, nor could you argue that those with the least experience have nothing to offer. Could you say with any confidence that a critic's eighty-fifth review of *Hamlet* would always be more interesting than their first? Or that the first review by a future Clurman, Shaw or Tynan would have no merit? All critics have to start somewhere.

My point is not to diminish the value of expertise. Everyone has a right to an opinion, but that doesn't mean every opinion carries equal weight. The philistine who bluntly asserts, 'I know nothing about art, but I know what I like', would be unlikely to provide us with insight or elucidation. The democratic mood of our times and the self-publishing spirit of the internet have made us suspicious of elitism, but we can't disguise the fact that some people just know more about certain subjects than others. These people may be our democratic equal, but that doesn't mean we can't learn from their deeper understanding. Any passer-by in the street may have an opinion about your hair, but when you get it cut, you'd expect the stylist to be trained. Likewise with a theatre review, you want a critic who's put a bit of thought into the matter.

The complication with theatre criticism is it's generally a self-appointed job, at least in English-speaking countries. University courses in the discipline are a relatively recent innovation and, as far as I know, no newspaper or website would insist on an academic qualification. I happen to have a degree in drama, a great grounding for the job, but no editor has ever asked me about it. Nor have they queried my lack of journalistic qualifications. In my experience, this is typical. Critics come from all kinds of educational backgrounds and are united only in their passion for theatre. That means there's a blur between hobbyist and expert, and an uncertainty about where opinion ends and expertise begins. When you ask a doctor for an opinion, you assume they have pretty good grounds for their answer. With a critic, it may just be an opinion.

Harold Clurman produced a twelve-point list of 'the complete critic's qualifications'[2] and you may find it makes intimidating reading. His list of requirements included knowledge of 'the greater part of classic and contemporary drama as written and played' and of 'the history of the theatre from its origins to the present'. He also said the critic should have 'long and broad playgoing experience – of native and foreign productions' and he recommended working in the theatre in some capacity. That's in addition to having a deep knowledge of the culture as a whole. Clurman ticked the boxes: he studied in France, helped set up the Group Theatre in New York and worked as a director as a well as a critic. How many other critics could claim to have the same kind of practical and intellectual breadth?

For the journalist critic, there is a competing pressure. As we have seen, the critic is often expected to be an educated expert, someone like Clurman with a deep understanding of the history of the artform, the careers of the artists and the technicalities of the staging, as well as with an illuminating perspective on the production's wider cultural context. Running parallel to this is the contrary expectation that the critic should be speaking up for the ordinary theatregoer. This critic is the voice in the stalls letting people know whether a show is worth the ticket price – what we called the critic as consumer guide. It's surely not possible to fulfil both of these expectations at the same time, but you may feel that's what's being demanded of you. All you can do is strike a balance somewhere between the two. If that's the case, what level of expertise should you aim for and how can you learn more?

How much research is too much?

Let's think about the amount of research you could put into a single show. Imagine *War Horse* was touring to your town. Staged by the National Theatre of Great Britain, the play is about a horse taken away by the army to help on the battlefields of France during the First World War. If you were diligent, you could read Michael Morpurgo's original novel and, perhaps, his *Private Peaceful*, also set during that conflict. For extra background knowledge, you could study a few history books on the war – at least a dozen were published in the centenary year of 2014 and there are several more solely on the subject of animals during wartime. To ensure you had the same field of reference as your readers, you would watch Steven Spielberg's movie adaptation of the story. Your research into the production could include a study of Handspring Puppet Company, which has a history in Cape Town dating back to 1981, as well as of co-directors Marianne Elliott and Tom Morris (a sometime critic). It'd be useful to have a knowledge of other productions that had combined actors, puppets and live music, as well as an awareness of plays such as *Oh! What a Lovely War, Journey's End* and *Observe the Sons of Ulster Marching Towards the Somme* that have dramatized the conflict. You could request a copy of the script and, like an embedded critic, you could sit in on rehearsals and interview the creative team. Any of this research could give you fascinating insights and would equip you to do the job of critic as educator.

On the other hand, there is the risk of becoming disconnected from the experience of the regular theatregoer. If you were not careful, the trade-off for all this knowledge could be your failure to be surprised, to be drawn into the production's imaginative world and to be open to the spontaneity of the live event. If – and I stress 'if' – it meant you ended up as all head and no heart, would you be in a position to react in an emotional way?

Research checklist

The conscientious critic will have knowledge of:

- the previous work of the creative team
- the history of the producing company and of the presenting theatre
- the science, history, philosophy, aesthetics and politics that underpin the show
- (for new work) the inspiration behind the show, as well as other work that has tackled a similar theme
- (for classics) the script, the production history and any academic commentary
- (for adaptations) the source material and other adaptations

It would be nice to be able to give a definitive answer to this conundrum, but I don't believe there is one. A large part of the audience who go to see *The Lion King, Billy Elliot: The Musical* and *The Full Monty* on stage will be there because they loved the movies. The same is true of adaptations of classic novels. If the critic went into any one of those shows being unfamiliar with the source material, they would be incapable of answering many of the questions that their readers would be asking. How does it differ from the original? What were the solutions to the inevitable problems of adaptation? What is lost? What is gained? To be able to answer these questions, you have to do your homework, but you have to do it with care. If you read the book or see the movie too close to seeing the adaptation, you can find the source material eclipsing the reinterpretation. The impression of the original can remain so vivid that you can't see the production in its own terms. For both you and the reader, it can be hard to tell whether you are reviewing the original or the adaptation. The best way round this is to do your research as far in advance as possible to allow yourself time to get a level-headed perspective on the background material as well as on the show itself. If you see the film in January with a view to reviewing the adaption in March, you'll know the territory but won't be so overwhelmed by the original that you can't keep the two things apart in your mind.

Clearly, that's not always practical and, for a critic at any stage in their career, there will always be times when their knowledge is not as broad as they would like. It may be preferable to have the knowledge, but when you find yourself at a loss, it is better to declare what you do know instead of bluffing about what you don't. These days, it's usually possible for the critic to catch-up with DVD box sets, YouTube videos and plays in print, but nobody can know everything and there will be times when you get caught out. Seattle critic Brendan Kiley wrote a mea culpa on The Stranger with the title 'If I Read More Plays, I'd Be a Better Critic (Or, I Regret Not Doing My Homework)'. He'd realized eighteen months too late that the Satori Group's *Fabulous Prizes* by Neil Ferron was 'clearly a response' to Enda Walsh's *The Walworth Farce*. Only when he saw Walsh's earlier play did he realize the similarities:

I remain enthusiastic about Satori Group (who are devoted to bringing original works into the world) and Neil Ferron (who's lately taken to directing music videos), and I expect to see more good stuff from both of them. But if I had done better homework as a critic, and had some working knowledge of *The Walworth Farce* a year and a half ago, I would've watched *Fabulous Prizes* with slightly different eyes.[3]

Not only would he have watched with slightly different eyes, he would have given his readers a richer insight into what Kiley was doing. It was, however, an understandable gap in his knowledge. Although Walsh's play had had successful runs on both sides of the Atlantic, it was not so well known that you could have expected every critic to be familiar with it. Unless the company had marketed *Fabulous Prizes* as a response to *The Walworth Farce*, there must have been many critics and audience members in the same position as the critic. But even though Kiley seemed unduly harsh on himself ('it's always uncomfortable to be publicly slapped in the face with your own ignorance'), we should applaud his willingness to learn. Given that people value expertise so highly, every critic should make it a lifelong ambition to increase their knowledge – of theatre, of society, of politics, of technology, of history, of everything. Being a theatre critic is one of those rare jobs that is a continual education.

How to learn more

So assuming we think research is a good thing, is there a right and wrong way of going about it? Michael Bogdanov would say there was. In 1996, the director took issue with the critics in an article in the *New Statesman*.[4] He had staged a production of Goethe's *Faust* for the RSC in Stratford and was convinced the critics, faced by a relatively unfamiliar play, had turned en masse to the Penguin *Introduction* for 'common literary warmth'. He totted up the number of times identical phrases had cropped up in their reviews and found seven instances of 'redemption and optimism', six of 'majestic awe', five of 'soaring poetry' and fourteen of 'awe' on its own. He believed that in Germany, any critic would have known Goethe wrote much of the play in *Knittelvers* or doggerel (i.e. not soaring poetry) and, in modern times, none would have thought optimism an appropriate word to use about a play in which the protagonist's megalomania had uncomfortable parallels with 'Germany's imperialist ambitions of the past 100 years'. His implication was that the UK critics had done only the shallowest of research and had almost universally come away with misleading ideas. To engage properly in the production, he wrote, they should have read the play, preferably in the original. In the absence of that, he found no analysis of textual choices nor any consideration of how he had gone about staging a play regarded as unstagable. His complaint, in other words, was not to do with whether or not the critics had liked the show, it was that they hadn't fully answered our first question: what were the theatremakers trying to do?

If Bogdanov's complaint was valid, then maybe it's time to send the critics back to college. What would they learn there? If you didn't know anything about the courses in dramaturgy and dramatic criticism at the Yale University School of Drama, you might imagine a group of students furiously turning out theatre reviews all day long. Take a look at the course outline,[5] however, and you get a different picture. Yes, as you'd expect, there are the criticism workshops which students must take in each of their six terms, but they are far from being the only element in the three-year programme. 'The aim is to impart a comprehensive knowledge of theater and dramatic literature — a knowledge necessary to the dramaturg, the writer and editor, and the teacher', runs the brief. Consequently, the would-be critics take classes in subjects such as translation, adaptation, dramatic structure and issues in twenty-first-century performance. 'Topics for written examinations, theater history case studies, and dramaturgical casebooks must . . . reflect breadth of study across time periods, genres, movements, etc', says the course website, going on to suggest that areas of study may include:

major historical periods such as Greek, Jacobean, French seventeenth century, modern, contemporary; important dramatists or other figures such as Aristotle, Artaud, Euripides, Shakespeare; basic dramatic genres such as tragedy, comedy, melodrama; significant theoretically or critically defined movements such as romanticism or symbolism.

That's a lot of knowledge and it's a particular challenge to the theatre critic to take it all in, starting with 3,000 years' worth of drama – not just plays, but dramatic movements and performance styles. It's a history you have to work at to learn about; unlike some artforms, you don't come across it while casually flicking through the radio and television channels. There's no theatrical equivalent of Spotify that you can have playing in the background while you get on with other things. Because it's not in the air, you have to go out and discover it and seeing lots of theatre is crucial to widening your vision. It's important that you do so because part of a production's context is all the plays that have ever gone on before. If theatremakers are building on this tradition, the critic needs to be writing about it too. Reading books about directing, acting, playwriting, storytelling, lighting and design will further add to your understanding.

Theatre touches on all aspects of society and all fields of knowledge. A critic needs to know not just about theatrical genres and movements but about politics, philosophy, sociology, science, literature . . . 'What's the best book to read to learn how to be a film critic?' asked the film critic and filmmaker Mark Cousins on Facebook. His answer was surprising: 'Roger Fry on Paul Cezanne.'[6] By choosing the work of an art critic writing about a painter, Cousins was acknowledging both that film is a visual medium and that no artform exists in isolation. Film, like theatre, is a reflection of the world around us and the critic needs to know about that world. A theatre critic with a grounding in visual art would bring an extra layer of interpretative skill to the job, but they'd also have a richer field of reference for knowing not just about Chekhov, but also about Chaplin, Chagall, Chomsky, Chandler and

Chumbawamba. Acquiring such knowledge can't happen over night. It is a lifetime's work and the best the critic can do is to remain open, inquisitive and receptive.

What about Clurman's suggestion that critics should have experience working in the theatre? Writing in *American Theatre*, critic Tony Brown reflected on his experience taking a year-long sabbatical during which he spent several months as a dramaturg for Chicago's Lookingglass Theatre. He called it a 'fascinating experience',[7] but discovered not every critic was comfortable about being on the other side of the footlights. He interviewed Ben Brantley who told him he preferred to have as little to do with theatre people as possible. The *New York Times* critic made a habit of seeing a show and heading straight back home, keeping himself to himself and turning down any request to discuss theatre-related issues. Brantley said it was a policy that ensured he could never be called a 'compromised man'.

Brown contrasted that attitude with that of *New Yorker* critic John Lahr, who made no secret of staying the night with producer friends when he was away from home. 'Anyone who is not practiced in the art of the theatre has no qualifications to write about it',[8] he said. For himself, Brown said he operated somewhere between the two positions, 'a middle path between absolute objectivity and absolute immersion'. Both extremes have their pros and cons. If objectivity is even possible, it would free critics of partisanship, which is admirable, but deny them an insider's insight, which could be a weakness. Immersion, by contrast, may be good for describing the mechanics of what's going on, but flawed when it comes to providing a cool-headed perspective.

Even the most reclusive of critics would agree that a basic understanding of how a production is put together aids the job of interpretation. A theatre critic with a grasp of how acting, lighting, set, sound, dramaturgy and all the other contributing skills are executed is likely to have more to offer than the outsider who naively responds to the effects with no comprehension about how those effects were achieved. There's no requirement for the critic to be especially skilled in any theatre craft (a music critic doesn't need to play the violin to recognize a virtuoso performance), but it can be an advantage to understand the principles behind those crafts. Brown said his stint as a dramaturg didn't affect how positive or negative his reviews were, but he did think it had given him a 'better aim and more discrimination in selecting targets'.

In 1989, Michael Billington was invited by the RSC to direct a group of actors at London's Barbican. He chose *The Will*, a one-act comedy by Pierre de Marivaux, and gamely went into rehearsals. Among the things he said he learned were that directing was a process of 'constant adjustment', that rehearsals were fun and that the director's job was not to impose emotions but to help the actors discover them. As for how it would change him as a critic, he said: 'I shall resume my aisle-squatting a bit more aware of the collaborative process of theatre; aware that things we, as critics, so confidently ascribe to the director, are often the result of the spontaneous combustion of rehearsal.'[9] Like spending time as an embedded critic, getting hands-on experience in this way can make you 'a bit more aware', a little more sensitive to the way choices are made and executed, and a touch more alert to the various skills at play. In the next chapter, we'll consider how to keep people reading not by what you say but in the way you say it.

EXERCISE

Read three reviews that have been published about the same production. Identify the phrases in each that tell you more than you could learn simply by watching the show. This could include anything from the name of the playwright to the critic's mental associations. How much has the critic researched, how much is comment and how much is cross-referenced to other things? What did you learn for each of the reviews?

Notes

1   Trewin, J.C. (1987), *Five & Eighty Hamlets*, Hutchinson.

2   Clurman, Harold (1994), *The Collected Works of Harold Clurman*, Applause.

3   Kiley, Brendan (1 January 2014), 'If I Read More Plays, I'd Be a Better Critic', on The Stranger (www.thestranger.com/seattle/if-i-read-more-plays-id-be-a-better-critic/Content?oid=18548985).

4   Bogdanov, Michael (15 November 1996), 'Vicious, excretory, arse-licking, arrogant. We are talking about critics, who else?', in the *New Statesman*.

5   Yale University School of Drama (2013–2014), Dramaturgy And Dramatic Criticism (MFA And DFA).

6   Fry, Roger (1927), *Cezanne: A Study in His Development*, Macmillan.

7   Brown, Tony (September 2001), 'A critic under the influence', in *American Theatre*.

8   Ibid.

9   Billington, Michael (1993), *One Night Stands*, Nick Hern Books.

6
HOW TO FIND YOUR VOICE

Stepping out in public

Every critic is a performer. Just as an actor has to hold an audience, keep them gripped, leave them waiting for more, so the critic has to draw in the reader, interest them and engage them. Because your focus as a theatre critic is on the entertainment provided by others, you may not realize that you too are expected to entertain. But that's what's happening. It doesn't matter if you have the most brilliant insight, the most fascinating analysis, the most revolutionary contribution to make to the art of theatre, it will count for nothing if you can't keep them reading. 'It is axiomatic to say that the best critics are also the best writers',[1] wrote John W. English in *Criticizing the Critics*. 'Conversely, excellent critics are never bad writers.'

When we considered all the reasons someone may choose to read a review, one of them was simply to pass the time. Imagine a passenger on a train with an hour before their stop and nothing but a newspaper to occupy them. They turn to the arts page and come across your review. They are many miles from the theatre, they have no intention of seeing the performance – perhaps they're not even a theatregoer – but they are willing to be diverted for as long as you can keep them amused. They will alight upon your review just for something to read.

There are examples where virtually the sole intention of a review is to fulfil this function. Under the heading 'Winner's Dinners', the late Michael Winner was capable of writing an 800-word restaurant review in *The Sunday Times* in which he dedicated just a paragraph or two to the meal. More than 500 words into one piece about London's up-market Nobu, he interrupted himself: 'I bet by now you're saying, "This is meant to be a food column, Michael. Did you eat? If so, are you going to tell us about it?" Oh well, if you insist.'[2] Even then, his description of what he ate could not have been called analytical: 'All the food was good', he wrote. This was not a dereliction of duty. Far from it. Winner knew the vast majority of his readers would never venture near the restaurant concerned. He also knew they loved to be entertained by his gossipy, anecdotal prose. He'd write about the guest he was dining with, the actors he'd worked with and the latest jokes he'd been told. For those who liked him, reading a Winner article was an end in itself.

At this extreme of the spectrum, the thing being reviewed is of secondary importance; it's an excuse for the writer to exercise their journalistic gifts as an entertainer. It's like Alfred Hitchcock's MacGuffin: a plot motivation that justifies the action but is not in itself of any particular interest (you don't need to know what the baddies have stolen as long as you understand the good guys have to get it back).[3] British journalists such as Julie Burchill, writing about pop culture, A.A. Gill, writing about television, and Jeremy Clarkson, writing about cars, take a similar approach. The pop culture, television and cars act as a jumping-off point for whatever else is on their minds. They are very present in their writing.

Previously, we lumped such writers under the heading 'critic as ego' and suggested their contribution may not be in the best interests of either the theatre profession or the craft of criticism. But there is a trade-off. On the one hand, it is true that a lot of the most entertaining writing tells you more about the reviewer than the show. The work of art becomes the equivalent of the fall guy in a comedy double act; it is the butt of the joke, something that exists not on its own terms but as a way of making the writer look clever or funny. If you make yourself the main subject, you'll find it harder to answer our first question, 'What were the theatremakers trying to do?' Your ego will be too preoccupied with itself to be bothered about anyone else's motivations. On the other hand, the reason many of these journalists command the highest salaries is that, as technicians, they know how to entertain their readers. That is not a skill to be taken lightly. 'I have always held that the lighter, the frothier, the more amusing you make your reviews, the more you will be read and the more the theatre will gain',[4] said Alan Dale in the 1920s. 'If there is room for [humour] in *Hamlet*', asked George Jean Nathan, 'why shouldn't there be a place for it in criticism of *Hamlet*?'[5] Those two were writing in the era of the Algonquin Round Table, the New York lunch club attended by playwrights, actors, journalists and wits including theatre critics Dorothy Parker and Alexander Woollcott. As Kevin C. Fitzpatrick pointed out in his introduction to *Dorothy Parker: Complete Broadway 1918–1923*,[6] the internet has turned Parker into a 'gin-soaked quote machine' – and a frequently inaccurate one at that – but to read her reviews for *Vanity Fair* and *Ainslee's* is to appreciate her flair for breezily entertaining writing; a reflection, as often as not, of the breezily entertaining shows she had been watching.

Famed for his acerbic reviews, the larger-than-life Woollcott, who was the model for Sheridan Whiteside in *The Man who Came to Dinner*, was master of the entertaining put-down. 'Mrs Patrick Campbell is an aged British battleship sinking rapidly and firing every available gun on her rescuers',[7] he wrote towards the end of the actor's career. He began one review: '*Number 7* opened last night at the Times Square Theatre. It was misnamed by five.' Done well, such writing can go on to outlive the play that inspired it. Reading it can be an end in itself. A few decades later, this is how Bernard Levin began his *Daily Express* review of *Out of This World* by Giuseppe Marotti:

Strictly speaking, I cannot swear that being kicked in the stomach by a horse would be an experience preferable to seeing this play . . . because I have never been kicked in the stomach by a horse.

But I have seen this play, and I can certainly say that if a kick in the stomach by a horse would be worse, I do not wish to be kicked in the stomach by a horse.

And I can certainly add that, unpleasant though the prospect of being kicked in the stomach by a horse may be, I would certainly rather be kicked in the stomach by a horse than see the play again.[8]

EXERCISE

Write a 400-word review that uses the production as an excuse to amuse your readers. Putting yourself at the centre, feel free to say as much or as little about the show as you like. Perhaps you'll focus on a journey to the theatre, a minor detail in the plot, someone in the audience or a secondary character on stage – anything to entertain. How comfortable are you writing in this voice?

Making your point

In theory, Levin could have used that introduction to any play he strongly disliked; you had to read past the funny bit to find out what the show was like. But it would be wrong to assume that entertaining writing was incompatible with serious criticism. The job is to write well, think clearly and entertain. The reason Kenneth Tynan remains a towering figure among theatre critics many decades since his heyday on *The Observer* in the 1950s is not only because of what he had to say but because of how he said it. Like the Algonquin wits, he could be very funny, but humour wasn't the only way he made his writing stand out. Frequently, he took an unexpected approach that would grab the reader's attention. His review of *Requiem for a Nun* by the novelist William Faulkner at London's Royal Court in 1957 came in the form of a monologue spoken by the character of the stage manager in Thornton Wilder's similarly folksy *Our Town*. Under cover of this entertaining double parody, Tynan found a way of analysing the play's weaknesses just as he would have done normally:

'Course, Mr Faulkner don't pretend to be a real play-writer, 'n' maybe that's why he tells the whole story backwards, 'n' why he takes up so much time gabbin' about people you never met – and what's more, ain't going to meet. By the time he's told you what's happened before you got here, it's gettin' to be time to go home.[9]

Several shows he tackled in the form of dialogues. His review of Graham Greene's *The Potting Shed,*[10] a Christian allegory, was set ten years in the future when a failed drama critic was telling his psychiatrist about the day he lost his faith not in religion but in the theatre. To discuss Terence Rattigan's *Variations on a Theme*,[11] he imagined a conversation between himself and the playwright's apparently neglected muse. His 1958 response to *Krapp's Last Tape*[12] and *Endgame* was a spot-on pastiche of Samuel Beckett which encapsulated the playwright's frustrating genius.[13] Such instances foregrounded the talents of the critic in a way that could have been considered indulgent had Tynan not used the technique as a critical tool to comment lucidly on the productions in question.

In London, the two bloggers calling themselves the West End Whingers – aka Andrew and Phil – exploit the informality of the internet to create a kind of theatre writing that simply didn't exist before the twenty-first century. Although there is a critical content to their writing, there is also a conversational irreverence that would be frowned upon by a newspaper editor. They seek to reproduce the kind of cheeky banter that a theatregoer would indulge in with their friends. It is camp, funny and self-deprecating, as much about the writers as about what was on stage. Their targets are the ephemera of theatregoing: things critics have conventionally overlooked, such as the comfort of the seats, the respective moods of the two writers and the quality of the wine in the interval (their promise is to 'help you decide between the Merlot and the Marlowe'). When focusing on the performance, they frequently concentrate on aspects other critics would choose not to mention. Take this riff about Jude Law's trousers in Michael Grandage's production of *Henry V* at the Noel Coward Theatre:

What exactly was going on there? Phil went with Helen, a serene, intelligent and polite person, not normally given to noticing, let alone bringing up such indelicate matters, but it was the talking point of the interval.

His breeches are eye-wateringly tight round calf and thigh, then billowing substantially around his dress circle. Henry Five most modestly underestimates the case. Go along and say that you didn't notice and we will say you are myopic or possibly a liar.[14]

Aside from being very funny, that last comment raises an interesting challenge. If the West End Whingers were right and Law's trousers were 'the' talking point at the interval, shouldn't it be the critic's duty to allude to it too? Do conventional critics adhere to some unwritten code that compels them to avoid 'indelicate matters' or is it that the Whingers' relative lack of interest in our first question ('What were the theatremakers trying to do?') liberated them to write about aspects over which the theatremakers had little or no control? In this respect, it is significant that the two writers distinguish themselves from the professional critics, whose reactions they discuss as if they were somehow doing a different job. Michael Coveney called them 'two non-critics who seem full of trivial opinions',[15] an assessment that amused them enough to use as a slogan on their site. Their primary purpose is to entertain and, even though their opinions can be insightful, they choose not to position themselves as anything other than regular theatregoers, buying their own tickets, commenting on preview performances and writing when it suits them. It's as if they don't want to be taken seriously.

The creative response

The internet, of course, has ushered in new ways of discussing theatre. Only a few years ago, nobody would even have understood Megan

Vaughan's review of *Teh Internet Is Serious Business,*[16] Tim Price's play about hackers at London's Royal Court. On her Synonyms For Churlish blog, she took Tynan's review-as-dialogue technique and updated it as sixteen screen grabs of an imagined smartphone text conversation. She had one correspondent describing the play using only emoji ideograms – smiling faces, lipstick kisses, gold trophies – and the other replying with her critical interpretation. In other words, she reviewed a play about the digital age in the language of the digital age. Until recently, our vocabulary did not include 'smartphone', 'text conversation', 'screen grab', or 'emoji ideogram', and even the most imaginative critic had neither the technical capacity nor the publishing opportunity to express themselves as creatively as Vaughan did. Likewise, it is hard to think of a pre-digital equivalent of Eve Nicol reviewing festival shows using pictures of cats,[17] David Ralf creating a 'doodle review' of *No Place to Go*[18] at London's Gate Theatre for *Exeunt Magazine* or Jane Howard writing an 'almost live review' of Ivo van Hove's marathon Roman Tragedies for Australia's *The Lifted Brow* with updates every five or ten minutes.[19]

You can't imagine *The New York Times* beginning a review like this from Matt Trueman:

> I wasn't going to write about *Handbagged*. My pen dried up at the start of the show, meaning I've got no notes on Moira Buffini's play, and I went from the theatre to a particularly boisterous wedding, meaning I've got very few memories of it either. Professional's a meaningless term anyway, right?[20]

And neither can you imagine *The New York Times* continuing, as Matt Trueman did on his eponymous blog, by discussing what all the other reviewers had said about the play. Bloggers can set their own deadlines, can choose whether or not they'll even write about a show and can decide to focus on any aspect of a production that interests them. In Trueman's case, he was compelled to write after reading a set of other reactions and feeling 'not one of those reviews seemed to mention what *Handbagged*'s really about'. His subsequent reflections proved his opening paragraph to be disingenuous: notes or not, he went on to give a compelling argument about an aspect of the play he thought the other critics had missed.

EXERCISE

Instead of writing a conventional review, respond to a production in a creative way. Use the theme of the show to suggest the form your response takes. There are no limits: you can use words, dialogue, images, film, sculpture, performance, collaboration . . . whatever idea occurs to you. What are the strengths and weaknesses of your response?

Mind your language

Another playful approach is to let some quality in the show dictate the form and language of your review. Like some of the Tynan examples, it's a way of paying homage to the production while communicating something of its flavour to your readers. Wittily blending criticism and quotation, Ian Shuttleworth borrowed a line from Shakespeare when reviewing a production of *King Lear* starring Frank Langella at Chichester's Minerva Theatre for the *Financial Times* before its run in New York:

> However, some lines are so colossally integral to our sense of Lear that, textual variation notwithstanding, they should never be cut. Never, never, never, never, never.[21]

When Byron Bache reviewed a Melbourne staging of *The Pirates of Penzance* for the *Herald Sun*, he picked up on the nautical theme of the Gilbert and Sullivan operetta: 'The Production Company's mounting of the show is definitely seaworthy, but somewhere below deck it's taking on a bit of water.'[22] Switching to metaphor gives you a more colourful form of expression, one that reinforces the theme of the show as well as entertaining the reader. It would have been much duller for Bache to have written: 'The Production Company's mounting of the show is competent, but has some weaknesses', which is roughly what he meant. You do, however, have to be careful not to get carried away by your own conceit. If a nautical show wasn't taking on water, metaphorically or otherwise, it would be misleading to use such a phrase. The critic's wittiness should not be at the expense of truthful reporting.

On the right occasion, however, the language of the play can affect not just the odd sentence but the whole review. Having emulated the form of the Borders ballad for his gothic comedy *The Strange Undoing of Prudencia Hart*, playwright David Greig inspired more than one critic to write their review in verse. Here is a taste of the rhyming write-up by Daniel Janes for A Younger Theatre:

'It's difficult to know where to start
With the strange undoing of Prudencia Hart.'
So begins David Greig's eponymous revel,
In which a Scottish academic has a tryst with the devil –
And such is the potency of this heady Scots brew,
That said couplet could easily begin my review.
Since its 2011 premiere at the Tron in Glasgow,
The play's toured the world, from São Paulo to Chicago.
Only now, however, does it reach London's capital,
But it was well worth the wait, and the audience lap it all
Up.[23]

Janes, like Dan Hutton who did something similar on his blog,[24] took on the tasks, such as elucidation and commentary, they would perform in a normal review, but they did so in a way that was both eye-catching and reflective of the show itself.

Writing with confidence

Lively writing is one thing, but what makes a great theatre writer such as Harold Clurman and George Bernard Shaw is not just their wit and readability but their authority. Much of that is to do with the firmness of their opinions. Even when Tynan made a passing remark, it could have the revelatory force of an epigram: 'The English hoard words like misers; the Irish spend them like sailors',[25] he wrote in a review of Brendan Behan's *The Quare Fellow*. 'The history of twentieth-century drama is the history of a collapsing vocabulary',[26] he said in relation to another Behan play, *The Hostage*. These were startlingly forthright sentences that defied you to disagree. 'Get your facts right first',[27] said Shaw. 'That is the foundation of all style, because style is the expression of yourself; and you cannot express yourself genuinely except on the basis of precise reality.' For 'facts' you can substitute the word 'opinions': the more certain you are about those, the more certain your writing will be. The way you write can bolster or undermine your authority. If your grammar is faulty, if your sentences are inelegant, if your argument is unclear, if your style is laboured, the reader will have little reason to trust your judgement. The more confident your expression, the more persuasive your writing will be. An authoritative style, however, should not be a cover for unsound reasoning. If you adopt what Charles Marowitz called a 'tone of Olympian assurance'[28] while being insensitive to the work you're reviewing, you may simply come across as pompous and out of touch.

So what should a theatre review sound like? Should it have the seriousness of an academic essay or the throwaway air of a Facebook chat? Should the critic come across as an all-knowing expert or a friend in the foyer? To an extent, the answer will depend on the publication you are writing for. Before you write a word, make sure you have familiarized yourself with the way it addresses its readers. Is it polite or abrasive, formal or fun, pacy or pedestrian? Writing for different publications is the equivalent of talking to different people: you have the same thing to say, but you phrase it differently according to whether you are with your grandmother, teacher, best friend, a stranger or an overseas pen pal. You needn't lose your individual style, but you instinctively adapt to the circumstances.

Finding a voice that feels comfortable can take time, partly because you are not always sure who you are addressing and partly because you are being pulled in conflicting directions. If you want to be taken seriously, you're more likely to lean on the traditions of cool-headed academic analysis and authoritative broadsheet sobriety than the language of the street with all its hesitations, digressions and uncertainties. But if you want to be accessible, you'll keep it light and chatty. Getting the balance right requires confidence and experience; you know you're not writing an academic essay, but it takes time to figure out what exactly you are writing.

House style

Straight away, however, there are some practical measures you should take. As well as understanding the tone of the publication, you should pay attention to its house style. Do you write *Woman in Mind* or *Woman In Mind*? Monday 10 August or Mon Aug 10 or 10th August? Seventies or seventies or 1970s or 70s or '70s? Double or single quotes? US or UK spelling? If the publication has a style guide, ask for a copy and read it. Like being punctual, reliable and meeting your deadlines, you will win favour by making less work for the people commissioning you. If your editor gives you a word count, especially for a print publication but online as well, do everything you can to stick to it. This is for your sake as much as theirs. You may find it painful to remove your favourite phrases and most pertinent insights, but you will find it more painful still if a subeditor does it on your behalf in an effort to fit the copy into the available space. It will almost always seem as if they have distorted your meaning or disrupted the rhythm of your sentences.

From a stylistic point of view, there are a couple of points to bear in mind. In modern journalism, there is a near universal preference for writing reviews in the present tense. A cheap trick it may be, but it creates a sense of immediacy and of the play taking place in the moment. It also makes the review feel topical for the duration of a production's run; if Blanche Dubois strides upstage on the opening night of *A Streetcar Named Desire*, she'll probably still be striding upstage three months later. You will, though, run into occasional problems. Handling tenses can get tricky when you need to refer to a one-off incident, such as a heckle from the audience or an onstage mistake, that really won't happen three months later. In such cases, it's usually possible to switch from present to past and back again without causing confusion. Dorothy Parker began one paragraph in the present tense: 'Richard Bennett gives a most remarkable performance . . .' – and changed to the past for the next paragraph: 'There was only one thing that made *The Unknown Purple* decidedly more difficult the night I was there – that was the audience.'[29] Less certain is the dilemma faced by Peter Kirwan of the University of Warwick who pointed out that journalistic reviews opt for the present tense whereas 'academic reviews use the past'.[30] That created a conundrum for him when he set up a blog, Bardathon, that attempted to marry the two forms by combining the 'analysis of academic criticism with the quick format of the journalistic review'. If you find yourself in a similar bind, I can only wish you the best of luck resolving it, except to say whatever your solution, it should be consistent.

Did you notice I just made use of the word 'I'? If it jumped out, it's because of the widespread journalistic and academic practice of avoiding the first person. The approach is a legacy of the days when newspapers and journals would publish articles anonymously or under a pseudonym. This practice was almost universal until the late nineteenth century and the emergence of 'new journalism' with its leanings towards the literary and individual voice of the writer. The convention persists to this day when we can still see news reports credited to 'our foreign correspondent' and anonymous titles such as 'staff reporter'. It reminds you that the story is more important than the messenger, which is one reason many critics choose not to write themselves into their own reviews: avoiding the 'I' ensures they make the theatremaker the subject of each sentence and not themselves. It makes it easier for them to give weight to our first question, 'What were the theatremakers trying to do?' It's also a way of affirming their status as independent observers, looking in dispassionately from the outside, like level-headed social scientists rather than as engaged spectators in the audience.

If one of those uncredited nineteenth-century writers were to have used the first person, it would have raised a question in the reader's mind: 'Who is this "I" whose individuality is being asserted in this unattributed article?' If the journalist made personal judgements, it would raise a further question: 'How can I trust their opinions if I don't know who they are?' The introduction of the byline, the line at the start of an article giving the writer's name, resolved this tension, while making possible a more individualistic school of Romantic criticism. In the meantime, however, journalists had acquired a habit of writing in an impersonal manner, a style that persists even in our era of picture bylines.

But if you don't use the first person, what do you use in its place? There are several alternative phrasings available to you – instead of 'I', you can opt for 'you', 'one' or 'we' – and all of them provoke further questions. If you switch to the first person plural – 'We find ourselves in the Forest of Arden' – you have a good tool for suggesting a collective experience, but you raise the question about who this 'we' is. Is it everybody in the audience? Is it a more select group of people who share the critic's values and perspective? Or is it just the critic in disguise? If you opt for 'one' – 'One finds oneself in the Forest of Arden' – you raise a similar set of questions and risk alienating your readers by what sounds like pompous upper-class speech – acceptable for the royal family, less so for the Royal Court. Plumping for the second person – 'You find yourself in the Forest of Arden' – an approach popularized by the film critic Pauline Kael, can give the reader a sense of direct engagement, creating a tone of familiarity and inclusiveness, but taken literally, it assumes the critic knows how you, the reader, will react. Like 'we' and 'one', it's probably an undercover 'I'.

Which approach you take is a matter of personal preference. I'd recommend you write in the voice that most closely resembles your natural speech patterns, but you may have an editor who disagrees. Whatever you choose, you should assume a hidden 'I think' at the start of every review, if only as a matter of brevity. Readers understand that reviews express personal opinions so you don't need to remind them of the fact. The more personal or idiosyncratic your response, however, the more likely you are to need the first person.

Le mot juste

The advantages of a wide vocabulary are plain. The more words you can draw on, the more precisely you can express yourself. One of a theatre critic's jobs is to give an impression of what a show was like. And 'impression' is the key word. Compared with the thing itself, a review is a sketch, giving no more than a sense, a rough idea, a generalization of what it was like. Capturing the flavour of the music, an actor's manner of speech or the texture of the costumes is always an approximation. Choosing the right word, however, can make your review less approximate. There's no reason the right word should be fancy or obscure; it just needs to get you the furthest distance in the shortest time. Rarity alone is not a reason for choosing a word. The best writers have a facility with language, but they do not use it as a smokescreen to obscure a lack of anything to say. If you find yourself using a fancy or unfamiliar word, ask yourself whether it expresses your meaning or merely sounds impressive. If it's the latter, you should return it to the dictionary until you have a more honourable use for it. A technique that has been used as an exercise at the National Critics Institute at the Eugene O'Neill Theater Centre in Connecticut is to write a review without recourse to adjectives.[31] It can be tough to do away with your most sumptuous vocabulary (score out 'most sumptuous'), but illuminating to see how little meaning is lost. Someone once said that if you like the sound of a particular passage when you read over your work, you should cut it out. That may be too brutal, but you should be on your guard against phrasing that is more showy than meaningful. I'll leave you to pass judgement on Clive Barnes who wrote that Paul Zindel's *And Miss Reardon Drinks a Little* 'is nearly better than it is. But not quite nearly enough.'[32] Some may argue that criticism like that is nearly better than it is. But not quite nearly enough.

EXERCISE

Select a published review and go through it removing all adjectives and adverbs. What effect does it have on the meaning? Now go through the same review, this time adding adjectives and adverbs to every noun and verb. How does the writing change?

In his highly recommended book *Theatre Criticism,*[33] Irving Wardle gave a 'black glossary of critical terms' that, to his mind, plagued reviews. They were words that meant less than they seemed. He included 'controversial', 'stylized', and 'mannered', all of which can be used as a smokescreen: what was the controversy, what was the style and what was the manner? If you want to say a show was evocative, it would benefit the reader to know what it evoked. If it is atmospheric, what particular atmosphere do you have in mind? Be on your guard also for the language of arts managers who have devalued words such as 'innovative', 'diverse' and 'challenging', and will no doubt devalue others in future. Take a look at websites such as badtheatrecopy.tumblr.com and prbuzzsaw.com for a chastening reminder of how language can become meaningless through carelessness and over-use. You should be equally unsentimental about stock phrases that come too easily to you: clichés help when you're writing quickly, but they're not much use in describing precisely what a show was like. To avoid either trap – the tired or the exotic – know what you want to say, then find the words to say it.

In his 1946 essay 'Politics and the English Language', George Orwell distinguished between words of Anglo-Saxon origin and those of Latin or Greek. For clarity, choose Anglo-Saxon; for obfuscation, go for Latin. 'A mass of Latin words falls upon the facts like soft snow, blurring the outline and covering up all the details',[34] he wrote. Anglo-Saxon wasn't better than Latin in every case, he said, but he believed writers should say what they meant using the 'fewest and shortest' words. Orwell's advice was characteristically succinct, but you can spend a lot of time putting it into practice.

Even if you avoid jargon and cliché, it can be hard to say exactly what you mean. Critics are often good at conveying the thrill of a great performance, but less good at saying precisely what was great about it. They can tell us a performance made the audience cheer, that it was superior to another fine actor's interpretation and that it will be remembered for many years to come. Sometimes, they'll narrow it down by saying what the performance was not: not as bombastic as usual, less frenetic than you'd expect . . . but identifying exactly what it was can elude them. Take the often quoted line by Samuel Taylor Coleridge about the actor Edmond Kean: 'To see him act was like reading Shakespeare by flashes of lightning.'[35] In isolation, this creates an air of excitement (imagine acting that had the intensity of lightning!) but tells you nothing about what Kean's performance was like. For that, you have to check out Coleridge's previous sentence – less quoted, but more informative and actually giving an opposite meaning: 'His rapid descents from the hyper-tragic to the infra-colloquial, though sometimes productive of great effect, are often unreasonable.' Now, we have a much fuller impression of the actor, one who was prone to the extremes of a stormy night, both the flashes of lightning and the dark obscurity on either side. The more precise your use of language, the closer you will get to capturing the performance – and that's something you'll never stop working at.

However experienced you are, you can always improve your writing. Every time you find yourself enjoying an author, whether you're reading a novel, a review or an opinion piece, you should take time to ask yourself what made their writing so compelling. What combination of syntax, grammar, language, rhythm, humour, intellect, surprise, mood and emotion made you read on? Conversely, next time you find yourself drifting away and turning the page, force yourself to go back and investigate why the writer lost you.

If you have not formally studied journalism (and many working critics have not), there are many books that will give you a grounding. Among those on my own shelf are *The Nuts and Bolts of Writing* by Michael Legat,[36] *Waterhouse on Newspaper Style* by Keith Waterhouse,[37] and *Essential English* by Harold Evans.[38] Study books such as these and return to them every couple of years to refresh yourself. I won't attempt to offer grammatical tips here. For our purposes, let's focus on the journalistic questions that have most bearing on writing a review: how to grab the reader, how to keep them reading and how to organize your thoughts. Those are the themes of the next chapters, starting with the question of how to write your very first sentence.

EXERCISE

After you have written a review, study other reviews of the same production to see how different critics described the same things. What phrases stand out? What words best capture the moment? Compile a composite review that takes the best bits from all of them.

Notes

1   English, John W. (1979), *Criticizing the Critics*, Hastings House.
2   Winner, Michael (2 March 2008), 'From ridiculous to sublime', in *The Sunday Times*.
3   Hitchcock, Alfred (8 June 1972), 'Alfred Hitchcock explains the plot device he called the "MacGuffin"', on Open Culture (www.openculture.

com/2013/07/alfred-hitchcock-explains-the-plot-device-he-called-the-macguffin.html).

4 Miller, Tice L. (March 1974), 'Alan Dale: The Hearst Critic', in *Educational Theatre Journal*, Vol. 26, No. 1.

5 Nathan, George Jean (1928), *Art of the Night*, Alfred A. Knopf.

6 Fitzpatrick, Kevin C. (2014), *Dorothy Parker: Complete Broadway 1918–1923*, iUniverse LLC.

7 Teichmann, Howard (1976), *Smart Aleck*, William Morrow & Company.

8 Rigg, Diana (1982), *No Turn Unstoned*, Elm Tree Books.

9 Tynan, Kenneth (1975), *A View of the English Stage*, Davis-Poynter.

10 Ibid.

11 Ibid.

12 Ibid.

13 Ibid.

14 West End Whingers, (28 November 2013), 'Review – *Henry V*, Noël Coward Theatre', on the West End Whingers blog (https://westendwhingers. wordpress.com/2013/11/28/review-henry-v-noel-coward-theatre).

15 Coveney, Michael (11 August 2011), 'Whingein' in the Rain', on What's On Stage (www.whatsonstage.com/west-end-theatre/news/08–2011/ whingein-in-the-rain_7734.html).

16 Vaughan, Megan (23 September 2014), '*Teh Internet Is Serious Business*', on Synonyms For Churlish (http://synonymsforchurlish.tumblr. com).

17 Nicol, Eve (August 2013), edinburghfuringe.tumblr.com.

18 Ralph, David (November 2013), 'No Place to Go', in *Exeunt Magazine*.

19 Howard, Jane (28 February 2014), 'Roman Tragedies: an almost live re-view', on *The Lifted Brow* (https://www.theliftedbrow.com/liftedbrow/ roman-tragedies-an-almost-live-review-by-jane).

20 Trueman, Matt (26 October 2013), 'Review: Handbagged, Tricycle Theatre', on Matt Trueman's blog (http://matttrueman.co.uk/2013/10/ review-handbagged-tricycle-theatre.html).

21 Shuttleworth, Ian (11 November 2013), '*King Lear*', in the *Financial Times*.

22 Bache, Byron (31 October 2013), '*The Pirates of Penzance*', in the *Herald Sun*.

23 Janes, Daniel (16 July 2013), '*The Strange Undoing of Prudencia Hart*', on A Younger Theatre (http://www.ayoungertheatre.com/review-the-strange-undoing-of-prudencia-hart-royal-court-theatre).

24 Hutton, Dan (16 July 2013), '*The Strange Undoing of Prudencia Hart*', on Dan Hutton (http://dan-hutton.co.uk/2013/07/16/the-strange-undoing-of-prudencia-hart).

25 Tynan, Kenneth (1975), *A View of the English Stage*, Davis-Poynter.

26 Ibid.

27 Shaw, George Bernard (1955), *Advice to a Young Critic*, Brown, Watson Limited.

28 Marowitz, Charles (1986), *Prospero's Staff*, Marion Boyars.

29 Fitzpatrick, Kevin C., editor (2014), *Dorothy Parker: Complete Broadway 1918–1923*, iUniverse LLC.

30 Kirwan, Peter (2010), ' "What's past is prologue": Negotiating the authority of tense in reviewing Shakespeare', in *Shakespeare,* Vol. 6, No. 3.

31 Caggiano, Chris (20 July 2010), 'A theatre critic's manifesto', on www.chriscaggiano.com (www.chriscaggiano.com/a-theater-critics-manifesto.html).

32 Barnes, Clive (26 February 1971), 'Theater: Reardon sisters arrive; their troubles do not quite make a play Harris-Parsons team does best in cast', in *The New York Times*.

33 Wardle, Irving (1992), *Theatre Criticism*, Routledge.

34 Orwell, George (1946), 'Politics and the English Language', Benediction Classics.

35 Coleridge, Samuel Taylor (1823), *Specimens of the Table Talk*, Harper and Brothers.

36 Legat, Michael (1989), *The Nuts and Bolts of Writing*, Robert Hale.

37 Waterhouse, Keith (1989), *Waterhouse on Newspaper Style*, Viking.

38 Evans, Harold (2000), *Essential English for Journalists, Editors and Writers*, Pimlico.

7
HOW TO WRITE THE
FIRST SENTENCE

Taking the plunge

In the last chapter, we imagined the critic as a performer. If you are new to this role, you are now about to step in front of your public for the first time. You may well have some backstage nerves. The circulation of a newspaper could be in the tens of thousands. Your potential readership on the internet runs into the millions. It's like showing up at a very big party where you definitely want to look your best. Unsure what to wear, you throw all your clothes onto the bed and stare at them in bewilderment. Which outfit will make the right impression? Which one will make a statement about yourself? Which one will be intriguing enough to make people want to keep talking to you?

It's not that you have nothing to say, quite the reverse: you've got a wardrobe full of ideas and what's overwhelming is the decision about what to say first. There are all those readers out there and you don't want to lose them by appearing too dull, dowdy, extravagant, revealing, pretentious or old hat in your very first sentence. If you think about it too much, you can freeze with the journalistic equivalent of stage fright.

How you kick off is certainly important. This is what the novelist D.B.C. Pierre, author of *Vernon God Little*, said on the subject in a piece he recorded for BBC Radio 6 Music:

> The opening line is crucial. The opening line should have in it all the compelling reasons that the story exists. So it needs to intrigue us

and at the same time set the scene. My favourite first line of any book is from *The Tin Drum* by Günter Grass and that line is: 'Granted I am the inmate of a mental asylum.'[1]

He was talking about novels and short stories, but it's no bad ambition for a theatre review. What is the thing you can say that's going to intrigue and entice the reader enough to read on? There is, of course, no right answer, any more than there's a right outfit to wear for a party. You just have to plump for the one that instinct tells you will turn the most heads. Look at ten reviews of the same show and you'll find ten opening lines. Some may work better than others, but most, if not all, will do the job. In reality, partygoers don't actually laugh at your clothes. 'Opening lines have to pop into your head', said John Simon. 'Opening lines that you have to sweat and toil over are not going to be worth the sweat.'[2]

EXERCISE

Find a newspaper or magazine. Read the first line of every article. Which make you want to read more and which don't?

A good place to start is to think of the first thing you'd tell a friend about the show. Whether it's a stunning performance, a boring script, a miraculous scene change, a topical resonance or a fight breaking out in the grand circle, if it's significant enough to flag up to your friend, it's likely to be significant enough to flag up to your readers. Don't worry about all the other things you want to say: they will follow in due course, sentence by sentence, with the logic of your argument. The Roman critic Horace formulated the concept of 'in medias res' or 'into the middle of things', the idea that an author could intrigue the audience by starting half way through the story. He wasn't talking about reviews, but the same principle applies. On occasion, you will want to start at the beginning, as Lyn Gardner did with her *Guardian* review of Sarah Rutherford's *Adult Supervision* at London's Park Theatre:

> It's US election night 2008 and Barack Obama is about to make history. Uptight former lawyer turned full-time mum, Natasha – who, like Madonna, has plucked her adopted children from an African village – has invited some school-gate mums from her childrens' [sic] pricey private school to her house to watch as events unfold on TV.[3]

She introduced her review in the same way the play introduced itself, then continued in similar style for another paragraph before broadening things out to put the play in context and discuss her reaction to it. Piggybacking on the story of the play in this way can help the reader get a sense of what's at stake and is especially valuable for new and unfamiliar work. We'll consider this idea in more detail presently, but it is not the only way to go about it. Leap into the middle and see what you find, as Gardner herself did the following month in a review of *Eric and Little Ern* at London's Vaudeville Theatre:

> 'Where would you be without me?' asks Eric Morecambe. 'Be a comedian,' replies Ernie Wise. It's an exchange that gets to the heart of one of British comedy's greatest partnerships, Morecambe and Wise, who kept British TV audiences chortling and for three decades brought a little sunshine to their lives.[4]

The line she quoted might have come from any point in the performance, but for Gardner, it epitomized the whole show. Once you've made up your mind about what to say first, you still have to decide how to say it. For inspiration, let's look at a selection of approaches taken by critics writing at around the same time as Gardner in late 2013. First, we'll go to the *Toronto Star*, where Robert Crew used a drip-feed technique to compel the reader to move to the next sentence to find out more. The idea is to offer just enough detail to intrigue, but no more. Reviewing a play called *Tainted* by Kat Lanteigne, Crew kicked off with a stand-alone paragraph of just six words:

It is a heart-rending story.[5]

As a sentence, this was grammatically correct. There was a subject (*it*), a verb (*is*), an article (*a*), an adjective (*heart-rending*) and a noun (*story*). According to the rule book, this was a complete unit of meaning. But although technically it made sense, it left us with a question. The reader's only possible response was: '*What* is a heart-rending story?' Searching for an answer, they had to move to the next sentence. Crew then answered by explaining the historical background to the play (the giving of 'tainted blood' to haemophiliac patients in the 1980s), by which time the reader was hooked and he could go on to offer his assessment of the production.

Crew's opening question was implied – there was no question mark, but it felt like there was. Pat Donnelly on the *Montreal Gazette* created the same effect by beginning her review of Annabel Soutar's *Seeds* at the Centaur Theatre with two explicit questions: 'Why would a huge multinational company like Monsanto sue an ordinary Saskatchewan farmer for allowing certain innocent plants (not marijuana) to grow in his fields? And who was this wily farmer who fought back?'[6] Even if you had no interest in the play, it would be quite hard to resist reading on after a provocation like that. Think about the opposite approach and imagine a sentence that left no questions: 'Jane Smith's production of Shakespeare's *Macbeth* for the Queen's Players opened last night at the Royal Theatre for a three-week run.' This could be factually true, it could be grammatically in order, but the only question it would leave you with is 'So what?' Nothing in the way it was written would make you keep reading.

Sometimes, you can grab the reader simply by the authority of your opening statement. Paul Taylor, writing in *The Independent* about a production of Lope de Vega's *Punishment and Revenge* at the Ustinov Studio, Bath, set the stakes high from the start, making it plain that this was an event worthy of the reader's attention:

> No English director is a better advocate for the glories of Spanish Golden Age drama than Laurence Boswell – as he proves once again with the richly enterprising three-play repertory he has masterminded at Bath. The tragic centrepiece of the season is his darkly glittering and deeply engrossing production of *Punishment Without Revenge* (1631) – generally reckoned to be one of the greatest of the four hundred surviving theatrical works by the astoundingly prolific Lope de Vega.[7]

Taylor's experience earned him the right to express himself like this. Only by seeing enough Spanish Golden Age dramas directed well by Laurence Boswell (and presumably less well by other directors) could he justify his opening assertion. Crucially, he chose to express his view with total certainty; no ambiguity, no caveats, no qualifying adjectives, just a bold statement of fact. This in itself was the compelling reason to read on; even though his first sentence was a complete unit of meaning, its sense of importance made you want to know more.

Clare Brennan, writing in *The Observer*, managed to inform and intrigue in this opening sentence about a Manchester production of *All My Sons*:

> It hadn't occurred to me that there might be any issues attached to this Royal Exchange co-production with the black-led theatre company Talawa of American playwright Arthur Miller's 1947 play.[8]

In just thirty words, she managed to name both co-producers, give a pertinent detail about Talawa's 'black-led' nature, identify the name and nationality of the playwright and the date of his play. Not only that, but she compelled you to go on to her next line to find out about the unexpected 'issues' attached to the production:

Then I read the correspondence on the Exchange's website. People wondered whether the play would have to be directorially adjusted to accommodate a non-white cast. As far as I could see, Michael Buffong (who directed the award-winning production of Lorraine Hansberry's *A Raisin in the Sun* for the Exchange in 2010) has made no changes to the text, nor were any necessary: skin colour is not Miller's theme; ideological orientation is.

Once again with admirable concision, Brennan covered extensive ground in just seventy words, providing evidence of the discussion around the production (a visit to the theatre's website), an answer to her opening question (it was a non-white cast), further contextualization (the director's previous work) and an unequivocal statement of her critical position ('skin colour is not Miller's theme'). At each stage, she gave you enough information to be intrigued but too little to stop reading. Each sentence left you with a question. Sentence one: what were the issues attached to the production? Sentence two: what did it say on the website? Sentence three: were people right to wonder whether the play would have to be adjusted? By sentence four, you were hooked.

Perhaps you prefer a sprinkle of wit. Just as you might crack a little joke when you meet someone for the first time, so kicking off a review with some light humour may endear yourself to the reader. Responding to a rash of productions of Ibsen's *Ghosts*, Sarah Hemming in the *Financial Times* began in playful fashion:

> By some spooky coincidence, there are several *Ghosts* around at the moment.[9]

To anyone who knew Ibsen did not write haunted-house thrillers, Hemming's use of the word 'spooky' was funny. To anyone who didn't, it was still an intriguing sentence. She went on to make serious points about a serious drama ('a blistering endgame, the darkest hour before the dawn'), but not before drawing the reader in with a gently amusing introduction.

Reviewing a production of Eugene O'Neill's *Desire Under the Elms* in *The Irish Times*, Peter Crawley started with a critical argument that built up to a question:

> No matter how many people suffer in Greek tragedy, we can usually decide on a single tragic hero: Oedipus, blind and raging; Phaedra undone by her own hand; Medea avenged and inhuman.
>
> But who is the tragic figure in Eugene O'Neill's play, indebted to the ancients, from 1926?[10]

Under cover of this rhetorical structure, Crawley set the twentieth-century play in the context of its classical forebears. Not only did he engage his readers in a debate, he informed them of the terms of that debate by taking them on a brisk trot through the stories of Oedipus, Phaedra and Medea before introducing the idea that O'Neill was doing something slightly different. In this way, Crawley primed his readers for an analytical discussion about the nature of the drama, one that, most likely, would take the whole of the review to play out.

Here is an example of two opening sentences in which opinion and description were interlocked. Writing in *The Australian*, Chris Boyd leapt straight in with an opinion that conveyed a tremendous amount about the nature of a Melbourne Theatre Company production:

> EDDIE Perfect's new play, *The Beast*, is chaotic, offensive and incredibly indulgent – no surprises there – but the atom-splitting chaos is controlled and self-sustaining, the offence is given to hypocrites and snobs, mostly, and the writerly indulgence is utterly delightful. Well, mostly delightful then.[11]

By twisting the expected meanings of his own words, Boyd established a sense of the production's excitement and the complex, contradictory effect it had on the audience. You would want to read on to discover how such oppositional forces played out in practice. The critic's task was then to explore the implications of the provocative introduction in greater detail.

How you choose to kick off your review will determine the shape of what follows. If you set up an expectation, at some point you will have to fulfil that expectation or, for effect, turn the expectation on its head. Consider this first line in a *Guardian* review by David Cote of the 2013 Broadway run of Harold Pinter's *Betrayal*, starring Daniel Craig and Rachel Weisz:

> Mike Nichols and his cast get so much wrong in the Broadway revival of Harold Pinter's *Betrayal* (1978), let's start with what goes right.[12]

In just twenty-four words, Cote managed to tell us the name of the director, playwright, play and approximate location, express a forthright critical opinion and, even better, give an indication of the structure of the review to follow. Immediately, you knew he was going to tell you about the production's strengths and you knew also that at a certain point, he would put the boot in. The plot of a thriller has a similar tension: although all is going swimmingly, we're on the edge of our seats because we know something bad is about to happen. We have to read on. In the next chapter, we'll look at how to keep people reading on by considering some of the ways you may structure a review.

EXERCISE

Write the opening paragraphs of three reviews of the same production, each between 50 and 100 words. The first will try to grab the reader with an arresting opinion, whether or not it does justice to the show. The second will be all about you as the writer and next to nothing about the production. The third will express your honest reaction in a punchy tabloid style. Which works best?

Notes

1 Pierre, D.B.C. (14 September 2013), 'How to Tell a Good Story', Three-Minute Epiphany, BBC Radio 6 Music.

2 Napoleon, Davi (spring 1997), 'John Simon, The Art of Criticism No. 4', in *The Paris Review*.

3 Gardner, Lyn (22 October 2013), *'Adult Supervision'*, in *The Guardian*.

4 Gardner, Lyn (20 November 2013), *'Eric and Little Ern'*, in *The Guardian*.

5 Crew, Robert (27 September 2013), *'Tainted* is no *Angels in America*: review', in the *Toronto Star*.

6 Donnelly, Pat (1 November 2013), 'Theatre review: *Seeds'*, *Montreal Gazette*.

7 Taylor, Paul (21 October 2013), 'Punishment Without Revenge', in *The Independent*.

8 Brennan, Clare (6 October 2013), *'All My Sons'*, in *The Observer*.

9 Hemming, Sarah (6 October 2013), *'Ghosts'*, in the *Financial Times*.

10 Crawley, Peter (6 October 2013), *'Desire Under the Elms'*, in *The Irish Times*.

11 Boyd, Chris (8 October 2013), 'Eddie Perfect's *Beast* comes alive', *The Australian*.

12 Cote, David (28 October 2013), *'Betrayal'*, in *The Guardian*.

8
HOW TO STRUCTURE A REVIEW

Making the news

Standard news reporting practice is to lead with the most important facts. As the article goes on, the journalist adds information in decreasing order of relevance and answers the questions known as the five Ws – 'who, what, why, where and when?' – as quickly as possible. Thus:

Caledonian 'tyrant' slain

King Macbeth is dead. Palace sources have confirmed that Lord Macduff slaughtered the warlord yesterday in a battlefield clash near Dunsinane. It was the culmination of a hard-fought campaign to end the king's dictatorship. Eyewitness reports suggest Macduff's victory was swift, bloody and decisive, and that Macbeth died fairly. 'They say he parted well and paid his score,' said Earl Siward, who was present at the scene.

The killing brings to an end the regime of terror instigated by the former Thane of Cawdor. It paves the way for the ascension of King Malcolm who paid tribute to his forces' bravery on the battlefield: 'Thanks to all at once and to each one, whom we invite to see us crown'd at Scone,' he said.

Macduff had been gathering forces against Macbeth for several weeks. The leading Scottish noble has promised to display the dead king's head on a pole above a sign saying: 'Here you may see the tyrant.'

Formerly known as the Thane of Glamis, Macbeth came to prominence after his military success in the war against Norway and Ireland. He was made Thane of Cawdor under the auspices of the late King Duncan. He assumed the title of King of Scotland following the suspicious murder of Duncan at his Inverness castle. Insiders say Macbeth had been encouraged in his murderous ambitions by his wife who recently committed suicide after a period of mental ill health.

This structure, often described as an inverted pyramid, gets straight to the point with the headline (*Caledonian 'tyrant' slain*) then fills in more and more details as the article goes on. In this example, the first three sentences tell us who (*Lord Macduff*), what (*slaughtered King Macbeth*), where (*a battlefield . . . near Dunsinane*), when (*yesterday*) and why (*to end his dictatorship*). The reporter can add facts, quotes and background information for as long as there is space. When space gets tight, a newspaper subeditor can cut sentences from the bottom up, getting rid of the least important information, safe in the knowledge that the most essential part of the story, being at the top, will remain intact. Look at the example above and see how many sentences you can remove from the bottom before the article becomes meaningless.

Whatever structure the critic uses, a valuable principle to learn from the news report is the importance of those five Ws. They are essential to give your reader a sense of the event you're talking about. It is common for some of this information, such as the name of the play, the address of the theatre and the dates it is running, to be included at the start or end of the review. But before you can build your argument, you will also need to give some indication about the nature of the production (what it was like, what it was about) and about the theatremakers responsible for it.

In certain publications, theatre critics may be expected to structure their reviews using the same inverted-pyramid technique. If the review is to be published alongside regular news reports, an editor may want it to compete for attention in the same terms. This can feel awkward because, unless the auditorium catches fire, a theatre performance does not have the man-bites-dog shape of a typical news event. Somehow, from the mass of emotions you have experienced and ideas you have processed, you have got to say something direct and to the point. It means combining your news sense and your critical judgement to decide on the most important aspect of the production. Sometimes there will be an obviously newsworthy aspect, such as the presence of an A-list celebrity in the cast. More typically, you will find yourself turning your own opinion into the main event.

EXERCISE

Write a 200-word review of a production as if it were a news report. Lead with the most important aspect, which could either be a fact about the show or your opinion of it, and answer the five Ws – 'who, what, why, where and when?' Do you find this approach liberating or constraining?

Classical structures

Some publications don't necessarily demand a news style, but they do expect their critics to get reasonably swiftly to the point. With this in mind, some critics have a preference for an Aristotelian rhetorical structure more in common with an academic essay: an arresting introduction, the development of an argument, then a conclusion. Michael Billington of *The Guardian* will often state an opinion in his opening paragraph, explore the production in his subsequent paragraphs, then restate his opinion in different words at the end. It's a way of organizing your thoughts and of making it clear to the reader the direction you are going to take.

Other publications formalize this further. Look at the reviews in *Variety*, the US entertainment trade magazine, and you'll see every opening paragraph, or lede, setting out the key facts and opinions in less than 100 words. The rest of the review will analyse the production in greater detail but is unlikely to spring any surprises. Take this lede from a *Variety* review by Karen Fricker of *Punk Rock* at the Lyric Hammersmith:

> This riveting new work confirms Simon Stephens as one of the most important and exciting British playwrights working today. The premise of 'Punk Rock' could be glibly summed up as 'The History Boys' meets Columbine, but this hardly does service to the compassion, insight — and theatrical panache — of Stephens' approach. What initially feels like an exploration of the everyday horrors of contemporary adolescence slowly reveals itself as a story of exceptional violence. The writer's perfectly calibrated setup leads auds to some of the biggest, most complex questions of our times: how do these things happen, and what can be done?[1]

In exactly 100 words, Fricker conveyed her opinion along with a sense of the production's context, importance, narrative, style, relevance and thematic context. In the 600 words that followed, she returned to each aspect to fill in the detail, including further plot description, direct quotation and a dramaturgical analysis. Anyone reading only her lede would get a good impression of the production's key points, while anyone intrigued enough to read on would gain a richer understanding. Although *Variety* has a precisely formulated house style (extending to its own slang: note Fricker's use of the abbreviation 'auds' for audiences), its critics still have considerable freedom to prioritize those aspects of the event that seem most pertinent and to keep people reading through the force of their argument.

Starting with a strong opinion can give your review certainty and drive. It does, however, pose two risks. The first is you may lose your readers after the first couple of sentences because they've found out all they need to know (the inverted pyramid structure allows readers to move on after a sentence or two unless they're particularly interested in the story). The second is that any equivocal comments you go on to make may be overshadowed by the force of your opening remarks. The boldness of your first line could give a misleading impression of the show as a whole.

Going with the flow

Alternatively, you may prefer to withhold your most strongly held critical opinion until last in order to give the review a dramatic twist. Your structure might go: 'this aspect was good, that aspect was good, but it was all undermined by this other aspect which was bad'. Equally, it could go: 'this aspect was poor, that aspect was mediocre, but it was all redeemed by this other aspect which was fantastic'. Such approaches allow the critic to break free of a tick-box mentality, dealing with each element in turn in a formulaic way, and to build their review around a central narrative-like argument, illustrating it with observations about acting, design, direction, music and so on along the way. Done well, this discursive approach can feel more organic and readable. You focus on the thing that strikes you most forcibly about the production and deal with the 'score-keeping' only as and when it seems appropriate for your argument.

You could think of the review as the story of your encounter with a performance and, like any storyteller, you need to use whatever means you can to keep people reading. With his looser approach, the critic can't ignore the five Ws completely (the reader still needs to know what the article is about), but they can delay answering those questions until it suits them. Unlike the news reporter using the inverted pyramid, the critic often keeps the most important piece of information until last and may withhold opinions for dramatic effect. As a consequence, many will tell you tales about their reviews being rendered pointless by news subs straying onto the arts desk and chopping out their crucial last paragraphs. As long as that doesn't happen, there's a reasonable chance someone may keep reading until the end.

The close-up and the long shot

John Ford's classic western *The Searchers* opens with a woman coming to the door of her isolated homestead and looking out on an open plain. We see the whole landscape in long-shot: the arid sands of Monument Valley, the defiant sandstone buttes and the clear blue sky. It's an awesome sight. Only once we've taken in the big picture do we notice a man – John Wayne – approaching us on horseback from the middle distance. In cinematic terms, this is an establishing shot, an image that shows a character in context, one that tells us not only about a cowboy, but also about a cowboy's environment. Having shown the entire canvas, the filmmaker is then free to focus in on the details.

The same storytelling technique can be used when writing a review. The critic starts with the big picture, perhaps in the form of some broad observation, topical reference or historical overview. Then, with the context established, they hone in on the specifics of the performance. Here is a brilliant example from Chris Jones in the *Chicago Tribune*:

> I was listening to the radio Saturday afternoon as I drove to the Steppenwolf Theatre Company: Reports were coming in of the shooting in a shopping mall in Nairobi, Kenya. A kids' cooking competition had been going on. 'A lot of children were involved,' I heard a reporter for *The Daily Telegraph* say, dryly, as I locked my car. He was not exaggerating. By Sunday morning, it was clear several children had died, and a 2-year-old was among the wounded.
>
> Here in Chicago, of course, you do not have to look to Africa to see children impacted by violence and war: 3-year-old Deonta Howard was shot in the head Thursday night in Cornell Square Park, less than 12 miles from Steppenwolf.

Children have always died in wars, and, make no mistake, there is a war going on within Chicago city limits. And children have always watched adults they love die — or be imprisoned, tortured, transported, gassed, chased away, exiled or otherwise removed from their lives.[2]

It was only on his fourth paragraph that Jones even mentioned the play he was writing about: *The Wheel* by Zinnie Harris in a production by Steppenwolf Theatre. He opened in far-away Kenya and that day's news of a massacre in a Nairobi shopping mall. In his second paragraph, he focused in to a scene not far from the theatre where a child had been shot in the head a few days earlier. In paragraph three, he kept the distance broad with a generalized comment about war and the death of children. Only then, with the scene set, did he bring us into the theatre.

Observe the way Jones took us from the universal to the particular, finding common ground with readers before positioning an unfamiliar production in a way we could understand. The danger of the long shot is in the critic never fully connecting with the production. If you spend too long in generalized discussion about the play's themes or its historical context, you may find it hard to respond to the energy of the specific event. Jones avoided that trap by zooming in with every paragraph; rather than continuing to talk in abstract terms about children dying in far-away wars, he brought us ever closer to the show. Critics who get stuck in long-shot mode, by contrast, can sound like they weren't even at the performance and will fail to do justice to the live event.

To avoid this risk, you could take the opposite approach. To stick with the cinematic terms, this is the close-up. A prime example is the opening sequence of Stanley Kubrick's *A Clockwork Orange*. After the credits, the face of Malcolm McDowell fills the screen. We get a detailed view of his unblinking expression, the exaggerated eyelashes painted around his right eye, the bowler hat tilting down and the malevolent grin. For the moment, we know nothing about where he is sitting and who he is with; only as the camera zooms out do we piece together his place among a gang of delinquents sitting in the futuristic Korovo Milk Bar. The equivalent for a theatre critic is to begin with an arresting image and work outwards. After seeing David Tennant in the lead role of *Richard II* by the Royal Shakespeare Company in Stratford, Louis Wise began with the smallest of details in his *Sunday Times* review:

> First, the hair. *Richard II* may be a gem of a history play, a triumph of poetry, a very English tragedy, but David Tennant's king stuns us, first and foremost, with a wonderful brown weave cascading down his back. And if it's just hair, it's apt: luxuriant, self-indulgent, slightly absurd (to the modern eye, anyway), it's a nice encapsulation of Richard of Bordeaux's reign. As he quaffs wine and scoffs sweeties, depleting his nation's coffers because God says he can, he's a medieval pop star, a divine brat manipulating the system. It's Florence and a particularly mean Machine.[3]

When it works, this technique can bring a tremendous immediacy to a review. The reader is thrown right into the thick of the action and has to make sense of the production from the inside out. It provokes a question that demands an answer ('Why is he talking about hair?') and, in its tight focus, creates a vivid impression. The trick for the critic is spotting just the right detail that will epitomize the production as a whole. Wise's conceit would quickly have run aground if he hadn't been able to sustain the connection between Tennant's hair and 'Richard of Bordeaux's reign'. That's the thing that was missing (for deliberate comic effect) from the West End Whingers review that focused on Jude Law's trousers. You can imagine audiences talking in the interval about Law's trousers and Tennant's hair, but it's unlikely Law's trousers shed much light on the production as a whole. That being the case, it would be fine to mention them in a description of the actor's performance, but problematic to use them as a foundation for a review.

The trousers and the hair are examples of a close-up on an actor's appearance, but you can engage the reader by focusing on any small detail, be it a gesture, a piece of stage business, a single line or a verbal exchange (do make sure to quote accurately for fear of offending the playwright). It doesn't happen in every performance, but sometimes a single moment leaps to your attention that seems to epitomize something bigger: an actor's charisma, a director's interpretation, a play's deepest themes. It's as if you have seen the string of DNA that gave the production life. As long as you can make the connection between the micro and the macro, the close-up could be the technique you need.

Between the extremes of the long shot and the close-up, you'll find many more perspectives. The performance itself will be what triggers your decision to take one approach over another. That's because theatre criticism is a practical art. It can't happen in isolation or in the abstract. You can't decide in advance how you will write about it or what you will say. It exists in response to something else. For this reason, the next chapter looks at the challenge of keeping your wits about you so you can respond to a live artform in the moment.

EXERCISE

Write the opening paragraph of a review – around 100 words – which begins by describing a small detail: perhaps a line of dialogue, an actor's gesture or a moment in the staging. Now write a second opening paragraph about the same production, this time starting with a general observation about the play's theme or the nature of the theatre. Which approach works the best?

Notes

1 Fricker, Karen (9 September 2009), '*Punk Rock*', in *Variety*.

2 Jones, Chris (22 September 2013), 'Joan Allen on a roll through the years', *Chicago Tribune*.

3 Wise, Louis (27 October 2013), '*Richard II*', in *The Sunday Times*.

9

HOW TO WRITE IN
THE MOMENT

The alert critic

It's the start of the Edinburgh Festival Fringe. We're in a studio theatre on Princes Street. The room is empty apart from a chair in the middle of the stage. The audience is starting to come in. There's still a bit of time to wait, but I notice the young critic in front of me has a notepad and is writing something down. The show has not even begun. What can he possibly have written? I lean forward and take a peak over his shoulder. He has written one word.

'Chair.'

It makes me laugh. There's no way this note could be of any help when he comes to write his review. He may as well have written 'curtains' or 'floor' or 'audience'. Equally, there's a big part of me that sympathizes with him. I don't think I've ever sat down at the start of a show without some small sense of alarm. Will this be the show that leaves me with nothing to write? As a critic, you're there, primed and ready to respond, but until the show starts, you have no material to respond to. You have no way of knowing whether the chair will turn out to be significant. Reason may tell you it will be of no importance whatsoever, but for a while, it is all you have to go on. Imagine the horror of having to file 300 words of intelligent and insightful copy and all you have to write about is a chair.

Even twenty minutes into a production, you may still have this feeling. Unless it's a production of Ionesco's *The Chairs*, the absurdist play in which an elderly couple fill the stage with more and more chairs, you will have realised the chair has no special significance, but you may still find yourself at a loss to know what is significant.

Theatremakers often take their time before showing their hand. They tease you with their evasions, try to intrigue you with withheld information and add suspense by offering more confusion than clarity. It can mean the actors have been talking for ages and you still can't figure out what's motivating them or what they're going to say next. You have little sense of what's important and what's not. The show is speeding by and it feels like you can't even tell what is happening, let alone what you think of it.

Such anxiety is normal. It's the equivalent of an actor's backstage nerves. Your uncertainty shows you are focusing and paying attention. So what if the chair proves not to be significant? At least you were prepared for it to be so. After all, you could argue that a show begins as soon as you encounter the architecture of the building, the atmosphere in the foyer, the pre-show music (or lack of it), the level of the house lights and so on. All of those factors contribute to the production's meaning in some way, so why not the chair? The question at this stage is about how great their contribution will be. It's impossible to say, but if that makes you nervous, you can take solace in the fact that everyone – critic or not – always has an opinion at the end of a performance, even if it is that they didn't understand it. At the start of a performance when anything is possible and the show could go in any direction, your feeling of panic is only to be expected.

Theatre is a live art. It happens in the moment and it can only be reviewed in the moment. It is not literature. You cannot read it and re-read it. All you can do is experience it. In this, the critic has a lot in common with a comedy improviser. Both have certain ways of preparing, of keeping their creative muscles flexed, of making sure they are fresh and ready to work, but neither can do the job until the performance takes place. Improvizers can practise word-association techniques, but they cannot rehearse the specific instant of inspiration that will make their performance special. That will depend on the mood of the room, the suggestions made by the audience, the responses of the other performers – all factors over which they have no control. Likewise, critics have ways of getting up to match fitness: depending on the show, they could choose to read the script, watch the movie it is based on, research previous productions, interview the director or recall shows they have seen by the same creative team. Any of these may prime them to be responsive, but none of them is a substitute for the moment-by-moment experience of seeing the show live.

Preparing yourself

Theatre is fluid. I mean this in two ways: first, that it is live and no performance is ever exactly the same as the last; and second, that it is constantly affected by the world outside. This means you can't write about theatre without being aware of the context in which it takes place. And you can't write about context until you experience it for yourself. There is no preparation you can do to forecast the difference between a performance on a humid Wednesday afternoon in the Toronto Fringe Festival and a glamorous red-carpet premiere on Broadway – even if they feature the same actors in the same play. How could you know in advance that a particular scene will suddenly resonate with one of today's headlines? Extensive reading will not help you capture that one-off event when an actor improvizes their way out of an unscheduled technical gaffe. A veteran critic may have seen *Macbeth* a hundred times, but will never have seen this *Macbeth* staged in this particular room on this particular day before this particular audience. Above all, there is no way you can predict how you will feel about any of this; your emotions, your intellectual engagement, your irritation and your joy are all unknowns. You can't do your job until they do theirs – and that lack of control is either invigorating or scary depending on your temperament.

So how do you train yourself to respond in the moment? You may be tempted, as I was when I had to write on-the-night reviews for the first time, to have a snappy opening paragraph at the ready, something written in advance that could help you as your 11pm deadline races towards you. Technically, this is possible: you just need to think up something generic about the play or the company, something specific enough to be interesting and general enough to work in all circumstances. Almost invariably, however, it will be second-rate. It will never match the sense of purpose of the review you write when you leave yourself open to the event itself. Your job is to be reflexive, to comment not on what you expect to be there, but on what you find. You can guess, you can have your suspicions, but until the final curtain, you don't know for sure what the most remarkable thing about the production will be. It could be a poetic turn of phrase, a moving performance, a heart attack in the audience, an absence, a presence, a piece of choreography, an idea, something you are reminded of, some magical combination of all these things working together . . . you can only wait and see. To do otherwise is not to be true to the performance.

Not knowing can make you feel vulnerable, but if you trust your instincts, listen to your inner reactions and try, at all costs, to be honest about your response, then you can turn that vulnerability into creative energy. Like the improvizer, you forget about a script and free yourself to work with the material you find.

How to take notes

All of this means there's likely to be a lot of ideas buzzing around your head by the end of a performance. When you start writing, you're going to have to impose some kind of order on them, deciding what's important and what's not, what helps you make your case and what doesn't. During a stimulating show, you can find yourself desperately trying to keep hold of all these ideas, sometimes to the exclusion of the rest of the performance. It is unwise to dedicate all your mental energy to remembering some detail from the first scene only to realize it contributes little to your understanding of the production as a whole, but it is easy to let that happen.

Taking notes is one way to cope with this information overload. Say what you like about the critic who wrote down the word 'chair', but at least he didn't have to think about it again. He could concentrate on the rest of the show with a clear mind. Critics have different attitudes to taking notes. *The Guardian* critic Lyn Gardner writes copiously, especially during the Edinburgh Fringe when she can finish the day with a backlog of five shows to review. She relies on her written reminders because she has so much information to process. *Scotsman* critic Joyce McMillan likes to scrawl on her programme, making little remarks in the margins. For myself, it depends on my mood and the nature of the show. Often, I find note-taking helps me concentrate. I rarely refer back to the notes when I come to writing the review, but they are a good way of focusing at the time. Once you've made a note of something interesting, you can shift your concentration to something else. I find it particularly helpful to make notes about visual aspects of a performance, especially if reviewing dance or physical theatre. Personally, I find it harder to recall the abstract elements of a production, so a note about the music, lighting, costumes or choreography can be helpful in the same way as writing down an illuminating quote from the dialogue. The longer a piece I have to write, the more detail I know I will need – especially dates, place names, job titles and the like – and the more likely I am to make notes of that nature.

At other times, however, I take no notes at all. This is usually when I am feeling confident enough to immerse myself fully in the production, trusting that only when I emerge will I be in a position to see what is most interesting, affecting and significant. If I am given a script, as often happens today with new plays, I know I'll be able to find quotes or check technical language later if necessary, so I can get on with enjoying the play.

The danger of note-taking is getting so absorbed in your own intellectual world that you forget to engage emotionally with the performance. You cease to be a participant in a communal experience and become a detached observer, sitting in judgement like a clear-headed scientist objectively noting down chemical reactions as they take place in a test tube. This is to risk missing much of the point of theatre. Sure, there is an intellectual element and dispassionate analysis has its place, but so too does laughter, provocation, shock, anger, sadness and any other emotion you care to add. Stand back from this and you deny yourself the reason you and your readers go to the theatre in the first place. You can strike a balance between your objective and subjective reactions, but you do need to have both. Certainly, you should never let yourself get so preoccupied with note-taking that you stop watching the play altogether.

EXERCISE

Go to two shows close together. Choose mainstage productions so you won't be too self-conscious about bringing out a notebook. Commit yourself to making lots of notes in one and none in the other. Write a 250-word review within 24 hours of each performance and think about the differences. When were you most in the moment? When were you most precise? Which show was easier to recall? Did you refer to the notes as you were writing? Did you miss them when they weren't there? Did making notes affect your enjoyment of the show?

Causing a scene

Important too is the role of theatre as a communal event. It is a live artform that needs an audience. To understand what's going on, the critic must be part of the congregation, not watching from the wings.

This is especially the case with theatre in small studio spaces and even more so with promenade and site-specific performances. Here, the scribbling critic is likely to draw the energy of the room towards themselves, distracting from the main event. To pursue the laboratory analogy, they risk creating the observer effect, the phenomenon by which a scientist skews the results of an experiment in the act of watching it.

There are times when the advantages of allowing yourself to experience the performance in the moment outweigh the disadvantages of having to rely on memory when you come to write about it. That was a lesson learnt by Lyn Gardner who ended up on the front row (the only available seat) of an intimate one-woman production of Jennifer Tremblay's *The List* by Stellar Quines on the Edinburgh Fringe. Ten minutes into the show, actor Maureen Beattie stepped forward and removed Gardner's pen and paper. Many critics would have been affronted, but Gardner realized Beattie was right, as she later explained in a blog:

> The dynamics of the space, the powerful subject matter and my front-row location all combined to make my note-taking a very unwelcome distraction. Beattie took decisive action with minimal fuss and, at the end of a magnificent performance, returned my pen and paper with grace and a smile.[1]

To her great credit, Gardner had given the production an enthusiastic four-star review which made no mention of the interruption, only that 'the really magnificent thing is Maureen Beattie's mesmerising and thrillingly unforgiving performance'.[2]

When to write your review

Staying alive to the moment during the performance should make it possible to communicate some of the production's spontaneous energy in your review. Unless you have an unusually good emotional recall, the longer you wait before writing, the harder it is to do this. A review written against a deadline on the same night as the performance may be short on reflection, but it's likely to better convey a sense of the dynamics of the show and your passion for its strengths and weaknesses. The pressure of writing in this way can be scary, but once you get over your fear, it can be a satisfying way to work. These days, my deadline is normally 10am the following day, still close enough for the memory to be fresh but not so close that I depend on an adrenalin rush to get it done. When I wake up in the morning before starting to write, it can feel like my subconscious has been busy making connections, putting things in perspective and making sense of things that had puzzled me. The resulting review will perhaps be a fraction less heated, but also more considered. My experience waiting for longer periods, such as for a weekly round-up or a festival overview, is that some of the detail and urgency fades, while highlights come into perspective and broader connections are made. The writing isn't necessarily better or worse, but it does have a different pace and texture.

Every critic will have their own preferences, but a lot of the time the decision is made for you. This is as true for traditional newspapers, where overshooting your deadline by a matter of minutes can land you in trouble, as it is on the internet, where the pressure is on to attract web traffic as soon as possible after the press night. A lot of the more creative blog responses, the kind that offer deeper critical commentary and unexpected connections, necessarily take longer to appear, but with major shows, it's common for the first reviews to go online by lunchtime the next day. If you want to be part of the race to publication, you have little choice but to get your thoughts in order quickly. That can be alarming, but you'll be surprised what's possible under the pressure of a deadline.

For a more speedy response still, you may turn to Twitter. Within minutes of the final curtain, you can use the micro-networking site to fire off an instant reaction and set a discussion in motion. It's a tempting thing to do but it's worth exercising some caution. Twitter has many things going for it, but nuance is not among them. The 140-character format is perfect for the thumbs-up/thumbs-down school of criticism, but limited if you want to say something of any complexity. Before you press the 'Tweet' button to circulate your hilarious but damning one-liner, ask yourself if you would want it to be your definitive word on the show. Funny and smart it may be, but do you want it to be the first thing audiences and theatremakers learn about your opinion?

If you're anything like me, even you won't know what your opinion is until you have thought it through in the form of a review. By blasting out the first thing that comes into your head as you leave the theatre, you could saddle yourself with a superficial reaction that does no justice either to the show or to yourself. You're on safer ground if you loved the show and have something positive to say about it, but a negative opinion may come across as gratuitously rude or misleadingly one-sided.

The open and interactive nature of social media means that although a tweet may read like the kind of casual remark you'd say to your friends in private, it is published in the public sphere and is very likely to go straight into the inbox of the very people you are writing about. That means, like anything you write, you have to be prepared to stand by it.

If you want to make a quick social-media splash, a more restrained approach would be to comment on some distinguishing aspect of the production that would remain true whatever your opinion: 'Third show I've seen this week with a farmyard animal on stage' . . . 'Audience mobbing the stage door and blocking the traffic for a glimpse of their favourite celebrity' . . . 'Slowest interval drinks service in the country' . . . Any of those might pick up a few retweets, but none would box you into a corner before you had started writing. You would then be free to tweet again either once you had written your review or, better still, when it was online and you could send out a link.

In the next chapter, we'll look at the process of transforming the reactions you've had in the moment into opinions that you're comfortable about expressing in public.

Notes

1 Gardner, Lyn (16 September 2012), 'Lyn Gardner on the unwelcome distraction of note-taking', in *The Guardian*.
2 Gardner, Lyn (29 August 2012), '*The List*', in *The Guardian*.

10
HOW TO WRITE OPINIONS

Speaking out in public

As you have read this far, I'm going to make a few assumptions about you. I know you are literate, because you are reading a book. For the same reason, I suspect you are well educated. And, as you have an interest in the arts, I imagine you are attuned to the sensibilities of others. I think you're a decent, well-meaning sort, liberal-minded and easy-going. I'll go further and deduce you are not given to insulting people. You don't go out of your way to start a fight. If you are irritated by a friend's behaviour or concerned they are causing offence, you will either ignore them or try to deal with the matter in the least confrontational way. Unless you are possessed with extra reserves of confidence, unless you are unusually assertive, unless you are prepared to get as good as you give – and I don't think you are any of these things – you will not blurt out every niggle, irritation and complaint that goes through your head. I think this is what you are like.

If my assumptions are right, the first time you write a theatre review, you'll need to readjust. Suddenly, you'll find yourself saying in public what you were reticent to say in private. Whether you are offering praise, straight description or condemnation, you'll be using language that is a lot less circumspect than you'd use in everyday life. This can be a bit of a shock.

It's one thing to go to a show with a friend and share your opinions on the way home. With your friend, you won't mind being ribald, off-colour, passionate, irreverent, irrelevant, emotional, right or wrong. It's just a conversation. No big deal. It's quite another thing, however, to broadcast those same opinions in public, suspecting strangers and maybe even the artists themselves will be reading. Now, not only do you have the responsibility of talking directly to the theatremakers, but you yourself will be exposed. In this situation, you are as vulnerable as the artist; you're putting your opinions on the line and inviting the ridicule of anyone who cares to read you. Are you really so stupid as to think that? Is this the best analysis you have to offer? How can we give you any credence when you express yourself so clumsily? Call yourself a critic?

The moment you do call yourself a critic, you pass from the private realm into the public. You go from the person you are at home to the person you want the world to think you are: cool, sophisticated, articulate and intelligent. Out go the off-colour jokes and the wrong-headed judgements; in comes a new level of seriousness.

Here is a selection of negative comments lifted from published reviews: 'what is hard to credit is the general incompetence of the staging'[1]; 'a group of spotty sixth-formers might just about have got away with an abomination like this as an end-of-term show in the mid-Eighties'[2]; 'anyone who loves theatre will want to run screaming with horror at the sheer ineptitude of the enterprise'[3]. Take each of them in turn and imagine yourself saying the same thing directly to the artists' faces. Would you have the nerve? If you couldn't say it to their faces, could you justify saying it in print? Would it be cowardly to use your privileged position as a critic to say things that would be contentious if you said them in person? Or would it be a dereliction of duty to pull your punches?

The word 'critic' has its derivations with the Ancient Greek 'kritikos', related to discernment or judging, and 'kritos', related to picking out and choosing, so expressing an opinion is locked into the job. What would be the point of a critic who didn't say what they thought? To answer the question, it helps to remind yourself who you are writing for – the theatregoer, the casual newspaper reader, the random internet browser, the cultural completist, the future academic – none of whom care about the sensitivities of the performers. They want to know what the show was like, what they've missed, what it says about the world or whether they should see it. To find that out, they don't need you to be rude – making a judgement is not the same as handing out a punishment – but they do need you to be honest.

The literary critic Marcel Reich-Ranicki, who was noted for his forthright style, said: 'Clarity is the politeness of the critic. Directness is his obligation and his job.'[4] His argument was that you can be as polite as you like in daily life, but in a review, you have to get to the point. A critic is not employed to give blandishments. Even with the decline of the omnipotent critic handing down judgements from above and the rise of the more democratic forms of social media, the basic job of making judgements is little changed. And even if you prefer criticism not to be adversarial, you still have to be rigorous in your assessments.

EXERCISE

Think of something you disliked about the last show you saw. Write a sentence that expresses your view in a tone of contempt and ridicule. Now express the same sentiment in a spirit of understanding and support. How many different ways can you rewrite the sentence? Which would you be happiest publishing?

Telling it like it is

If expressing opinions is unavoidable even for those critics who take the most collegiate and supportive approach, then the greatest ambition must be to tell the truth, or at least, the truth as the critic perceives it. At the time it is published, a bad review hurts: it can wound a director's ego, damage the actors' morale and threaten business. These are the irritations a theatre company has to deal with, hence the anger, but they are temporary and probably not as bad as they seem at the time. In any case, not only are they not your concern, but there is no reason to suppose you have written something the artists didn't know already. You shouldn't flatter yourself that you have shown special insight in your damning review. Deep down, the theatremakers have a better sense of the strengths and weaknesses of their work than anyone. How could they not? They've been analysing it for weeks, if not months or years, making refinements, glossing over inconsistencies, adding, improving, reworking. Perhaps they lack the critic's disinterested perspective, but in all other respects, they'll know everything about the complex collaborative mix that makes perfection an honourable but unattainable goal. They will be fully aware of the difficulty of their task and the gulf between their ambition and their attainment. Not every show can be equally good. Inevitably some productions work better than others. It would take an unreflexive artist to think otherwise. It's really no big deal for a critic to point that out.

If critics wriggle out of expressing an opinion by narrowing their focus or retreating to the purely descriptive and impressionistic, they are shirking a key responsibility of their job. Not only would they be misleading readers, but they would be encouraging complacency in an artform they profess to love. The message may be unwelcome, but if you can show yourself to be consistent as a critic, to write each review without malice, to attempt as true a reflection of what you felt as possible, then even those whose work you haven't liked will eventually appreciate that you are in earnest. They will value the honesty of your viewpoint, if not in relation to their own work, then at least in relation to someone else's. As Oscar Wilde said, 'there is only one thing in the world worse than being talked about, and that is not being talked about',[5] and artists would rather be taken seriously than be flattered or, worse, ignored.

Goodbye social life

Let's assume this is what we want. That means, in the short term, the clarity and directness Reich-Ranicki talked about may lose you friends, especially in the close-knit world of theatre. People are likely to think of you as a destructive force even if most of your reviews are positive, something director Marshall W. Mason discovered in the mid-1990s when he sidelined as a critic on the *New Times* in Phoenix, Arizona: 'I learned that even though more than 75 percent of my reviews were favourable, the perception was that I was terribly mean, even vicious',[6] he wrote. He'd have sympathized with Stanley Kauffman who spent an eight-month stint as theatre critic on *The New York Times* in 1966. During that time, the backer of a show he had disliked sent him a letter enclosing toilet paper. It was, he said, 'not fresh'.[7]

Even in a big city, the profession is relatively small and, for better or worse, there is every chance you will soon bump into the people you have been writing about. With a live artform such as theatre, critics run into actors, directors, designers, musicians and admin staff every time they go out. Those people will also make their feelings known on Twitter, sometimes in response to your own tweets – and you might have to take a deep breath before deciding whether or not to tweet back. Some of them will accept you are just doing your job and will understand that criticism goes with the territory. If you're lucky, they won't take it personally. Others will feel slighted that, as they see it, you have trashed them in print (sometimes even the most innocuous phrase can sting) and want to confront you about it. You admire the actors who say they don't read their reviews (it shows a healthy independence of mind), but you will come across as many who can quote the most damning notices verbatim as if they've been carrying them around like a cross to bear.

It means, whether you like it or not, you should be prepared to say to someone's face anything you have said in print. And you have to be prepared for them not to like what they hear. That's why having a thick skin is an asset to a critic. If you want people to like you, you're

probably in the wrong job. At the very least, you should be prepared
to be criticized by the people you have criticized. However hard you
try to capture the truth of your experience, you will not always get it
right. If plays can be criticized then there's no reason reviews shouldn't
be criticized too. You can always improve. As Samuel Beckett said:
'Try Again. Fail again. Fail better.'[8]

Making your mind up

In this respect, self-awareness is an asset. Try to question not only the
performance you are reviewing but also your own reaction to it. If a
show makes you angry, what does it tell you about yourself? Are you
angry for clear critical reasons or because the production makes you
feel threatened and unnerved? Perhaps the show has provoked you in
exactly the way it intended. Or perhaps not – it's always hard to tell,
but when you look back at the outraged critical opinions of the past,
they often tell you more about the mores of the day and the prejudices
of the critic in question than about what the theatremakers were trying
to achieve.

All of us are capable of hiding our true motivations behind a rational-
sounding argument, often without realizing. Instead of revealing our
animal prejudices, hates and fears, we'd rather present our more
sophisticated side to the world. It's why you're more likely to hear
people saying they were bored by a sex scene than admitting to
having been turned on by it. In similar circumstances, you should ask
yourself whether you are taking cover behind an intellectual
smokescreen and concealing your true responses. I've chosen the
example of anger or outrage, but the same applies to any reaction you
may have, from laughter to tears.

This capacity for self-reflection is important given the very act of
forming an opinion is contentious. I often leave the theatre uncertain
about what to think, my head full of the possibilities a production throws
up but not yet reconciled to what it all means. At such times, it is only

in the process of writing the review, giving myself time to contemplate, reason, and argue, that I discover my opinion. What is surprising is how resolutely I stick to that opinion from then on. If I read a differing opinion, I'm convinced the other critic has got it wrong. I'll regard them as an idiot. How could they possibly think that? This is in spite of my own initial uncertainty, an uncertainty that suggests I could easily have arrived at many different opinions, including theirs. No doubt the other critic will be thinking the same in reverse about me and my review.

As the developmental biologist Lewis Wolpert said in *Six Impossible Things Before Breakfast*, 'beliefs, once acquired, have a kind of inertia in that there is a preference to alter them as little as possible'.[9] Wolpert proposed an evolutionary reason for this: once you have come to the opinion that a fire burns or an animal bites, you have a distinct advantage in sticking to that opinion. If you changed your mind every time you faced danger, you'd be dead. Our ancestors prospered by forming an opinion, learning the lesson and consistently putting it into practice. As a species, we seem to apply the same principle to all opinions, regardless of whether they are based on life-threatening empirical evidence (fire is always hot) or something less rational such as a belief in horoscopes, political parties and the merits of a show. All of those beliefs tend to be arrived at on impulse, by a hunch, going on a gut feeling, but are just as hard to shake off as a belief in something demonstrably true. That doesn't necessarily mean they are wrong (you'd be nowhere as a theatre critic without your gut feelings) but, being rationalized after the fact, they are subjective and open to challenge. The more you can be aware of this, the more supple your critical muscles, the more elastic your response and the more truthful to your actual experience.

Getting opinions in proportion

None of this is to suggest you have carte blanche to say whatever you like. Being honest is not the same as being rude. Take an example dreamed up by *Daily Telegraph* critic Charles Spencer, author of a series of crime novels about a hard-drinking reviewer, Will Benson, who has a job on the fictional *Theatre World*. In the first of the series, *I Nearly Died*, Benson does a hatchet job on a production of *Romeo and Juliet*. When his review, dashed off in the heat of the moment, appears in print, he realizes he has failed to sound the right note: 'Written in rage, but read in tranquillity, it was bad tempered rather than amusing, patronizing rather than wittily detached.'[10] Benson has made an honest attempt to capture the flavour of the evening (despite his regret, he does not change his low opinion of the show), but on this occasion, his skills as a journalist have failed him. It happens to us all.

Mastering the power of language is like being given the keys to a high-performance car. We've all seen people's personalities change when they get behind the wheel. Your mild-mannered neighbour becomes the aggressive tailgater, flouting the speed limit and intimidating other drivers. Thanks to the anonymity of the internet, much the same thing happens online. People who are civil and considerate in real life turn into belligerent trolls, leaving provocative remarks on blogs and malicious comments on Twitter. As a critic, you cannot hide behind an avatar or the shaded windows of a speeding car, but you do have the facility – and a kind of social permission – to express yourself with a force that other audience members do not.

Just as if you were driving a high-performance car, you have a responsibility to go about your business with care and attention. There is no Green Cross Code to consult, but you should be aware of the rules of the road. The entertaining writer can be like the speeding driver, offering thrills, exhilaration and danger, but veering wildly from the route of the sensible critic, a dull but safe motorist who reaches the destination without incident by sticking to the prosaic truth. Your ambition should be to take the best of both approaches. There's nothing wrong with making a joke, but if the gag is at the expense of the truth, if it says more about you and your hilarious sense of humour than it does about the reality of the production, then you could lose more than you gain.

Jokes stand out, but you need to take care of all the language you use. With a dictionary's-worth of words at your disposal, you have the capacity to write a high-octane report that is exciting to read while bearing little resemblance to the actual highs and lows of the production. Was an actor's performance miserable or was it merely mediocre? Did an ensemble hit Everest-like heights or was the achievement more hill-like? If you bring out the superlatives in one review, proclaiming a career-best performance, the greatest play of the decade or the finest ensemble in the country, what ammunition will you have left to describe the next good show that comes along? As critic Annegret Märten has pointed out,[11] it seems every actor who takes on Hamlet in a major London production is praised by someone in superlative terms: 'David Tennant is the greatest Hamlet of his generation'[12] ran the headline above a *Guardian* article; '[Rory] Kinnear's prince at the National is the most anticipated of his generation'[13] claimed an introduction to an article in *The Times*; while producer Sonia Friedman, announcing the casting of Benedict Cumberbatch as Hamlet, called him 'one of the most gifted of his generation'.[14] The coincidence of these virtually identical phrases tells us as much about the desire of critics to find a modern-day Shakespearean hero on whom to lavish praise as about the reality of the actors' achievements.

The most extreme language makes the most dynamic review, but to maintain credibility, you have to say what you mean. No real discernment takes place when everything is either damned or lauded. To capture in words the emotional intensity of the best theatre is a great achievement; to make your review more exciting than the event itself is to lie. The more you can stay true to your experience, encapsulate your thoughts and express your contradictory impulses, the more honest a reflection of the event your review will be. To write compellingly about the shades of grey in between the extremes is a worthy aim.

The subjective voice

On a practical level, most critics jealously guard their opinions until they've written their reviews. It's considered bad form to talk about the show with other critics during the interval or immediately after the final curtain, partly to avoid the charge of collusion and partly not to be influenced by other people's opinions. It's hard to be true to your own still-solidifying responses if you have other voices buzzing around your head, especially when those voices are not in agreement with your own. Personally, I apply this rule not just to other critics but anyone I might be seeing the show with. It makes me a lousy date but it means I can write with some degree of clarity. In this respect, I'm with Razumihin in *Crime and Punishment* who said: 'To go wrong in one's own way is better than to go right in someone else's.'[15] That's a personal choice and not true of all critics, and even I will make exceptions. When writing a Sunday newspaper round-up, for example, I've sometimes taken the opportunity to reflect on reviews published during the week and to situate my own opinions in relation to what others have been saying. Such a technique is common among bloggers, who are often more interested in wide-ranging discussion than polarized opinion. There's a case to be made that a collegiate approach to reviewing may actually be beneficial, as Lyn Gardner suggested in a *Guardian* blog: 'Might not hearing or reading other perspectives on a show actually enrich your views and deepen the conversation that you try to start around the show?'[16]

The approach you take will depend on your temperament and the nature of your review, but unless you want to make yourself unpopular, I don't recommend you spend the interval asking the other critics what they thought.

How to write positive reviews

Writing positive things about a show is not taxing. When you're racing against a deadline, it's easier to throw a superlative or two in the direction of the theatremakers than to get under the skin of a production. If you're going to speak negatively of a show, you'll want to explain your reasoning – it's bad enough delivering bad news without coming across as reckless and misanthropic. If you're going to be generally benign, the pressure is off: who's going to complain about all those nice things you've said? Follow this reasoning to its conclusion and you'll end up with a review that is cheery but bland. The challenge, then, is to be critically rigorous as well as enthusiastic. It means being precise and arguing a positive case as persuasively as you would a negative case.

It also means risking some embarrassment. If you rave about a show that everyone else turns out to be indifferent towards, you could be made to feel foolish. How naïve, how gauche, how exposed you will appear for expressing your passion so honestly. What will it mean for your credibility and your professional standing? The easier option is to affect an air of cynical detachment, awarding praise where it is due but at no emotional risk to yourself. It's also the least honest option. For a truer response, you need to trust your instincts and give your enthusiasms free rein.

At the same time, it can be difficult to get a sense of perspective. When you love a show, it's natural to reach for the superlatives. You want to pass on your enthusiasm in as bold a way as possible. The bolder you are, the more punchy your writing and, you hope, the more persuasive it will be. If you overplay your hand, however, you could end up sounding less persuasive. Loving a show is one thing, making unsustainable claims for it is another. Robert Cushman of Canada's *National Post* and an eight-times winner of the Nathan Cohen Award for Excellence in Theatre Criticism wrote that *After Miss Julie* at the Storefront Theatre 'with the possible exception of *The Double*, is the best show in Toronto'.[17] If he hadn't been up to speed with all the key shows in Toronto, he would have been on shaky ground. It would have been easy for any reader who had seen a better show to call his bluff. As it was, he wrote with the authority of someone who knew the terrain. In an email, I asked him if he found it harder to write in absolute terms the older he got and if he'd advise caution for those with less experience. He replied:

> Yes, I guess as I get older I do get more careful about making sweeping statements – about declaring things incomparably good (or bad). On the other hand, it means that when something stands out, it really stands out. To younger critics: I don't know that I'd advise 'caution' exactly – youth is the time for making bold statements – but it's good to try and make clear what your standards of comparison are: i.e. how much you've actually seen.

How to write lukewarm reviews

The force of a strong opinion, whether negative or positive, will provide the animating energy you need to power through a review. With something passionate to say, you can concentrate on your argument and let the other details follow in its wake. Much harder is to write interestingly on something you are indifferent towards. With a show you neither love nor hate there is too little at stake to get worked up about. The challenge is how to avoid boring the reader with your tepid response. When he worked as a book reviewer, George Orwell found himself 'constantly INVENTING reactions towards books about which one has no spontaneous feelings whatever'.[18] He questioned the value of writing anything about such books, but was compelled to do so by the journalistic system. This facility to respond imaginatively to middling material is, however, what distinguishes the professional critic from the amateur. As the majority of work lies somewhere between the extremes of the brilliant and the dire, critics are more likely to find themselves in this situation than not. You don't want to damn with faint praise but you don't have much reason to shout about it either.

Aping Orwell and inventing reactions is not the ideal way to go, but you're likely to find yourself leaning on some of the strategies we looked at in Chapter 3. In the role of critic as theatrical analyst, you will seek out those distinctive elements of a production where they exist and give them due credit. In the role of critic as educator, you will situate the production in its social and cultural context. And in the role of critic as ego, you will engage with the show in a lively and entertaining manner, taking care not to overstate your case: writers who are fond of hyperbole tend to be more exciting than reliable. By taking seriously our first question – 'What were the theatremakers trying to do?' – and by always assuming that what you see on stage is deliberate, you will be helped in those cases where you have no compelling answer to our third question – 'Was it worth it?'

How to write negative reviews

In an interview in *The Harvard Advocate*, the novelist Dave Eggers warned his readers off becoming critics: 'I was a critic, and I wish I could take it all back, because it came from a smelly and ignorant place in me and spoke with a voice that was all rage and envy.'[19] It was good advice to the extent that if you are writing bad reviews because you hate your chosen artform, it is time to think again. A voice that is 'all rage and envy' will eat you up from the inside and your reviewing days will be numbered. You simply won't be able to maintain the energy to go and watch all those shows before the cynicism defeats you.

A more likely scenario is that your negative reviews come from loving theatre not hating it. When you know how good theatre can be, you will be at best disappointed and at worst angry with productions that fail to live up to your ideal. The best bad reviews come not from a 'smelly and ignorant place', but one that is high-minded and aspirational. When you react intensely against a production, however, the pressure is on to explain yourself. Unless you are happy to appear like an arrogant and condescending bully, you need to express not just your anger but a rationale for that anger. To attack a show makes you susceptible to counter attack, so you need to present a reasoned argument rather than a series of entertaining putdowns (which isn't to rule out entertaining putdowns).

You should also question your own reaction: if it is especially intense, could the show have hit some vulnerability in your own psychological make-up? In which case, is your attack a way of defending yourself? Michael Billington always regretted his hostile first-night review of Sarah Kane's *Blasted* ('Far from crying, like the man in front of me: "Bring back the censor", I was simply left wondering how such naive tosh managed to scrape past the Court's normally judicious play-selection committee'[20]) and later suggested that his 'initial incomprehension' had prevented him from giving an 'honest assessment of its virtues and faults'.[21] If you have a strong reaction, what does it say about you?

Staying within the law

If you choose to comment negatively, it is important to understand the distinction between saying a performer acted badly and saying a performer can't act. To say a performer acted badly is the critic's legitimate assessment based on the evidence of the show. It's perfectly possible (even common) for a good actor to make decisions that lead to a bad performance. It's the critic's job to say so. To claim a performer can't act, however, is problematic in two ways. First, it is speculative: how could a critic know the actor was unsuited to all roles? And second, it could damage the actor's reputation and their employment prospects: who would want to hire an actor who couldn't act? Depending on the libel and defamation laws, you could be sued for saying so. Do not treat my comments as watertight legal advice: make sure you know what the law is in your country.

When it comes to expressing opinions, critics in the US have the Constitution's First Amendment on their side: 'Congress shall make no law . . . abridging the freedom of speech, or of the press.' Precedent was set in 1901 at the Supreme Court of Iowa where the Cherry

Sisters, a much derided vaudeville act, had taken a complaint against the *Des Moines Leader*. Contemporary reports suggest this variety act fell into the so-bad-it-was-good category. Audiences and critics alike would delight in ripping it to pieces. Each performance was greeted with a hail of rotten vegetables from the stalls, followed by merciless reviews in the press. Their shows sold out, but for all the wrong reasons. *The Des Moines Leader* had republished a damning review by Billy Hamilton, editor of the Odebolt *Chronicle*, of 'Something Good, Something Sad'. Hamilton was far from alone in condemning their song-and-dance act, but the sisters sued the publishers for $15,000, claiming the review had been 'severe and satirical' and had held them up to ridicule.

When the case came before Polk County District Court, the judge ruled that: 'Any performance to which the public is invited may be freely criticized. Also any editor may publish reasonable comments on that performance.' It was a decision upheld in the Supreme Court and which protects critics in the US to this day. Subsequent legal rulings have made it clear that opinions are neither true nor false, they're just opinions, and as they are constitutionally protected, even a bizarre or unreasonable opinion must have the right to expression.

In England and Wales, theatre reviews are protected by the principle of fair comment which, in 2010, became known as 'honest comment' and, in 2013, 'honest opinion'. To defeat a defence of honest opinion, a claimant would have to prove a critic did not hold the opinion and, as the law allows the opinion to be prejudiced, exaggerated and obstinate, that is not easily done.

The principle of fair comment does not put critics above the law, however. It is possible to defame someone in a theatre review just as it is in any piece of writing. Opinions may be considered fair comment, but there is no such protection for facts. You can say what you like about the play, but if you made an unseemly allegation about the private life of the playwright or the health-and-safety record of the theatre without the facts to back it up, you could land yourself with a court case. In such an instance, you would have strayed beyond commenting on the production and damaged the reputation of an individual or an organization.

Whether or not a legal action is successful, the proceedings can go on for years and will make no one happy but the lawyers. Even if you acted within the law, your publication may insist on its lawyers double-checking all your copy until the case is settled. You should be scrupulous about not getting yourself in the same situation. In any case, it's worth considering whether you want to be the sort of critic whose reviews are seen as 'prejudiced, exaggerated and obstinate'. Being cruel may raise a laugh, but it may also be destructive, cynical and too easy. Bad reviews are a corrective to the upbeat hype of the theatrical publicity machine and they contribute to a fruitful public discussion about artistic standards, but if they reveal more about the critic than the work being criticized, their value is questionable.

EXERCISE

Write a deliberately damning 250-word review in which you dismiss every aspect of the production in the rudest of terms. Now give the same show an unequivocal rave review. Which approach feels most comfortable? Which is most true?

Notes

1   Billington, Michael (20 September 2013), 'Much Ado About Nothing', in The Guardian.
2   Walker, Tim (14 December 2012), 'Julius Caesar', in The Sunday Telegraph.
3   Gardner, Lyn (12 September 2013), 'Afraid of the Dark', in The Guardian.
4   Associated Press (18 September 2013), 'Marcel Reich-Ranicki dies at 93; influential German literary critic', in the LA Times.
5   Wilde, Oscar (1891), The Picture of Dorian Gray, Ward Lock & Co.

6 Mason, Marshall W. (2006) *Creating Life on Stage*, Heinemann
Educational Books.

7 Kauffmann, Stanley (November 1991), 'Album of a theatre critic' in *The
American Scholar*.

8 Beckett, Samuel (1983), *Worstward Ho*, Calder Publications Ltd.

9 Wolpert, Lewis (2006), *Six Impossible Things Before Breakfast*, Faber and
Faber.

10 Spencer, Charles (1994), *I Nearly Died*, Victor Gollancz.

11 Märten, Annegret (13 June 2014), 'Reviewing across cultures', presented
at Adapting, Performing & Reviewing Shakespearean Comedy in a
European Context.

12 McCrum, Robert (9 January 2009), 'David Tennant is the greatest Hamlet
of his generation', in *The Guardian*.

13 Nightingale, Benedict (25 September 2010), 'Rory Kinnear's Hamlet: an
icon of our times', in *The Times*.

14 Denham, Jess (26 March 2014), 'Sherlock's Benedict Cumberbatch to
play Hamlet on London stage in 2015', in *The Independent*.

15 Dostoyevsky, Fyodor (1866) *Crime and Punishment* (trans Constance
Garnett), Wordsworth Classics.

16 Gardner, Lyn (2 September 2013), 'Should critics talk to each other?', in
The Guardian.

17 Cushman, Robert (23 November 2013), 'Robert Cushman: The riveting
After Miss Julie may be the best show onstage now in Toronto', in *The
National Post*.

18 Orwell, George (3 May 1946), 'Confessions of a book reviewer', in
Tribune.

19 Garner, Dwight (15 August 2012), 'A critic's case for critics who are
actually critical', in *The New York Times*.

20 Billington, Michael (20 January 1995), '*Blasted*', in *The Guardian*.

21 Billington, Michael (2007), *State of the Nation*, Faber and Faber.

11
HOW TO GIVE STAR RATINGS

Numbers versus words

It's thanks to the critic as consumer guide that star ratings have become ubiquitous. By giving every review a number, usually on a scale of five, sometimes ten and occasionally seven, the critic indicates the degree to which a show is worth seeing. A single star tells you to avoid; five tells you not to miss. I know few critics who like the system (they hate their work being reduced to a number), but I also know few who don't use their stars in conversation. 'How many stars did you give it?', we will ask each other. Sometimes you'll even come across critics discussing their rating in the body of a review: 'Despite certain weaknesses, the reason this scrapes into the four-star category is . . .'

This isn't hypocritical. We can all see that stars function as a handy shorthand, one we'll even use from time to time, but we're also aware of their limitations. The weakness is that if ratings make sense at all, it is primarily in terms of consumer-centric reviewing. The critic who presupposes that all theatre is interesting and who values its capacity to stimulate philosophical thought has no use for stars – how could one idea be more valuable than another? Even on a more mundane level, the star rating is a crude measure of a production's worth. If it were only a matter of answering our second question – 'How well did they do it?' – the stars would be an adequate approximation, although there would still be the uncertainty about what the consumer wanted. But if you expect the rating also to answer the third question – 'Was it worth it?' – it ceases to be meaningful. A show that achieves its mediocre ambition gets three stars. A show that fails to achieve its grand ambition also gets three stars. Personally, I would much prefer to see the noble failure than the average success (the first is worth the effort, the second less so), but at first glance, the reader would assume the two three-star productions were in the same middling category. The stars can't tell you that a dreary production is essential viewing because of an exceptional actor – nor can they convey any of the nuances, caveats and juxtapositions that words make possible.

It doesn't help that websites, magazines and newspapers rarely provide a definition of what the stars mean and, when they do, there is no agreement from one publication to another. Do two stars mean 'bad' or 'not bad'? One website used to express its verdict in terms of the number of glasses of Scotch whisky you'd have been better off drinking if you weren't seeing the show. Counterintuitively, this meant five glasses of whisky was the equivalent of one star in another publication, while one whisky was a rave. Not surprisingly, it dropped the system, but audiences are still left with the problem of deciding how one publication's seven stars relate to another publication's five stars, not to mention all the half-stars and decimal divisions they'll come across. Even if they looked at it mathematically, the 20 per cent range for each star rating covers an ambiguously large area. Three stars could be anything from 41 per cent to 60 per cent; four stars could mean 61 per cent or it could mean 80 per cent. As a result, readers have got to decide whether the rating tells them anything useful at all. In *The List* magazine's survey of 5,678 reviews in eighteen publications covering the 2014 Edinburgh Festival Fringe, it reported that 76 per cent were split evenly between the three- and four-star categories.[1] The reader could make special efforts to see the shows that got five stars, amounting to 10 per cent of all reviews, and they could discount the 14 per cent of one- or two-star reviews, but that still left an undifferentiated mass of worthwhile shows in the middle. If the vast majority of shows get three or four stars (the average was 3.4 stars), it suggests the rating system's main function is to reassure the reader that they haven't made a terrible mistake. When the critics deem eight shows in every ten to be worth seeing (three stars and above), the only way to tell one from the other is to read the words.

We can complain all we like, but for as long as our consumer-orientated culture persists, stars are not going to go away. That being the case, the critic as consumer guide must learn to use them with care. If you're writing for an editor, ask them what they think each star rating means and use that as your guide. A complaint made frequently against inexperienced critics is they are too quick to lavish five stars. In their rush of enthusiasm, they fail to discriminate between the excellent and the merely very good. If in doubt, you should err on the side of caution: four stars is a pretty good recommendation and a three-star show should be worth seeing. Before you award five stars, ask yourself whether the show really is the best of its kind. Likewise before you give one star, be sure to persuade yourself that the show has no redeeming features. It's best to put out of your mind the suspicion that people are more likely to read a review with a high or low rating. One press officer half-jokingly suggested to me that critics should be bolder in their opinions and never give anything three stars. Choosing between a two or a four would force the critics to show their colours and make readers take notice. It's a tempting proposition, but although that same press officer has now become a prominent playwright, I haven't had the guts to put it into practice even for him. The reality is that most shows are neither exceptionally brilliant nor exceptionally awful. They can be accomplished, entertaining and worthwhile, but on balance, they're just somewhere in the middle. Your three-star review may get you ignored, but it's likely to be closer to the truth.

Be wise to the phenomenon of star inflation. This happens when you see two shows in close succession, the second better than the first. If you have already given four stars to the first show, the temptation is to give five to the second. It's very easy to fall into this pattern, but using one show as a benchmark for another will inevitably get you tied in knots. A banana is a four-star fruit. So is an apple. That is not to say the experience of eating a banana has anything in common with the experience of eating an apple. Try to keep the stars rooted to the show's own ambitions (our first question) and responsive to the context in which it takes place. Giving four stars to a $3m Broadway musical does not mean you think the experience is the same as seeing a four-star profit-share drama by a group of recent graduates. One is a banana, the other is an apple.

Once you've got to grips with the rating system, you can start playing against the stars to draw out aspects of the production that run counter to your overall assessment. In a two-star review, you can afford to accentuate the positive; in a four-star review, your explicit endorsement gives you licence to talk about weaker elements. If stars were expressed as a percentage, each one would cover a big range. There is a lot of territory between 41 per cent and 60 per cent, all of it covered by a three-star rating. Your words in conjunction with the star rating allow you to say whether it's a generally good three-star experience or a weaker one. Taken on their own, the words for a strong three-star review may actually seem more positive than those for a weak four-star review. For that reason, you often hear perplexed theatremakers saying, 'We got a three but it read like a four'. They may literally be right: because there are so many borderline occasions, a critic may swither between one rating and another until the last minute without feeling the need to change a word. An example of this is when you like the play but don't care for the production. Thinking as a consumer guide, you are reasonably certain that someone seeing the play for the first time will get a lot from it. Thinking as a critic, you know they could get even more from it with a better production. If it's a one-star production of a five-star play, you could end up with the worst of both worlds by settling for a middling three-star rating, even though giving a one or a five could be misleading. As a rule of thumb, you could say the stars relate to the production if it's a staging of an old play, whereas they better reflect the ideas of the playwright or the creative team if it's a new work. Inevitably, your words will do a better job than the stars.

Finally, depending on your publication, you don't necessarily have to regard star ratings as consumer advice. Instead, you can put yourself in the role of critic as judge and treat them like a grade from a teacher. A one-star 'avoid' becomes 'poor effort'; a five-star 'don't miss' becomes 'well done'. The distinction is subtle, but in certain circumstances, it can free you from the unknowability of the box office and focus your attention on the quality of the work itself. You may feel more comfortable giving three stars because the show was a pretty decent effort than four stars because you imagine the audience will enjoy it. Thinking like this can also help keep star-rating inflation in check.

EXERCISE

Choose four of five published reviews. Read them once then read them again, this time imagining a different star rating. How much is your reading coloured by your knowledge of the rating? How clear is the relationship between the critic's words and the rating they have given? How easy is it to change the rating without seeming to alter the critic's meaning?

Notes

1   *The List* (August 2014), 'Top rated shows of 2014'
    (www.edinburghfestival.list.co.uk/top-rated/year:2014).

12
HOW TO WRITE ABOUT ACTING

The art of precision

Writing about actors comes less easily to many critics than writing about plays. That's partly to do with literary training. From a young age, most of us have been taught how to analyse character, language and plot, all of which are expressed in words, the same words we use to write our reviews. The actor's contribution can be harder to pin down, despite them being centre stage and despite them being what drives most people to the box office. They present the critic with two challenges. The first is to gauge what they have brought to a role, to pick apart how much of the character is theirs and how much is the playwright's (was Olivier's Hamlet indecisive or should that epithet belong to Shakespeare's Hamlet?). The other is to find a form of words that does justice to their craft. Unlike a script on a page, the actor's work is not containable; it takes place before our eyes in time and space, involving gesture, physicality, spatial relationships, movement, diction, rhythm and pace. It is fast, fluid and fleeting, resistant to mere words. The task for the critic is to find the form of words that gets close.

It is easier to convey a general impression of the effects of a performance than to give an accurate idea of what an actor did. Frequently, we give the reader a sense of our enthusiasm or displeasure while leaving them with no idea of the nature of the performance. The eighteenth-century critic who told us that *Hamlet*'s closet scene 'excited our Admiration',[1] that John Kemble gave 'one of the finest pieces of Acting' since the days of David Garrick and that the audience gave 'universal Plaudits' left us with nothing about what Kemble did to excite the admiration, what made his acting so fine and why he merited the audience's plaudits. In this, he is not alone. Today, often because of the pressure of space, critics frequently summarize a performance with a single adjective – 'excellent', 'indifferent', 'funny' – without ever getting to grips with what made it so. Here, by contrast, is the early German physicist Georg Christoph Lichtenberg describing a production of *The Merchant of Venice* starring Charles Macklin as Shylock that he saw during a visit to England a few years earlier in 1775:

> The first words he utters, when he comes on to the stage, are slowly and impressively spoken: 'Three thousand ducats'. The double 'th', which Macklin lisps as lickerishly as if he were savouring the ducats and all that they could buy, make so deep an impression in the man's favour that nothing can destroy it. Three such words uttered at the outset give the keynote of his whole character. In the scene where he first misses his daughter, he comes on hatless, with disordered hair, some locks a finger long standing on end, as if raised by a breath of wind from the gallows, so distracted was his demeanour. Both his hands are clenched, and his movements abrupt and convulsive. To see a deceiver, who is usually calm and resolute, in such a state of agitation, is terrible.[2]

Not only did Lichtenberg give a vivid impression of Macklin's performance, he also described what effect the actor's choices had. All these years on, it is fascinating to learn in such precise detail how Macklin stressed the words, wore his costume and held his body, but Lichtenberg went one step further by identifying what emotional impact these details created ('as if raised by a breath of wind from the gallows'). His snapshots were not random but judiciously chosen to explain how the actor conveyed meaning and engaged the audience.

He also made it plain that the actor's craft is not a literary phenomenon but a performative one, just as dependent on physicality, gesture, choreography and spatial relationships as it is on language and delivery.

It is this kind of detail that distinguishes the most vivid writing about acting. To achieve this effect, you need to pay close attention to detail at the same time as taking in the bigger picture. A detail is of most value when it points to a more general truth. It's all very well to observe an actor repeatedly raising an arm above her head, for example, but it's more purposeful if you can say what that gesture conveys about her character or state of mind. You need to combine your observational and interpretative skills as you take in the actor's speech, movement, demeanour, gesture and emotional state, all the while being aware of everything else taking place on stage and the greater movement of the production. You'll never get it exactly right, but you'll never tire of trying.

EXERCISE

Write a 300-word review that focuses on a single actor, paying close attention to the choices they make (and those that they don't), the way they convey meaning and how they interpret their role. Look too at their appearance, movement, physicality and vocal presence.

How to define good acting

Complicating the matter still further is the question of fashion and taste. First you must identify what it is the actor is doing on a moment by moment basis. Perhaps you'll find a key in Constantin Stanislavski's theories about acting: what is at stake for the characters, what are their objectives, how urgent is their predicament and how does it

change according to circumstance? Secondly, however, you must
weigh this up against your ideas of what constitutes good acting.
From the beginning, critics have taken it upon themselves to call for
improvements in acting standards. Think of Hamlet's advice to the
players or the work that is done in today's drama schools. Good
acting, however, is not a fixed thing, but a fluid, culturally agreed – and
sometimes contested – norm. Critics often profess to liking an actor
for their trueness to life, but how actors achieve that truth is always
changing. The eighteenth-century critic mentioned above praised
Kemble in his performance of Hamlet for using 'every Exertion to make
the Character a true Copy of Nature'.[3] Writing about Edmund Kean
playing Richard III in 1814, Lord Byron said: 'Life – nature – truth
without exaggeration or diminution [. . .] Richard is a man and Kean
is Richard.'[4] Stark Young praised Laurette Taylor in the role of Amanda
Wingfield in the Broadway debut of *The Glass Menagerie* in 1945 for
her 'naturalistic acting of the most profound, spontaneous, unbroken
continuity and moving life'.[5] All three comments sound very like Sarah
Hemming in the *Financial Times* in 2011 praising Ian Rickson's
production of *Hamlet* starring Michael Sheen for plunging us 'into a
nightmare that feels all too real'.[6] One was a 'true copy of nature', one
was 'truth without exaggeration', one was 'spontaneous, unbroken
continuity', and one was 'all too real', but that isn't it to say the
performances of Kemble, Kean, Taylor and Sheen were in any way
alike. Look at a Hollywood film from the 1940s, a silent movie from the
early days of cinema or, better still, some archive footage of an actor
on stage and you'll get a sense of how our tastes have changed over
time. It's reasonable to assume that people half a century from now
will look back at the popular acting of our era and find it strange and
stylized. Where we see emotional truth, they will see artifice. Tastes
change all the time, sometimes more rapidly than others, and it is at
those points critics bring the debate into the open.

Even the preference for acting that is a 'true Copy of Nature' is
contentious. The naturalistic school of performance pioneered by
Stanislavski as he staged the plays of Anton Chekhov may appeal to

you more than the declamatory style of an earlier era, you may even be able to make a good argument about why, but you could never prove scientifically that copying nature was, by definition, better than exaggerating nature, distorting it or ignoring it altogether. There is no objective right or wrong.

You can imagine similar debates in every era. Did Steven Berkoff find a poetic truth through his grotesque and exaggerated gestures or did he merely draw attention to his Lecoq-schooled technique? Was Marlon Brando being true to life in *On the Waterfront* or was he just mumbling? Did Ricky Gervais bring the sitcom a step closer to the way people actually speak in *The Office* or did he just introduce a new set of mannerisms? Approaches to acting that first strike us as fresh and naturalistic usually turn out to be as artificial as the approaches they replace. That's not a bad thing; it's normal for art to be in a state of renewal. Actors must convince us of the truth of a situation by artificial means. As long as we accept the artifice, they can do their job. But when the rules change, one generation's bravura performer becomes the next generation's old ham. The critic is on hand to mark the changes.

EXERCISE

Write a 300-word review of a classical production that focuses primarily on the actors. Use trueness to life as your benchmark for success. Now review the same show on the assumption that good acting is based on diction, oratory, verse-speaking and a non-naturalistic use of movement. Which review does the production most justice?

How to treat actors with respect

Of all the theatrical elements that a review can focus on, acting feels like the most personal. Today's critic is comfortable making negative comments about the work of playwrights and directors, but more cautious when it comes to actors. To draw attention to weak performances away from the central roles seems like bullying. Unlike the rest of the creative team, it is the actor who has to go in front of an audience night after night. They are exposed and vulnerable, so unless they are throwing the whole production off the rails, it feels more humane to keep quiet about their deficiencies. This is partly because it can be tricky to distinguish between, on the one hand, the actor as a flesh-and-blood human being and, on the other, the choices the actor has made. Just because an actor is accomplished and much loved doesn't mean they are incapable of making decisions that take them to an artistic dead end. It's your job to comment on their decisions, but although you don't intend your comments to be personal, they can easily come across as such. You often feel compelled to explain that your remarks are about what the actor did in this particular performance, not about their capabilities in general.

Actors, of course, are there not only as the end product of a series of choices and not only as their characters, but also as themselves – they can't escape their height, their weight, their skin colour, their voice and their facial mannerisms. Indeed, the physical presence of the actors may make a significant contribution to the meaning of the play: it would be hard to stage *Laurel and Hardy*, Tom McGrath's affectionate tribute, without a tall, thin actor and a short, portly one. But how much is it acceptable for the critic to comment on that? The answer depends a lot on your cultural context. Henry Bate, writing in *The Morning Post* in 1778, was unimpressed by a Covent Garden performance of Nicholas Rowe's *The Tragedy of Jane Shore*. He had this particular complaint about the actor in the lead role of one of King Edward IV's mistresses: 'Mrs Yates's figure is grown rather too plump, and majestic, for the delicate Jane Shore.'[7] Today, you can just about imagine 'plump' being used as an adjective but never as a matter of critical judgement. First, we would find it hard to argue that plumpness was, in itself, an obstacle to playing a part (who's to say Jane Shore has to be 'delicate'?), and second, we would be too aware of the incendiary public debate about body image – especially women's body image – to risk singling out an actor in such personal terms (curiously, this is not always the case in criticism of opera and classical dance where tradition seems more likely to dictate what characters should look like[8]). In 1820, Leigh Hunt wrote at length about his admiration for the 'very prettiest leg we ever saw on the stage'.[9] It belonged to Ann Maria Tree, who played Viola in a production of *Twelfth Night*, and the critic insisted he had licence to write about it because 'such subjects are eminently critical'. By this point, he had already commended her acting, which was 'sincere, unaffected, and graceful', but he was not shy about discussing the impression her physical appearance had made on him, especially as it conformed with his society's expectations of the feminine ideal.

Going against the grain in twentieth-century criticism, John Simon had a tendency to make comments of this nature and was criticized for doing so. 'Diana Rigg is built like a brick mausoleum with insufficient flying buttresses', he wrote in *New York* magazine in 1970, a remark the actor included in her anthology of the 'worst ever theatrical reviews', *No Turn Unstoned*,[10] despite her initial 'dismay and hurt'. About Liza Minnelli in *The Act*, he wrote:

> I always thought Miss Minnelli's face deserving – of first prize in the beagle category. Less aphoristically speaking, it is a face going off in three directions simultaneously: the nose always en route to becoming a trunk, blubber lips unable to resist the pull of gravity, and a chin trying its damnedest to withdraw into the neck, apparently to avoid responsibility for what goes on above it.[11]

When Minnelli's agent, Sabina Harbison, complained to him that he should have judged the actor on her performance alone, he stuck to his guns: 'if we are allowed to invoke aesthetic criteria where other things presented on stage are concerned, why should faces be taboo?' His attitude raises many awkward questions. Whole books could be written about the sexual politics of the male critic gazing at a female body on stage and passing judgement. That's not to say the actor's physicality should be out of bounds. On the contrary, the way the performers control their bodies is central to the theatrical event. Think about how a production provoked a strong reaction from you at a particular moment and it may well be nothing to do with the script or the setting and everything to do with the actors' physical presence.

Without necessarily resorting to the kind of language used by Simon, the critic should be able to acknowledge the variety of shapes and sizes on stage and to identify the attributes that mark them out. In the case, for example, of *Untitled Feminist Show* by the American theatre director Young Jean Lee, the variety of shapes and sizes of the six naked performers was the whole point. In Toronto's *Globe and Mail*, Kate Taylor described them thus: 'Some of them are lithe and lean; others are gloriously fleshy; none of them conform to *Vogue*'s idea of a good swimsuit model.'[12] By using the adjective 'gloriously', Taylor found a way of referring to the fleshiness of the bodies that didn't reinforce swimsuit-model stereotypes. 'Their imperfect beauty', she went on, 'is a bold statement about the objectification of women.' As a critic, she was duty-bound to describe that imperfect beauty because that was what the show was about. A critic who was interested in the politics of representation may choose to take a similar approach to every play they see, challenging stereotypes and questioning casting choices.

Everything on stage carries a meaning and those meanings, even when they are related to the personal attributes of the actor, could be relevant to the critic's interpretation. If a black actor and an Asian actor were cast as twin sisters in a play set among the all-white British aristocracy of the eighteenth century, the critic would have to decide whether such 'colour-blind' casting was simply part of the playful logic of theatrical pretence or whether the director was making a statement about race (or the nature of sisterhood, or whatever). When Lee Breuer cast Mark Povinelli, who is 3ft 9in, as Torvald Helmer and Maude Mitchell, who is 5ft 6in, as Nora Helmer in *Mabou Mines DollHouse*, he was asking questions about the relative status of the different sexes. It wasn't a coincidence that the men in this version of Ibsen's *A Doll's House* had the most power and the least physical stature – it was central to the directorial concept. Not to have mentioned it for fear of offending the actors would have been to miss the point. Equally, had you been reviewing Povinelli in another production, one in which no such concept existed, you may have thought it gratuitous to mention his height. What matters is less what the actors look like than the meaning of what they look like.

EXERCISE

Write a 400-word review that examines how the actors' personal attributes contribute to the mood and meaning of the production. Consider their relative heights and weights, the way they walk, the way they hold themselves, their accents and intonation, their faces and physical features, their age, gender and race. Could you publish your review without causing offense?

How to write about movement

The challenge remains about how to capture the living, breathing, three-dimensional, dynamic flow of an actor's performance into something that makes sense to the reader. This is especially the case when trying to describe more obviously choreographed sequences. Even those theatre critics who are not called upon to review classical ballet or modern dance are frequently required to comment on theatre that incorporates similar skills, whether it is the big-top skills of Cirque du Soleil, the crossover work of dance-theatre companies or the whole sub-genre of physical theatre. Today, many of the most conventional rep theatres will employ a movement director from time to time, and it's important for the critic to develop a vocabulary that does justice to their work. It's not merely a question of describing the physicality of a performance, it's also about defining how the movement contributes to the production's impact. Natasha Tripney succeeded in doing both in her 'Interval Drinks' review of *Coriolanus*, starring Tom Hiddleston, at London's Donmar Warehouse:

> The choreography of the early fight scenes is slick and physical – Coriolanus and his enemy hurl each other about the stage, dashing each other to the floor – but it's almost too slick, and there are times when you find yourself marvelling at the technical effort involved, at the clank of cutlass on cutlass, at the force with which the punches appear to land, rather than feeling any sense of the rawness and mess of warfare. (Though, at least, when they finally cast their weapons aside and grapple on the floor you do get a glimpse of this).[13]

Many writers would have observed the energy of the fight scenes and left it at that. Tripney, by contrast, not only did justice to the production's muscularity, creating a vivid sense of what the cutlass clanks and forceful punches were like, but went further by identifying the way in which the physicality, to her mind, fell short of the 'rawness and mess of warfare'. She left you with an impression of choreography that was technically accomplished and exciting in its own way, but not resonating as strongly with the theme of the play as she would have liked.

A fight scene, like a trapeze routine, will always leap out as an example of controlled movement, but the critic also needs to find ways of encapsulating the more subtle choreography of an actor's performance. Describing Bryan Cranston as president Lyndon Johnson in Robert Schenkkan's *All the Way* at Broadway's Neil Simon Theater, Charles Isherwood did this by means of a simile in his *New York Times* review:

> . . . while Mr. Cranston doesn't have the towering stature of the man he's portraying, he still seems to be looking down at everybody

onstage from a great height. With his wide mouth often agape in a devouring, almost sinister smile, Mr. Cranston's Johnson often looks like a snake rising threateningly above a mouse as he prepares to make a meal of it.[14]

Not only did Isherwood give us an impression of what the actor looked like ('wide mouth often agape . . . sinister smile'), but he found an animalistic image that, in its power and cruelty, illustrated the nature of the character he was playing. The simile added to the reader's understanding of what the performance was like. We understood that Cranston was not literally imitating a snake, but that something in his demeanour suggested the idea of a poised and poisonous, predatory beast. That's why, if you're going to make a comparison, it should be relevant to the material you are describing. Had Cranston reminded Isherwood of some other creature – a bird taking wing, a galloping horse, a sleeping cat – he would have found it harder to make the connection to a play about 'one of the great manipulators of men'. A spurious comparison would have confused the reader.

EXERCISE

Write a 300-word review of a theatre production as if it were a piece of choreography. Shut yourself off to what the actors are saying and focus on their spatial relationships, their movement around the stage and the rhythm of their gestures. How much information is conveyed in this way?

How to write about famous faces and flashy acting

Mention of Cranston raises another question. Isherwood knew many readers would be attracted to his review to find out about the star of

Breaking Bad, which had recently completed its fifth and final season. Likewise, many people in the audience would have felt an affinity with the actor simply through watching him on television. Fame can have a distorting effect both on a performance and on the way it is written about. When a big-name actor is cast, you suddenly notice people taking an interest in theatre who've previously paid it no heed. Your editor allocates extra space to your review. Everyone wants to know what the famous face is like.

Irrespective of whether Cranston's performance was the most interesting aspect of *All the Way*, Isherwood had a journalistic imperative to focus on it. Had Cranston been in a minor role or if he had been the least impressive actor on the stage, Isherwood would still have had to devote space to him. In this case, the casting seemed to have been theatrically as well as journalistically justified, so there was no contradiction.

More ambiguous, according to Michael Billington, was the case of Angela Lansbury when she was cast as Madame Arcati in Noël Coward's *Blithe Spirit* at the Gielgud Theatre in 2014. It had been nearly 40 years since the Hollywood star had been seen on a London stage and her presence was regarded as an event. In the print edition of *The Guardian*, Billington's review ran on a news page and was nearly twice the standard length. The critic observed it was Lansbury's face on the posters and publicity, and it was her the audience had come to see. She gave 'good value',[15] he thought, and her performance was 'perfectly credible', but he felt the emphasis on her – not in Michael Blakemore's production itself, but in the hullaballoo around it – created a misleading impression of what the play was about: 'Coward's 1941 play is not called Madame Arcati, nor is it about spiritualism. It is really about a subject that haunts all Coward's best comedies, which is the perils of long-term commitment.' To Billington's mind, the real star of the show was Charles Edwards in the part of Charles Condomine. With another cast, the critic may have made Edwards the primary focus of his review; here, he had to deal with Lansbury's news value first. As a journalist, it was his responsibility to do this: a substantial percentage of his readers would have contextualized the production in the same light and would have expected Billington to do so too. None of this was Lansbury's fault; actors have control over their performance but little over their public perception. In this case, if we are to agree with Billington's analysis, it was as if the public, aided and abetted by the marketing department, had skewed the meaning of the play.

Even then it's hard to say how much of Cranston's charisma was attributable to his fame and how much to his innate acting abilities. Isherwood said his 'heat-generating performance galvanize[d] the production' and that even when he was off stage, the show 'retain[ed] the vitalizing imprint of his performance'. Clearly, Cranston got the part in *Breaking Bad* because he was very good, so it's no surprise he was very good in *All the Way* (although not every screen actor adapts well to the physical and vocal demands of the stage), but when it comes to the response of audience and critic, it is impossible to strip out the influence of celebrity on their judgement. There's a thrill about seeing a famous person which exists independently of what they actually do on stage. When this is true of a good actor, just think how more so it must be with an indifferent one. If the reason for their stardom is to do with their gifts as an actor, you will have plenty to get your teeth into. But if they are famous for being famous and have no particular talent beyond their charisma, you can find yourself having to dissect a performance you might otherwise have passed over with no comment.

In the same way that your eye is drawn to a star, so it is attracted to a certain kind of acting that is impressive in the moment but may not actually be in the best interests of the production as a whole.

C.E. Montague highlighted the opposite approach in his description of the restraint of the actors of Dublin's Abbey Theatre, a technique he called 'spiritual austerity':

None of them rants or flares, trumpets or booms, or frisks about when he had better be quiet, or puts on intense looks for nothing . . . They know how to let well alone; they stand still when others would 'cross stage to right' to no purpose.[16]

He concluded from seeing such a tight-knit ensemble in action that 'each part is played, in a sense, by them all'. It was an opinion reinforced by seeing a performance in which one of the best actors was ill, yet her understudy achieved much the same effect because her 'poignancy lay in the way the rest looked at her, from simple, held-in attitudes of wonder and apprehension'. This is a highly perceptive observation about how a theatrical effect is achieved and it reminds you that the acting that most readily catches the eye is not necessarily the best; indeed, it can even be detrimental to the overall impact of a production. For a critic, it can be hard to find a way of praising the actor who appears to be doing the least but is actually making the most valuable contribution. 'In a world of things overdone, like the stage, mere quietude has the value of epigram, like a thing soberly said in a newspaper',[17] wrote Montague. To think more deeply about the actor's art, you will find many an insight in books such as *A Dictionary of Theatre Anthropology* by Eugenio Barba and Nicola Savarese, *An Actor Prepares* by Constantin Stanislavski and *True and False* by David Mamet.

EXERCISE

Write a 500-word review of a production with a large cast. Focus on the ensemble, questioning how seamlessly the actors play together. Do they seem like atomized individuals or contributory parts of a bigger unit? If your attention is called to one actor more than another, is it in the best interests of the production? Is there someone on stage who is quietly contributing more than you realize?

Notes

1   Gray, Charles Harold (1931), *Theatrical Criticism in London to 1795*, Columbia University Press.

2 Lichtenberg, Georg Christoph, trans Margaret L. Mare and W.H. Quarrell (1938), *Lichtenberg's Visits to England as Described in his Letters and Diaries*, Oxford.

3 Gray, Charles Harold (1931), *Theatrical Criticism in London to 1795*, Columbia University Press.

4 Moore, Thomas (1838), *Life, Letters, and Journals of Lord Byron*, John Murray.

5 Young, Stark (1948), *Immortal Shadows*, Hill and Wang.

6 Hemming, Sarah (11 November 2011), *'Hamlet'*, in the *Financial Times*.

7 Agate, James (1932), *The English Dramatic Critics 1660–1932*, Hill and Wang.

8 See: MacAulay, Alastair (3 December 2010), 'Judging the bodies in ballet', in *The New York Times*, and Ellis-Petersen, Hannah (20 May 2014), 'Anger in opera world at "cruel" criticism of female soprano star's appearance', in *The Guardian*.

9 Houtchens, Lawrence Huston and Houtchens, Carolyn Washburn, eds (1950), *Leigh Hunt's Dramatic Criticism 1808–1831*, Geoffrey Cumberlege.

10 Rigg, Diana (1982), *No Turn Unstoned*, Arrow Books.

11 Simon, John (2005), *John Simon On Theatre 1974–2003*, Applause Theatre and Cinema Books.

12 Taylor, Kate (13 February 2014), *'Untitled Feminist Show*: when nudity is not enough', in the Toronto *Globe and Mail*.

13 Tripney, Natasha (2 January 2014), *'Coriolanus'*, on Interval Drinks (http://intervaldrinks.blogspot.co.uk/2014/01/coriolanus-donmar-warehouse.html).

14 Isherwood, Charles (6 March 2014), 'Washington Power Play', in *The New York Times*.

15 Billington, Michael (18 March 2014), *'Blithe Spirit* review: The play's the thing in a fine Noël Coward revival', in *The Guardian*.

16 Montague, C.E. (1911), *Dramatic Values*, Methuen & Co.

17 Ibid.

13
HOW TO WRITE ABOUT PLAYS

Getting the right idea

In 1977, playwright Edward Albee made this assertion:

> It seems inevitable that almost everyone has been encouraged until
> the critics feel that they have built them up beyond the point where
> they can control them; then it's time to knock them down again.
> And a rather ugly thing starts happening: the playwright finds
> himself knocked down for works that quite often are just as good
> or better than the works he's been praised for previously.[1]

Albee was far from being alone in thinking this and described a
recognizable phenomenon. Many artists have experienced the same
arc of initial welcome followed by mounting acclaim followed by
backlash. Politicians go through a similar thing: think of the trajectories
of pretty much any prime minister or president. They are deliriously
welcomed into office and supported through their early phase, until
suddenly the magic fades and the polls swing against them. For
someone at the sharp end of this process, it must be bewildering.
Their reception seems to bear no relationship to anything they've
done. This is why Albee's analysis has a touch of conspiracy theory
about it. It was his attempt to make rational sense of otherwise
inexplicable behaviour. But does his explanation hold up? Are critics
really such inadequate human beings that they need to control the

artists they write about? Is this need so great they are prepared to knock the artists down even at the expense of responding truthfully to their work? And are the critics so much in league with each other that they will all go through this destructive process at exactly the same time?

None of this rings true to me. A more likely explanation is that as human beings, we love novelty. When we find something new, we rush to embrace it. The first appearance of a talented playwright, actor, director or designer can generate a wave of enthusiasm – from audiences as much as critics. For the artist, the acclaim is unexpected and delightful and they can only assume they've been doing something right. So they stick to what worked and do it some more. With any luck, there'll be sufficient public excitement to carry them through another production or two. After that, however, they are no longer new. They can only be a novelty once. The audience will find it difficult to relive their initial excitement. What was once unexpected now seems predictable. The promise of the early work, all that giddy expectation of an unknown future, is replaced by the reality of the work as it actually is. The artist is the same person and their latest work may well be as good if not better. What has changed is the audience. There's no conspiracy. It's just human nature to get bored and move on to something newer and shinier. The best you can ask for is a critic perceptive enough to see weak points when the hype hits and lasting value when it fades.

The phenomenon Albee described is true of artists in all disciplines – musicians talk about their difficult second album – but it can be felt particularly acutely by playwrights because they are so often the generators of the ideas that drive the whole event. If their worldview becomes familiar, if their language loses its sheen, if their argument repeats, then there's only so much their collaborators can do to recreate the sense of surprise and discovery. Growing pains notwithstanding, many playwrights do go on to sustain a career and it is often their work above all others that the critic focuses on. In the case of a new play, the critic is likely to be most interested in the playwright's ideas and the way they are expressed. Especially if the review is short, they will relegate acting, directing and design to brief mentions, so they can get their teeth into what the dramatist is saying. The balance shifts a little in the case of collective, devised, physical and experiential theatre, but even then, the critic tends to prioritize the ideas being expressed over the manner of their expression. Once the play becomes established, the critic is more likely to focus on the other theatremakers because the interpretation of the ideas has become most interesting.

How to write about plot

When you invite a friend to the theatre, they'll usually want to know what the show is about. You have two ways of answering. The first is literal: 'It's about two men waiting for a man called Godot.' The second is metaphorical: 'It's about the meaninglessness of life.' (If you're feeling facetious, there's a third: 'It's about 90 minutes.') In critical terms, the metaphorical answer is the more interesting. It's the one that gets under the skin of a performance to reveal what lies beyond the surface details: *King Lear* is about arrogance, *Hamlet* is about indecision, *Macbeth* is about ambition, and so on. If you are moved by Hamlet's dilemma, it is not because you connect literally with the story: you are not a prince in medieval Denmark and your father has not been killed by your mother's new husband. No, you are moved because you are affected on a metaphorical level. You know, for example, what it is to be abandoned and betrayed or to have conflicting loyalties to two parents. The surface details of the plot, which may have no equivalent in your life, give you access to ideas, emotions and dilemmas that are fundamental to your being. We need the literal meaning so we can discover the metaphorical meaning.

That leaves the critic with a challenge. How do you write about the interesting stuff in your review without leaving the reader behind?

If you were reviewing *Waiting for Godot* and jumped straight in with a treatise on existential despair, you would alienate any reader unfamiliar with the play. They wouldn't understand why you were writing on that topic and wouldn't be able to relate it to the production. They'd be lost. Equally, you would bore your readers into existentialist despair if you attempted to give a detailed breakdown of the action on a line-by-line basis. You are writing a response to the production, not trying to copy it. A review is itself a story, but it is the story of the critic's encounter with a play and not the story of the play itself (although the two may overlap). Despite this, it is quite common – especially in film reviews – to find dense plot synopses that list everything that happened as though it were a news report. For the reader, such compacted information can be hard to process. A story that has unfolded over two or three hours in the theatre easily becomes impenetrable when boiled down to a couple of paragraphs. It's hard to keep up with who was doing what to whom – still less to care. And because you don't care, it can be hard to see what relevance this bald synopsis has to the critic's interpretation. That's frustrating because, as we have seen, the interpretation is the interesting bit.

The solution is to give just enough plot information to keep the readers on board, but not so much you overwhelm them with detail. You want to orientate them in the world of the play and provide them with enough information to make sense of your arguments, but you gain little by giving them a blow-by-blow account. There is no formula. In some cases, such as *Cinderella* and *Romeo and Juliet*, it may be reasonable to give no plot information whatsoever because you could assume your readers had enough cultural knowledge to get by with the broadest memory-jogging phrases: 'the rags-to-riches fairy story' or 'the tale of star-cross'd lovers'. In a review of *Cinderella*, you could spend a lot of time talking about Ugly Sisters and missing slippers and how poor Cinders gets to the ball, but more interesting would be to analyse the journey from childhood to maturity, from servitude to independence, from poverty to riches, from innocence to self-knowledge or whatever else strikes you about this enduring tale.

Likewise, *Romeo and Juliet* works in front of an audience because of the constant narrative interruptions to the young lover's plans; we hope they succeed, but they are repeatedly thwarted, by parents, by rivals and by circumstance. You could retell that story blow by blow in a review, but more illuminating would be a discussion of themes ranging from the impetuosity of youth to the divisiveness of tribalism. In other cases, especially with new and unfamiliar plays, the deeper meanings may be hard to grasp unless they are rooted in the action of the play. Here, critics have to draw on those aspects of the plot that best illustrate the points they want to make. There's no need to explain everything that happens, just what is pertinent.

On a technical level, there are two schools of thought when it comes to dealing with plot information. One is the drip-feed approach in which the critic withholds the information until it can be put to best use in their critical argument. The other is to dedicate a paragraph or two entirely to the synopsis. Usually coming towards the start of the review, the passage may include some production details, such as the names of the actors, but is generally free of colour or interpretation. Kenneth Tynan sometimes employed a variation of this approach by focusing exclusively on plot but relating the events in a tone that hinted at his critical attitude. In his review of *Guys and Dolls* at the London Coliseum in 1952, a show he called a 'young masterpiece', he used the language and rhythms of Manhattan to give an impression not only of what happened but the manner in which it happened:

This particular fable takes place in and around New York City, where many of the citizens do nothing but roll dice all night long, which is held by one and all, and especially the gendarmes, to be a great vice. Among the parties hopping around the neighbourhood is a guy by the name of Nathan Detroit, who operates a floating dice game, and Miss Adelaide, his ever-loving pretty, who is sored up at this Nathan because after fourteen years' engagement, they are still nothing but engaged. Anyway, being short of a ready scratch, Nathan lays a bet with a gambler called Sky Masterson, the subject of the wager being whether The Sky can talk a certain Salvation Army doll into joining him on a trip to Havana.[2]

He kept up this pastiche of Damon Runyon, on whose short story the musical was based, for several sentences more. 'Hopping around', 'neighbourhood', 'ever-loving pretty', 'sored up' and 'ready scratch' were phrases he drew from the language of the production, clearly anachronistic in a British newspaper of the 1950s and all the more entertaining for it. Within this synopsis, Tynan also managed to slip in a suggestion that this is a plot we shouldn't take too seriously: the gendarmes may have considered rolling dice all night long a 'great vice', but it's unlikely the critic felt the same way.

Tynan often wrote reviews without mentioning plot at all. His famous rave about John Osborne's Look Back in Anger in 1956 told you that Jimmy Porter is a 'provincial graduate who runs a sweet-stall', that his wife leaves him, that he goes to bed with one of her friends, that they divide the Sunday newspapers between '"posh" and "wet"' and that there is a final reconciliation scene. Those scant details were as much as he needed to discuss what is, after all, a character-driven play. When he felt it appropriate to focus on plot, however, Tynan was able to illuminate an essential quality of the work concerned. By going into pedantic detail, for example, about the action of a show called The Glorious Days, a vehicle for Anna Neagle in 1953, he made it seem ludicrous. The writing was very funny – and the joke was on the show. It was a technique he had inherited from George Bernard Shaw who set the bar in his 1896 review of True Blue[3] by Leonard Outram and Stewart Gordon which described the comings and going on board a cruise ship at ridiculous length, implying the critic's opinion but withholding explicit comment until the observation that the audience was 'half white with its purgation by pity and terror, half red with a voiceless, apoplectic laughter'. Even good plays can be made to seem ridiculous by describing them in this blow-by-blow way, another reason to avoid too much unmediated plot description unless for comic effect.

There's much more to a play than plot, of course, so as well as making a study of books about narrative such as Christopher Booker's *The Seven Basic Plots: Why We Tell Stories*,[4] critics should aim to increase their dramaturgical powers by reading analytical studies such as David Edgar's *How Plays Work*,[5] Alan Ayckbourn's *The Crafty Art of Playmaking*[6] and Steve Waters' *The Secret Life of Plays*.[7] None of this should presuppose that theatre comes in only one form. The critic must be equally equipped to deal with performance that is non-linear, experiential or fragmentary, that rejects character and plot, and that owes more to the aesthetics of visual art than the conventions of the well-made play. There may be no similarity between Albee's *Who's Afraid of Virginia Woolf*, a three-hour domestic drama for four characters, and Forced Entertainment's *Quizoola*, a twenty-four-hour improvised question-and-answer session, but both fall under the theatre critic's remit. Only by asking our first question, 'What were the theatremakers trying to do?', can we treat all work, however disparate, with the respect Albee called for.

EXERCISE

Write a 500-word review based on a detailed breakdown of the plot. See if you can also express your opinions about the show at the same time. How difficult is it to provide something more than a synopsis?

Notes

1 Booth, John E. (1991), *The Critic, Power and the Performing Arts*, Columbia University Press.

2 Tynan, Kenneth (1975), *A View of the English Stage*, Davis-Poynter.

3 Shaw, George Bernard (1932), *Our Theatre in the Nineties*, Constable.

4 Booker, Christopher (2004), *The Seven Basic Plots: Why We Tell Stories*, Continuum.

5 Edgar, David (2009), *How Plays Work*, Nick Hern Books.

6 Ayckbourn, Alan (2002), *The Crafty Art of Playmaking*, Faber and Faber.

7 Waters, Steve (2010), *The Secret Life of Plays*, Nick Hern Books.

14
HOW TO WRITE ABOUT THE PRODUCTION

The art and craft of theatre

As we discussed in the last chapter, if you were writing about a new play, you would be expected to give not only an outline of the plot, but also an interpretation of what the plot meant. There is the literal meaning (who did what to whom) and, more interestingly, the metaphorical meaning (what it symbolized). The same should be your ambition when writing about direction, set and costume design, lighting, sound, music, choreography, movement and other production elements. A literal description of what it looked and sounded like does a valuable job in orientating the reader in the world of the production; a metaphorical description goes further by telling the reader what impression that world made and what it meant.

How to write about design

Writing about set, costume and lighting is not always the critic's first priority. Even designers would say their job is to support a production's central artistic thrust, whether that be the actors' performances, the playwright's script or the director's concept, and not to draw attention to themselves. Unless you were writing about a visually driven theatremaker such as the Russian designer-turned-director Dmitry Krymov, you might give a misleading impression if you focused on design at the expense of the performances. If the design is the aspect that makes the greatest impact on you, it makes sense to write about it, but the dominance of the design may signal weaknesses elsewhere in the production. Yes, the fireworks are pretty but what do they say about the show? In the 1980s when there was a boom in high-budget musicals, people would joke about coming out of the theatre whistling the set. If the main thing you remembered about the 1984 production of *Starlight Express* was not the songs of Andrew Lloyd Webber and Richard Stilgoe, but John Napier's £1.4m design with its multi-level roller-skating tracks thrusting into the stalls and circle of London's Apollo Victoria, it would have felt as though things were the wrong way round. The medium would have triumphed over the message.

Peter Brook called his landmark book *The Empty Space* because, when theatre is stripped down to its elemental state, it needs nothing more than an actor, a 'bare stage' and someone watching. He didn't say a 'decorated stage'. It's not that Brook regarded design as unimportant (on the contrary, Andrew Todd and Jean-Guy Lecat wrote a whole book called *The Open Circle: Peter Brook's Theatre Environments*[1]), just that only in relatively rare cases is design the production's motivating factor or its most active component. It would be odd not to mention design when reviewing a piece of puppetry or object theatre, or the work of visually minded directors such as Robert Wilson and Robert Lepage, but not so odd with a provocative new play that was full of intellectual ideas. That's why critics often relegate these supporting production elements to the later paragraphs or, when space is limited, make no mention of them at all.

Indeed, a quick verbal sketch of what set, costumes and lighting looked like is often sufficient to give an impression of a production's atmosphere. More revealing, however, is when you go a step further and analyse the choices of the designers. The audience may be affected only subconsciously by what they do, but by investigating the visual elements, you can reveal a lot about a production's meaning; despite my earlier comments, you can usually find substance in the style. When, for example, Zoë Wanamaker starred as the poet Stevie

Smith in Hugh Whitemore's *Stevie* at the Minerva Theatre, Chichester, Lyn Gardner saw meaning in a costume choice that was at once simple and significant:

> She stands before us, stooping slightly, in a shapeless red pinafore like an awkward, slightly wistful schoolgirl up before the headteacher. But something glints in this elfin, middle-aged woman's eye. The crimson pinafore may be a fashion disaster, but it's also a flash of defiance, even danger, in a drab world.[2]

Gardner understood that designer Simon Higlett had not grabbed Wanamaker's pinafore from the nearest costume rail, but had made a purposeful decision related to what the production was trying to express. In metaphorical terms, it was not a shapeless red dress but a 'flash of defiance', something that enriched the actor's interpretation. David Benedict made a similar extrapolation in his *Variety* review of *Coriolanus*, starring Tom Hiddleston, at London's Donmar Warehouse:

> The control of stagecraft is everywhere apparent, not least in the added, silent scene in which Coriolanus, released from public display and privately exhausted from battle, stands alone. Caught center-stage in Mark Henderson's ferocious white light, water from high above the set surges down onto Hiddleston's bloody body, spraying into the dark like sparks off steel. A magnificent image in its own right, it's actually making audiences see and feel the character's brutally defiant self-determination.[3]

Here, Benedict honed in on a striking image and described it in compelling terms. The actor was 'caught', the light was 'ferocious', the water surged, the body was 'bloody'. This sounded like a scene worth seeing. But look at the simile Benedict used: the water, he said, sprayed 'like sparks off steel'. That's an unusual description of water and it's a key to his interpretation of what the design meant. Earlier, he had described the 'diamond-bright gleam of attack-ready energy' in

Hiddleston's interpretation of Coriolanus, a character who is a formidable warrior. By using the image of 'sparks off steel', the critic made us see Coriolanus as something metallic, perhaps a sword or a lathe, reinforcing his air of invincibility. Having put this idea in our heads, Benedict was able to make the connection between 'a magnificent image in its own right' and 'the character's brutally defiant self-determination'. He demonstrated that this 'added, silent scene' was not just a pretty picture or a gratuitous display of stagecraft, but a considered contribution to the production's overall impact. He recognized that Lucy Osborne's set and Mark Henderson's lighting were not simply ornamental but central to the production's meaning.

On some occasions, the set may be symptomatic of some strength or weakness in the production as a whole. If so, it can be your key to discussing the show. In one extreme case, Bernard Levin sustained an entire review with a tedious (and therefore hilarious) item-by-item checklist of everything on the set. By describing the bourgeois drawing room of *The Geese Are Getting Fat* by Arthur Watkyn in excruciating detail, he implied that the production itself was dull and irrelevant: 'On the window seat there are three rust cushions and one pink one, the pink one having a fringe of bobbles.'[4] He continued in that manner for some 500 words. For Levin, the meaning of this design, or so we may surmise, was one of complacent domesticity, small-minded and superficial. He dismissed the play itself without writing a word about it (effectively skipping our first two questions and leaping straight to the third).

Lighten up

If the critic's vocabulary is stretched when writing about acting, it is equally the case when discussing the visual aspects of a production, especially when it comes to the technicalities of lighting design. On a Tuesday afternoon in Leeds, I joined members of the Association of Lighting Designers (ALD) en route to the pub after a successful conference discussion about what makes good lighting design and what makes award-winning lighting design.[5] I fell into conversation with John Bishop, whose CV includes stints in Canada, Denmark, Estonia, Poland and Wales, and we wrestled with this question of how you write about lighting. He told me he regarded the stage as an aquarium. The set designer decides what shape the aquarium will be and where it will be placed. The director decides what will happen inside the aquarium – how fast the bubbles will rise from the ornamental diver, where the tropical fish will move. When all that is done, the lighting designer comes in and fills the tank with water. This is what makes sense of the aquarium and its contents, bringing it into focus, giving it texture, shape, colour and depth. But on its own, it is meaningless. A tank of water is just a tank of water.

This is why it rarely makes sense for a theatre critic to write about lighting in isolation. It's conceivable you could write exclusively about an actor's performance – they did it all the time in the nineteenth century – and, today, it is not uncommon to focus almost entirely on the work of a playwright. But, with some major exceptions, it is logical to talk about lighting only in terms of its contributory role. To do anything else would be like describing a tank of water. It is wet, it is fluid, it is transparent, but what else?

After a pint or two in the Adelphi pub, Bishop alighted on another simile. When he's working on a show, he feels like a composer. In this scene, the director needs a minuet; the next scene calls for a foxtrot; what the scene after that requires is a tango. He designs the lighting according to the required mood, making sure there's the right musical balance – not too many woodwinds, just the right amount of brass, a fuller sound from the strings. Like the accompanist of a silent movie, he saw his job as a response to the other theatremakers.

That Bishop twice turned to simile in the one conversation strikes me as significant. Whether he was filling an aquarium or composing a score, he was operating in an art that doesn't lend itself to straight description. What words should critics use to make the attempt? At the ALD conference, Scott Palmer, author of *Light*,[6] a valuable study of how light makes meaning in the theatre, talked about the kind of lighting he most admired:

> In naturalistic theatre, you can appreciate a great creation of a sunrise or a morning light, but I'm much more interested in where lighting moves away from a requirement to replicate the real world and where it helps our understanding of the dramaturgical journey in the play, where lighting is not seen as subservient to the other elements but takes on its own character.

The answer for the critic is not about getting technical with talk about follow spots, LEDs and fresnels, but to write about this character. As with any other of theatre's contributory artforms, it is a question of conveying the meaning and emotional impact of the lighting. Just as the critic need not be skilled in vocal technique to describe the force of an actor's bravura soliloquy, so it is not a requirement to be a technical guru to describe the lighting designer's contribution. At the conference, lighting designer Mark Jonathan had described the way he dealt with the requests of directors. 'We'll sit in meetings with directors and designers and they use words that are nothing to do with lighting,' he said. 'I feel it's my job to take the word that the director uses when he talks about the play and turn that into lighting. In its simplest terms it might be light/dark, warm/cold, quick/slow.' If that's the process he goes through, the challenge for the critic is to do the same in reverse – to put into words the abstract moods, atmospheres and patterns that lighting creates subliminally.

Another panellist, Kelli Zezulka, had read through the back issues of the ALD's magazine *Focus*, which she edits, and extracted the adjectives and adverbs used to describe lighting. She made a 'wordle' or 'word cloud' from her findings. The words that were biggest, that is the most frequently used, were 'colour', 'transitions', 'punctuation', 'defining', 'drenching', 'vivid' and 'perfect'. Among the other words on the list were 'gleaming', 'dramatically', 'contemplation', 'devastating', 'beautiful', 'evoking', 'monochrome', and 'shadowy'. Anyone who's ever mentioned lighting in a review will recognize at least some of these words. But how many tell you what the lighting was actually like? 'Devastating', 'gleaming', 'monochrome', and 'shadowy' sound like good indicators – but many of the others are merely synonyms for 'good'. Can anyone define what vivid or perfect lighting looks like? (Should you be wondering, the word 'punctuation' was used at the Knight of Illumination 2013 Awards when Paule Constable won for *Barnum* at Chichester Festival Theatre 'for taking a hugely problematic script in an uncompromising space and using lighting to give it structure, punctuation and dramatic momentum'.)

Writing about design demands a keen eye, a sharp ear and precise language. Under pressure of a deadline, it is hard to resist words such as 'atmospheric' and 'evocative', even though these one-size-fits-all synonyms for 'moody' actually mean very little. To do the job thoroughly, you need to define what the atmosphere was, what quality was evoked and, indeed, what particular mood you had in mind. Pushing yourself to find exactly the right vocabulary will make your writing more compelling. It could also help you figure out how the design elements have contributed to the production.

To help get your descriptive and interpretive muscles into shape, take yourself to your local art gallery and write a review of an exhibition. You may be happy to describe a theatre set as 'blue' or 'red', but you're likely to need a wider palate of colour-related words for a series of paintings. Similarly, you'll need to find a way for your written language to convey a sense of the exhibition's textures, shapes, volumes, arrangements and juxtapositions. You'll also need to analyse its meanings and the way it makes you feel – all without the familiar beginning-middle-end plot structure of the theatre.

Spending time in galleries can also help you develop an understanding of the visual references made by designers. It's common for set and lighting designers to work together to allude to a great work of art – *The Last Supper* by Leonardo da Vinci and *Nighthawks* by Edward Hopper are favourites – or else they'll borrow cinematic images to take us into the world of a director such as David

Lynch or Terry Gilliam. Frequently, it is only the costumes that tell you the era when a production is set, so the more accurately you are able to distinguish, say, the fashions of the 1930s and those of the 1940s, the better you'll be able to tell if the show is supposed to be a comment on pre-war appeasement or on post-war austerity. *Survey of Historic Costume* by Phyllis G. Tortora and Sara B. Marcketti, an overview of western dress from the ancient world through the twenty-first century, may help in this regard.

EXERCISE

Write a 400-word review that focuses on what the production looked like. Go into as much detail as you can about costumes, set, lighting and movement, identifying textures, patterns, styles, moods and associations. Discuss how these contributed to the production's meaning.

How to write about music and sound

Much of the above applies equally to music and sound. Once you've visited an art gallery, you should try reviewing a classical music concert, testing yourself on your ability to find words for what you hear. As with lighting, capturing the meaning is more important that explaining every technicality. It's valuable to understand how an effect is achieved but it isn't always necessary to spell it out. In fact, unless you are writing for a specialist publication, too much erudition may bamboozle your readers. Today the ordinary reader will usually find they can read a review of a contemporary music concert or a classical ballet and come away with a reasonable grasp of what it was like. Indeed, when you read reviews of artforms with which you're less familiar, it's surprising how little specialist vocabulary the critics use.

Just as surprising, however, is how little effort many theatre critics put into engaging with music and sound when it takes a dominant place in a production (many opera critics are similarly poor at engaging with the staging). Just as a set and costume designer will give visual clues, so a music director may throw in a bit of Cole Porter to suggest the New York of the 1920s, some flamenco to indicate Spain or something anachronistic to disrupt the flow. Such references contribute to the meaning of the production and it pays to be precise about them. Yet a cross-section of reviews of a new Andrew Lloyd Webber musical, say, is likely to skirt past the songs in a perfunctory way in order to concentrate on the story, the performances, the staging and the themes. This, by Stewart Pringle in *Exeunt* writing about *From Here to Eternity*, is a relatively rare example of a critic not only analysing what the songs were doing but also contextualizing them in relation to other show tunes:

Composer Stuart Brayson has possibly written too many tunes, but quite a few of them really do work. 'G Company Blues' is a military riff on *Les Mis*'s 'Work Song' that it [sic] totally hummable and as stirring on the second reprise as it is in the opening minutes, and the similarly macho 'Thirty Year Man' makes Prewitt seem considerably more interesting than he actually is. Given how many scenes take place between the beaded curtains of a bar-cum-brothel, they're sorely lacking an evocative number like 'One Night in Bangkok' or 'The Heat Is on in Saigon' to snap the world into life, and the substitute 'Don'cha Like Hawaii' is no substitute at all. Top of the pile, musically speaking, is undoubtedly Lorene's solo solo [sic] 'Run Along Joe', which shows up Act II's 'Love Me Forever Today' as well as the title song for the emotionally Xeroxed nonsense that they are. It's a fantastic tune, with some of Rice's best lyrics, and Harrison absolutely nails it.[7]

As with descriptions about acting, the most vivid writing about music and sound is characterized by fine detail, telling you not only what it was like, but what effect it had. Away from musicals, it is most commonly the case that sound and music operate like lighting, subtly enhancing the atmosphere while the audience focuses its attention on the main action. The challenge for the critic is to listen out for this, to identify what the composer, musical director or sound director is doing, to find words to describe it and to analyse how it contributes to the overall effect. For insights into the sound designer's craft, you could try *Theatre Sound* by John A. Leonard.[8]

EXERCISE

Spend a night in the theatre noting down everything you hear. Start as soon as you arrive, paying attention to the chatter of the audience in the foyer, music played at the bar, phones ringing, pre-show announcements, as well the music and sound that is a deliberate part of the production. Describe how the things you hear, and the intervening silences, make you feel. How difficult is it to stay conscious of sound?

How to write about direction

Whatever aspect of the production you are writing about, you will frequently be faced with the question of attribution. You may observe a clever lighting effect, an underpowered actor or an emotive piece of choreography, but it's hard to be sure who to credit or blame. You may guess the lighting designer, the actor or the movement director were involved in some way, but it might just as easily have been someone else in the company who had the idea. Maybe a technician pressed the wrong button and accidentally stumbled on the lighting effect. Maybe the designer created a set that restricted the actor's movement so much that their performance was constrained. Maybe the cast improvised the dance sequence as a last-minute solution to covering a set change. The only way to correctly say who did what would be for the critic to interview everyone at length – and even then there's every likelihood they'd have forgotten. Luckily, there's a simple solution: when in doubt, you should praise and blame the director. They are the ones responsible for everything you see on stage. If you don't like the music, it was the director who commissioned the composer and approved the score. If the actor is terrible, it was the director who cast them. You may love the lighting designer's flickering shadows and autumnal colours (and no one will complain if you say so), but the director made the choice to keep it like that. In a collaborative artform, you can never know for sure who did what, but you can reasonably assume the event you have seen was the event the director intended you to see. With the possible exception of certain jointly devised productions in which responsibility is shared by the company members (or, at least, billed as such), this is how nearly all theatre has been since the decline of actor's theatre, the actor-manager and the people they used to call producers who were somewhere between modern-day stage managers and traffic police, making sure nobody bumped into the furniture. If only as a journalistic shorthand, it makes sense to talk of the director's production even though you are fully aware it was the sum total of many people's work. The director is the one person with an overview of every contributing element and, over the past century or so, we have become accustomed to watching theatre as if through their eyes. This is true whether we're watching a large Eastern European ensemble or a one-person show in which director, playwright and performer are the same person.

The advent of the director is, however, a relatively recent phenomenon and, as theatre is forever in flux, the alert critic should be ready for the balance to shift again. We only have to go back to 1918 to find British critic James Agate celebrating the primacy of actors and playwrights, and contending that 'the truth of the matter would seem to be that whereas acting is a great art and play-writing a great art also, there is no *art of the theatre* which combines the two'.[9] Had British theatre been more open to outside influence, Agate would have acknowledged the work nearly fifty years earlier of Georg II, Duke of

Saxe-Meiningen, whose company was renowned across Europe for its meticulous attention to historical accuracy, the quality of its ensemble acting and the unity of its stage picture. Agate should also have known that by the end of the nineteenth century, the influence of Saxe-Meiningen could be felt in the work of André Antoine in France and Constantin Stanislavski in Russia, both pioneers in theatrical naturalism. So too should he have been aware that, soon afterwards, Max Reinhardt had made the transition from actor to director and earned a Europe-wide reputation for his illusionistic productions at Berlin's Deutsches Theater, some with the designer Edward Gordon Craig.

But in British theatre, news was slow to arrive. As late as 1928, Ivor Brown was able to complain that 'dramatic critics rarely acknowledge the fact (for praise or blame) that such a person as the producer exists'[10] even when that person 'may have controlled the pitch and pace of the acting on which so much depends'. Brown, however, also had a worry, one that would exercise critics for decades to come. He speculated that 'it is possible that in our own time or in the near future the dramatist may need protection from the producer with flighty notions'. On the one hand, he recognized the importance of a director because 'discipline must be imposed from some source'; on the other hand, he thought of the director's job in terms of 'self-surrender to the purpose of the dramatist'. For that reason, he wrote warmly of Stanislavski and Harley Granville-Barker, but was sceptical about the total-theatre ambitions of Craig and withering about the burgeoning expressionist movement. The argument over whether a director should be an artist in their own right or a conduit for the playwright remains with us to this day.

In the 1950s, when the contribution of a visionary director was still considered a novelty, Eric Bentley wrote about Britain's Tyrone Guthrie who staged three otherwise unrelated plays, Thornton Wilder's *The Matchmaker*, Christopher Marlowe's *Tamburlaine the Great* and Luigi Pirandello's *Six Characters in Search of an Author*, during Broadway's 1955–56 season:

Three plays which are so different that they would prompt no comparisons at all, the one with the other, have blended in my memory of the three productions, into a single impression. For example, one of the memorably theatrical 'moves' is that of an actor's popping up between another actor's legs. *Tamburlaine? Six Characters*? Both! What can be done in one play can be done in another. Three plays can become one. The not only divergent but incommensurable personalities of Wilder, Marlowe, and Pirandello can be subordinated to the one personality of Tyrone Guthrie.[11]

Bentley seemed to relish the chance to observe a director's style as it manifested itself over three plays but, as a critic, his question was the same one raised by Brown nearly thirty years earlier: how satisfactorily could these playwrights be 'subordinated to the mind and art of Mr. Guthrie'? Wind the clock forward another twenty years, and Richard Gilman was asking that same question in *The New York Times*. This critic made the distinction between two types of directors: those such as Elia Kazan and José Quintero in the 1950s, who, 'for all their distinctive styles and notable energy', were 'measurably subordinate to the writers they had been hired to serve'; and those, such as Andrei Serban, Richard Foreman and Robert Wilson, who would 'place their own contribution on a par with the dramatist's and sometimes beyond'.[12] By contrast, he praised Peter Brook for a 1960s production of *King Lear* in which the director had stripped the play of 'all the conventional theatrical baggage' in a way that had allowed the 'language to shine through'. For his own part, Brook went on to make a distinction between a director who comes into rehearsals with a ready-made vision and the one who discovers meanings in the rehearsal room: 'A "directorial conception" is an image that precedes the first day's work, while a "sense of direction" crystallizes into an image at the very end of the process.'[13]

You'll hear similar arguments about twenty-first century directors – as Calixto Bieito, Rupert Goold and Katie Mitchell will attest. On the very same day in 2014, *The Guardian*'s two main theatre critics coincidentally set up camp on opposite sides of the debate. In a review of John Ford's *'Tis Pity She's a Whore*, Michael Billington lamented a 'spate of concept-driven classic revivals' and praised director Michael Longhurst for a production in which everything was 'driven by a desire to illuminate Ford's text rather than exhibit the director's ego'.[14] Lyn Gardner, meanwhile, wrote a blog in praise of Goold, Mitchell, Thomas Ostermeier, Ivo Van Hove and a generation of directors who had made it 'a great year so far for the reinvention of classics and modern classics'.[15] Both sides of the debate have their weak spots. Even if the traditionalists could demonstrate that a classic existed in a pure immutable form and that its author's intentions were beyond dispute, they couldn't argue that audiences' understanding of the play had remained static. *The Taming of the Shrew* is a different play because of feminism. Freud makes us see *Hamlet* in a new light. *Othello* is changed by centuries of colonial history. Theatre is a present-tense business and even the most hands-off director must make the play live for today. In that sense, it's not possible to stage a play as it was intended, because it was always intended as a blueprint for interpretation. As Gardner put it, 'the only way that Chekhov, Ibsen, Shakespeare and Miller will survive is if we recognise that all plays, even the most famous ones, are simply a suggestion for a performance, not a template for one that must be reproduced slavishly'. On the other hand, those who champion directors' theatre can't deny that, on occasion, the directorial concept is less interesting than the playwright's concept and that a director can suppress the play's richness by imposing an extraneous gimmick. Billington's complaint about directorial egos echoes Bentley's question about whether we should let directors 'take large scripts and make them small'. Wherever you come down in this century-old argument, you should approach your review with our first question in mind by asking what the theatremakers are trying to do. Whether their intention is to express the vision of the director or of the playwright (or, more likely, some combination of the two), you then have a framework to ask further questions about their achievement and purpose.

Like Bentley, you may find it takes three or four productions before you start spotting a director's signature characteristics. Some chameleon-like directors will forever elude you; they disappear into each new show in an attempt to let the playwright's voice be heard without interference. Writing about those directors can be hard; not because they are bad but because they are invisible. Others are more present and their visibility, like a spectacular lighting effect or a histrionic actor, makes them easier to write about, whether or not they have artistic merit. Wherever they sit on the spectrum from facilitator to auteur, directors make choices. It is those choices, the decision to stand back as much as the decision to step forward, that the critic analyses. With a grasp of theatre theory – Barba, Barker, Boal, Brecht and Brook, to name only the Bs – you will develop an understanding of the principles by which each director is operating. And with careful consideration, you will attempt to work out whether the director's choices have been to the benefit or detriment of the other elements.

Many a playwright will tell you how their work was misunderstood because of a director's inappropriate staging. Others will keep quiet because a director made their play seem better than it deserved. In such circumstances, when asking our first question, the critic must consider both what the playwright was trying to do and what the director was trying to do. If those things are in conflict, it will produce a more complex answer to the question of how well they did it. This is especially contentious when a play is new and its success rests on the first production. A perceptive critic will distinguish between the merits of the script and the merits of the interpretation. In the case of a classic, the critic can more easily identify the qualities the director has emphasized or underplayed. With a knowledge of the text and of previous productions, the critic can tell when, for example, a production of *Hamlet* draws out the theme of espionage, highlights the idea of madness or suggests there may be something incestuous about the relationship between Gertrude and her son. No two productions are the same and, even without changing a word, the director makes choices that, intentionally or otherwise, can only reveal different meanings. By identifying those choices, thinking through not only what happened but also what might have happened, the critic can shed light on the director's interpretation. After that, comes the process of deciding what effect the director's choices had on the production and of judging whether or not they were a success.

All this presupposes that the director, designer and technical team have total control over the way their work is received. But they don't. The theatre is a more complex and interesting place than that. The way you respond to a show, and therefore the way you write your review, will be influenced by many factors over which the theatremakers have little or no influence. They range from the weather outside the building to the history of the theatre company, from the state of the economy to the mood you are in. This is the subject of the next few chapters, starting with the one that may most justifiably be called the elephant in the room. It's about the audience and their unsung part in shaping a night at the theatre.

Notes

1 Todd, Andrew and Lecat, Jean-Guy (2003), *The Open Circle: Peter Brook's Theatre Environments*, Faber and Faber.

2 Gardner, Lyn (5 May 2014), '*Stevie*', in *The Guardian*.

3 Benedict, David (17 December 2013), 'London Theater Review: *Coriolanus* Starring Tom Hiddleston', in *Variety*.

4 Rigg, Diana (1982), *No Turn Unstoned*, Arrow Books.

5 'and the award for best lighting design goes to . . .' (29 April 2014), PLASA Focus, Royal Armories Museum, Leeds.

6 Palmer, Scott (2013), *Light*, Palgrave Macmillan.

7 Pringle, Stewart (28 October 2013), '*From Here to Eternity*', in *Exeunt Magazine*.

8 Leonard, John A. (2001), *Theatre Sound*, Methuen Drama.

9 Agate, James (1918), *Buzz, Buzz!*, W. Collins, Sons & Co.

10 Brown, Ivor (1928), *Parties of the Play*, Ernest Benn.

11 Bentley, Eric (2000), *What Is Theatre? 1944–1967*, Hill and Wang.

12 Gilman, Richard (2005), *The Drama Is Coming Now*, Yale University Press.

13 Marowitz, Charles (1986), *Prospero's Staff*, Marion Boyars.

14 Billington, Michael (29 October 2014), '*'Tis Pity She's a Whore*', in *The Guardian*.

15 Gardner, Lyn (29 October 2014), 'Daring directors are shaking up the classics – and making great theatre', in *The Guardian*.

15
HOW TO WRITE ABOUT THE AUDIENCE

Theatre as a social event

In 1709, we find writer and publisher Sir Richard Steele in the first issue of the *Tatler* describing a performance of William Congreve's comedy *Love for Love*. His first concern was not the play but who was watching it:

> There has not been known so great a concourse of persons of distinction as at the time; the stage itself was covered with gentlemen and ladies, and when the curtain was drawn, it discovered even there a very splendid audience.[1]

In addition to giving us the historically interesting detail that audience members would sit on the stage, Steele tells us much about theatre's social function in the early eighteenth century. The audience in London's Covent Garden were there to see and be seen. Writing at a time before the role of the journalistic critic had been established and therefore an important pioneer, Steele considered it part of his job to report on these 'persons of distinction'. Perhaps he even thought it was the most important part of his job in the 'illustrated journal of society and the drama' he had founded; it is, after all, the first thing he wrote about. A century later, the critic Leigh Hunt observed the same thing going on among his peers, whom he lampooned with heavy irony: 'When you criticise the performance of an old play, never exceed six or seven lines, but be sure to notice by name the Fashionables in the boxes, for such notices are indispensably requisite to sound criticism.'[2]

How different is theatre today? A twenty-first century critic may be less likely to refer to 'persons of distinction' in a review and, certainly, the social place of theatre has changed since Steele's day, but that isn't to say the audience plays no role. Now as then, the buzz of excitement increases in the presence of a celebrity (a modern-day 'person of distinction') and, even without a star name, we are social beings who can't help keeping an eye on the rest of the audience. On a first night, when critics are most likely to be present, the theatre will be full of actors' friends, board members, supporters of the company and familiar faces from the local arts community. They are likely to be in high spirits, to laugh vigorously (sometimes inappropriately) and to applaud enthusiastically. They will be very present – most likely, just as present as the 1709 audience for *Love for Love*.

Watching a live broadcast of a West End theatre production in my local cinema, I was struck by the pre-performance footage. While those of us sitting in the multiplex were quiet and attentive, the theatre audience we were watching on screen were noisy and sociable. They waved across the auditorium to friends, stood chatting rather than take their seats and had about them an air of heightened expectation that had no equivalent in the cinema auditorium. It reminded me that theatre is a social medium in a way cinema is not.

The role of the audience

The director Peter Brook said all that was needed for an act of theatre to take place was for a man to walk across an empty space '*whilst someone else is watching him*'.[3] In this most elemental definition, the act of watching is fundamental. A man walking across an empty space is not theatre. It becomes theatre in the presence of an observer. There is something about the liveness of theatre, the sense of it being an unrepeatable event, never quite the same, that spills into the audience. When we attend a performance, even if we go alone, we know our presence will, in some small way, help define the event; it wouldn't be exactly the same if we weren't there. The theatre critic should be sensitive to this. It isn't only what takes place on stage, it's also what happens in the auditorium that makes a piece of theatre.

Here's an example. It's a cold Thursday night in March and the crowds are pouring into the Edinburgh Festival Theatre for a pre-West End run of *The Full Monty*. The 1,900-seat auditorium is close to capacity and the audience is overwhelmingly female. There are a few men scattered around here and there, but for the most part, this is a girls' night out. Many have come in groups of four or more. I spot at least one hen party. For my sixteen-year-old son, it's an eye-opener; he's never seen an audience quite like it.

This is the demographic *The Full Monty* appeals to. In our collective imagination, we remember the 1997 movie as a raucous, feelgood comedy about male strippers. It tells the story of a gang of newly redundant steel workers who are so desperate for money and esteem they persuade each other to take part in an all-male Chippendales-style strip show. The audience they play to in their Sheffield nightclub is pretty similar to the audience that has shown up tonight in Edinburgh for Simon Beaufoy's stage adaptation of his original screenplay. There are many things we tend to forget about the movie, however. The image of these six ordinary working men getting naked (or going the 'full monty') to the sexy rhythm of *You Can Leave Your Hat On* tends to overwhelm our memory of the film's deeper concerns. Behind the laughter and the wish-fulfilment narrative, it is a serious study of unemployment, poverty, depression, sexual equality, impotence, suicide, body image and homosexuality. Whether the audience expects it or not, these are the themes Beaufoy is exploring in his play, produced by Sheffield Theatres (and defiantly not the Americanized musical version from 2000).

In the live theatre, this creates a fascinating tension. On the one hand, you have an audience that is out for a good time, determined to clap along to the shortest fragment of a familiar tune and wolf whistle as soon as an actor so much as touches the buttons on his shirt. On the other hand, you have a production, directed by Daniel Evans, that is equally determined to communicate the drama of lives devastated by industrial decline. It's as if the audience wants to leap straight to the famous final scene, while the company knows that moment must be earned. The instincts of Beaufoy and Evans are absolutely right in this respect. Their hunch is that only with the empathy and understanding developed over the preceding two hours will the closing striptease have an emotional impact. When it comes, it feels momentarily like the best final scene of any play ever. This is the prize the characters have worked for, the glorious achievement of a goal, and it is also just happens to be the reason the audience came out tonight. A scene that, earlier in the evening, would have been at best titillating, at worst crass, now becomes emotionally fulfilling.

To achieve this, Evans has had to take a firm control of the audience. At the start of the show, two men and a boy enter an abandoned steelworks. As they take in its vast and desolate scale, they look out into the auditorium and we feel a frisson of recognition that we are in the same space as the actors. The audience, however, is still excitable and prone to shouting out as if its members were watching an actual strip show. If the production doesn't nip those expectations in the bud, the actors will be working in opposition to the audience for the rest of the night. The solution comes quickly. Playing Gaz, actor Kenny Doughty, has a line about how quiet this once noisy factory has become. He holds out his arm to command silence so he can listen. It makes sense in terms of the script, but it has the effect of shutting up the audience. Everyone obeys his instruction to be quiet. In an email, Beaufoy told me:

> The line in question came up naturally as part of the writing process. In my research, a lot of steel workers spoke of how they had become prematurely deaf because of the noise. Another woman told of how ornaments would bounce along the mantelpiece with the thud of the hammers. So silence was a powerful message.

However, it quickly became apparent that as you say, we needed to re-set the audience's expectations. Curtain up, there was a party atmosphere that was very much all about the stripping. We needed to engage them in the characters and their plight in order that the stripping finale could really deliver emotionally. This line became the way of doing it. Kenny used it as a way of taking charge of the audience. He would hold that pause for as long as it took, until the audience was silent. From that moment on, control was back with the actors rather than a rowdy audience. It was quite a game of chicken on occasions . . .![4]

The result is that we realize this is a proper play and duly focus on what is being said. This is an example of a performance in which the audience is very present and, to an extent, helped determine its meaning. The exact same script would take on a different tenor if it were played in some arty studio before an audience who had never heard of the movie and therefore came with a different set of expectations. When the production reached London a year later, an online reader observed that Michael Billington in his *Guardian* review had seemed 'to be reviewing the auidience [sic]' as he had liked 'most of the component parts'.[5] This implied that the audience was not one of the component parts, yet Billington had argued specifically that it was: the 'actor–audience relationship' in the theatre, he said, made us 'complicit in the experience'.

Back in *The Empty Space*, Brook wrote about a touring production of *King Lear* he had directed that improved as a result of the 'quality of attention' brought by audiences between Budapest and Moscow, whose real-life experience connected them to the play's 'painful themes'. It then declined in quality in Philadelphia in front of an audience 'composed largely of people who were not interested in the play'. For better and then for worse, the actors modulated their performances in response to the different audiences. What was ostensibly the same Royal Shakespeare Company production was, according to the director, more subtle in eastern Europe and more crude in the US. Few critics have the privilege of travelling the world to observe these differences for themselves, but if they saw a way of identifying that 'quality of attention', it would be legitimate for them to take the audience into account in assessing the production's impact.

More than this, there are times when the audience makes such an impression that the critic will be compelled to make it central to the review. In February 1757, the unnamed critic of *The London Chronicle* described a production in Convent Garden of Aphra Behn's *The Rover*. It was a play that had been written, in the words of the review, in the 'dissolute Days of Charles the Second'.[6] The review said nothing about the production except that 'one of the Personages of the Drama takes off his Breeches in the Sight of the Audience'. What follows, however, gives you a vivid idea of what the occasion was like:

> The Ladies are first alarmed; then the Men stare: The Women put up their Fans. — 'My Lady Betty, what is the Man about?' — 'Lady Mary, sure he is not in earnest!' — Then peep thro' their Fans — 'Well, I vow, the He creature is taking off his odious Breeches — He-he — Po! — is that all? — the 'Man has Drawers on' — Then, like Mrs Cadwallador [sic] in the new Farce* — 'Well, to be sure, I never saw any Thing the Shape of it.' — Meantime, the Delight of the Male Part of the Audience is occasioned by the various Operations of this Phoenomenon [sic] on the Female Mind. — 'This is rare Fun, d — n me — Jack, Tom, Bob, did you ever see anything like this? — Look at that Lady yonder — See in the Stage Box — how she looks half-averted,' etc., etc. It is Matter of Wonder that the Upper Gallery don't call for an Hornpipe, or, 'Down with the Drawers,' according to their usual Custom of insisting upon as much as they can get for their Money.

> [*Mrs Cadwallader is a character in *The Author* by Samuel Foote, staged earlier in the same month.]

Here was a critic alive to where the real action was. They understood they were in a social hall of mirrors where everyone was keeping an eye on everyone else. They watched the women watching the stage. In hiding behind their fans, the women were indicating that they knew they were being watched by the men. Meanwhile, those men, who were also being watched by the critic, were getting as much fun from watching the women as they were from watching the play. As we experience it through the eyes of this critic, the theatre of the auditorium is even more fascinating than the theatre of the stage. This is especially the case, because the actor taking off his breeches had broken a social taboo. It was of secondary importance to know whether his performance was good or bad; the real interest was in the cultural significance of his action. The moment belonged to the audience.

That's not always a good thing. In 2005, the American Repertory Theatre invited Polish director Krystian Lupa to stage a production of Anton Chekhov's *Three Sisters* in Cambridge, Massachusetts. Although he cast American actors, he brought to the production a distinctively eastern European flavour and his own idiosyncratic approach. Actor Kelly McAndrew, who played Olga, told me about the effect this had on the audience:

> There were many performances where we lost up to half our house. Sometimes they would walk out right in front of us. In the fourth act, Krystian Lupa said to us, 'This is a new theatre that we are creating here called the theatre of waiting'. It's hard because you're looking at very long spaces where no one says anything. The audiences that stayed with it loved it. A lot of people commented on how much they enjoyed the time it took. In the published edition, Olga and Vershinin have a very brief exchange before Masha enters in the fourth act where there's a hint of love and things not necessarily working out the way that Olga wanted. It played for quite a long scene in our show. At one point, Frank [Wood, playing Vershinin] and I were facing the audience and it was Frank's turn to speak. I don't know how long had gone by – perhaps a minute and a half, maybe two minutes – and right as Frank was saying, 'Well, everything comes to an end,' somebody in the audience yelled out,

'Say something!' Some of the audience yelled, 'Shhh!' and some of the audience laughed.[7]

In the opening scene, the actors deliberately muttered their lines and kept the conversation on the cusp of inaudibility. For one audience member at the Edinburgh International Festival, where I saw it in 2006, this was unacceptable. 'We can't hear you,' she yelled in a crystal-clear English accent that would have put the queen to shame. 'We can't hear you,' she cried again for good measure. Unfazed by the intrusion, the actors did, momentarily, up the volume, but her intervention seemed to set off the other spectators into a frenzy of bad behaviour. It was one of the most distracting audiences I've ever sat in. If it wasn't the coughing or the squeaking hearing aid, it was the inappropriate guffaws from those who decided Lupa's interpretation was becoming comically overwrought (wrongly, to my mind, but that's another story). Having anything like a cool-headed response to the production with all this going on was almost impossible. As a consequence, I wasn't the only one who spent a good deal of my review discussing the audience. 'Although there is much to criticise, that doesn't excuse the philistinism of some Edinburgh spectators who greeted the last act with jeering derision',[8] said Billington in *The Guardian*.

The story echoes the experience of the actors who introduced *Waiting for Godot* to the English-speaking world in 1955. In his memoir, *I Know the Face, But . . .*, Peter Bull, who played Pozzo in the London premiere, recalled the 'waves of hostility' that 'came whirling over the footlights'.[9] Every night, he said, there was a 'mass exodus' from 'quite soon after the curtain had risen', not to mention 'audible groans'. As well as being depressing for the actors, this behaviour can't have escaped the notice of the critics. Some of them, indeed, were of much the same opinion as the audience ('I think myself justified in believing that a competent artist should be reasonably explicit',[10] said Ivor Brown), but famously, Harold Hobson of *The Sunday Times* swam against the tide: 'Mr Beckett has any amount of swagger. A dusty, coarse, irreverent, pessimistic, violent swagger? Possibly. But the genuine thing, the real McCoy.'[11]

The critic's voice in the crowd

History was on Hobson's side and his example shows us the value of holding your nerve. It may trouble our democratic instincts to say it, but the majority is not always right. If it were, we would have to agree that every long-running Broadway show was, by definition, better than every short-run fringe show. Critical judgement is not a straw poll or a popularity contest. Bad shows can succeed, good ones can fail. In the moment of performance, the critic is part of the audience and needs to be alive to the emotional pull of a production, but when it comes to writing a review, they can only stand apart from the crowd. They can write about what's going on inside their own heads but not inside anyone else's. Even if that were possible, there would be as many perspectives as there were people in the audience: how could the critic choose which to reflect?

Of course, critics aren't always right either, but their aim is more likely to be true if they trust their own instincts than if they try to second guess the audience. It's not impossible that someone who audibly groaned during *Waiting for Godot* in 1955 woke up the next morning with the realization they had seen something astonishing; a critic who based a review on their groans would be unable to account for any other reactions they may have had. As a matter of observable fact, they may report the audience's reaction and may add that people seemed to have enjoyed the production more or less than them – to go any further than that, however, would not be criticism but market research.

Judging the audience

The contradiction in writing about the audience is that you can only ever really write about yourself or, at least, your own perspective on their reactions. Kenneth Tynan effectively reviewed the audience when he took issue with the popularity of Eugene Ionesco, whose *The*

Chairs and *The Lesson* were staged at London's Royal Court in 1958 starring Joan Plowright, newly returned from Broadway:

> There was more in the applause than a mere welcome home. It had about it a blind, deafening intensity: one felt present at the consecration of a cult . . . This was an Ionesco cult, and in it I smell danger.[12]

In a similar vein, here is Leigh Hunt in the early 1800s, going into greater detail still as he complained about the audience's reaction to Mr Pope, a popular tragic actor whose bombastic style he detested:

> There is, however, an infallible method of obtaining a clap from the galleries, and there is an art known at the theatre by the name of clap-trapping, which Mr Pope has shown great wisdom in studying. It consists of nothing more than in gradually raising the voice as the speech draws to a conclusion, making an alarming outcry on the last four or five lines, or suddenly dropping them into a tremulous but energetic undertone, and with a vigorous jerk of the right arm rushing off the stage. All this astonishes the galleries; they are persuaded it must be something very fine, because it is so important and so unintelligible, and they clap for the sake of their own reputation.[13]

This is a superb description of the actor's technique and Hunt made his case very persuasively, but with what certainty could he account for the audience's behaviour? He seemed to have observed cause and effect (histrionic acting leading to audience applause), but it's quite possible the rest of the audience simply liked Pope's acting better than he did. Perhaps they didn't find it unintelligible at all. Perhaps they were unconcerned about their own reputation. Perhaps they had a taste that was different to Hunt's. Short of giving the audience a questionnaire, there's no way he could have known for sure – just as Tynan could not have proved that the 'blind, deafening intensity' of the applause for Ionesco was the sign of a cult. Hunt's analysis is plausible (I'm quite prepared to believe it), but it reminds me of the many times when my reaction has been at odds with the rest of the audience. If you're laughing and everyone else is stony-faced or, more typically, they're rolling in the aisles and you long to make a run for the exit, you naturally seek an explanation to account for it. Perhaps you'll find one as good as Hunt's, but you'll still be making a guess and the possibility remains that everyone else in the audience just likes it more than you.

Observing the laughter is one thing, but if you speculate too rashly about its causes, you may come across as a snob. The implication of sneering at someone else's laughter is that you somehow have better taste. We shouldn't imagine this is a phenomenon exclusive to the past. In *Reviewing Shakespeare*,[14] Paul Prescott pointed out that in the first few seasons of Shakespeare's Globe, the modern-day London theatre built to sixteenth-century specifications, critics would frequently make derogatory remarks about their fellow audience members. It was common for them to characterize the groundlings (who would be standing in the outdoors between the critics, usually seated, and the stage) as intellectually inferior, insensitive to Shakespeare's poetry and easily won over by a cheap gag or the opportunity to make a noise. In the reviews, foreign tourists, Americans in particular, 'often functioned as culturally incompetent counterpoints to the critic', according to Prescott who suggested today's critics were unsettled by the 'carnivalesque elements of popular theatre' in much the same way as their Puritan forebears. Presented like this, Shakespeare's Globe became a battleground in which critics defended their high-culture values against a perceived attack by low-culture elements. Prescott conceded that every theatregoer has at some point been distracted by other people in the audience, but nonetheless argued that the hostility of the critics 'stemmed from a number of deep-seated cultural presuppositions' to do with audience behaviour, Shakespearean performance style, popular cultural forms and class. These are the kind of things you will reveal about yourself and your values if you pathologize the audience as something other, somehow different to people like 'us'.

Taking the audience on board

Whatever the explanation, you can't blank out the audience. This is especially so on press nights when friends of the actors like to show their support in the most vocal way. Serious lines earn hearty chuckles, amusing lines win great guffaws. Already hyped up with first-night nerves, the actors may be further animated by the heightened atmosphere. You may, as a result, see a uniquely electrifying performance or you could see one with more nervous energy than depth. Either way, actors usually say they hit their best performances later in the run. In such circumstances, it may seem reasonable for the critic to take a step back, to screen out the more vocal enthusiasts in the audience and, perhaps, compensate for an excess of energy on stage.

There's merit in this idea, but there's no science to it. Only by seeing a show for a second time could you start to get a sense of the impact of the audience, but even that would be problematic. If your second audience was more muted, could you deduce it was more typical or might it also be an aberration? You have to respond to the event you witnessed – anything else is speculation. Somehow, you have to take the audience's influence on board, while keeping your wits about you. If you allow yourself to be irritated by the audience or irretrievably swept up in its enthusiasm, you may find it hard to keep a sense of perspective.

As a result, you won't always be in step with everyone else in the theatre. You can understand why producers and readers complain when a critic does not reflect the enthusiasm of the rest of the audience. For the theatremakers, it must be galling to hear laughter and applause every night only to have a critic – whose opinion is just one among many – respond in less laudatory terms. For audiences too, it can feel like their experience has been misrepresented by a critic's dissenting voice. It is easy to prevent this charge simply by acknowledging the audience in what you write. You rarely hear the argument in the opposite direction, however: would producers really be happy if every rave review drew attention to the audience's indifference?

Is the customer always right?

When this schism of opinion between critic and audience happens, as it frequently does, it can seem to be a throwback to the boxes-versus-galleries values embodied by Hunt's review. It isn't hard to characterize critics as elitist killjoys frowning on the ordinary theatregoer's pleasure, but that isn't really what's going on. The moment you call yourself a critic, your perspective changes. You are part of the audience, and you share many of the audience's pleasures, but you are there for a different reason. If you are laughing, it's your job to ask yourself why you are laughing. If you have a specialist knowledge, such as a close familiarity with the text of *The Two Gentlemen of Verona*, it's only right you should bring it to bear on the review. That's what George Bernard Shaw did after seeing a production of Shakespeare's play at Daly's Theatre in 1895: 'Let me hasten to admit that it makes a very pleasant entertainment for those who know no better. Even I, who know a great deal better, as I shall presently demonstrate rather severely, enjoyed myself tolerably.'[15] Shaw went on to take issue with changes to the scene order that he felt would have given the first-time viewer a misleading impression. He recognized such audiences would have enjoyed a 'very pleasant entertainment' but believed they could have had a more pleasant time still.

This is the critic's job – not to go along with the crowd but to speak for themselves and the greater good of the artform. In assessing a show's worth, only the critic as reporter and the critic as consumer guide would find it necessary to prioritize the audience's reaction. For any other kind of critic – judge, analyst, champion, educator, arbiter of taste, reformer, cultural commentator, social commentator, insider, ego and visionary – the audience is just one element among many or perhaps even of no relevance at all. In the next chapter, we'll look in greater detail at other contextual factors that affect the way you write, ranging from the mood you are in to the state of the economy.

EXERCISE

Write a 250-word review that focuses on the audience, describing the kind of people they are, what they add to the atmosphere of the event and how they react to the performance. Looked at this way, how much do they contribute to your enjoyment and understanding of the show?

Notes

1 Addison, Joseph and Steele, Richard (1817), *The Tatler, with Notes, and a General Index*, Desilver, Thomas & Co.

2 Hunt, Leigh (1807), *Critical Essays on the Performers of the London Theatres*, John Hunt.

3 Brook, Peter (1968), *The Empty Space*, McGibbon & Kee.

4 Beaufoy, Simon (8 September 2014), email to Mark Fisher.

5 Billington, Michael (26 February 2014), '*The Full Monty*', in *The Guardian*.

6 Gray, Charles Harold (1931), *Theatrical Criticism in London to 1795*, Columbia University Press.

7 McAndrew, Kelly (July 2006), interview with Mark Fisher.

8 Billington, Michael (31 August 2006), '*Three Sisters*', in *The Guardian*.

9 Bull, Peter (1959), *I Know the Face, But . . .*, P. Davies.

10 Brown, Ivor (1956), *Theatre 1955–56*, Max Reinhardt.

11 Shellard, Dominic (1995), *Harold Hobson: Witness and Judge*, Keele University Press.

12 Tynan, Kenneth (1975), *A View of the English Stage*, Davis-Poynter.

13 Hunt, Leigh (1894), *Dramatic Essays*, Walter Scott.

14 Prescott, Paul (2013), *Reviewing Shakespeare: Journalism and Performance from the Eighteenth Century to the Present*, Cambridge University Press.

15 Shaw, George Bernard (1932), *Our Theatres in the Nineties*, Vol. I, Constable and Company.

16
HOW TO WRITE
ABOUT CONTEXT

Lost in translation

Rob Drummond's *Bullet Catch*[1] is a one-man show based on a music-hall trick in which a volunteer shoots a gun at a magician. After the bang, the magician picks himself up off the floor and removes the bullet from between his teeth. In the closing moments of his theatricalized version, Drummond persuades an audience member to fire a loaded gun directly at his face. At the time of writing, he has survived every performance.

The production played successfully in Glasgow, on the Edinburgh Fringe and at the National Theatre in London. It was also warmly received by Charles Isherwood in *The New York Times*[2] when it played at 59E59 Theaters. But was he writing about the same show I had seen some months earlier? Yes, it was the same performer and yes, it was the same script, but close reading of Isherwood's review suggests that, in crossing the Atlantic, the production had taken on a different complexion. There are two details that persuade me of this. First, Isherwood observed that Drummond's Scottish accent lent a 'tinge of the exotic' to the performance; something, perhaps, that enhanced the mood of mystery and magic. Second, in a generally favourable review, the critic raised an objection to the idea of a gun being used as entertainment. It struck him as 'terrible taste' to have an apparently live firearm on stage when, in real life, innocent people were being slaughtered by guns every day. These are both legitimate observations.

They are honest reflections of what Isherwood thought and, quite possibly, what some others in his audience thought too. Even so, neither idea is likely to have occurred to reviewers in the UK. In the first example – the one about his accent – the difference is easy to explain. When *Bullet Catch* played on home turf, by definition, there could be nothing exotic about it. Only by travelling abroad, could it become so. Drummond had no control over this, yet the meaning of his work took on a different shade because it was being seen in a different context. At home, his Scottishness made him one of the crowd; abroad, it made him other.

Isherwood's observation about guns as entertainment is a little more complicated. Although it's not impossible to imagine a UK critic making the same complaint, it strikes me as unlikely. Just look at the crime statistics. In New York State, there are around fourteen times more homicides involving the use of a firearm per head of population than there are in Drummond's native Scotland. The annual state death toll of around 450 could fill six nights in Theater C, the New York studio space where *Bullet Catch* played. Viewed in this way, it would be understandable if American audiences were more sensitive to gun deaths than their Scottish counterparts. Firearm homicides are simply more present in the culture. It's possible, of course, that Isherwood's dislike of guns was unrelated to his country's homicide record. Maybe it was just his personal view. But on the basis that we are all shaped by the culture we live in, and on the basis that the right to bear arms is a contentious issue in the US, it's reasonable to assume his review reflected a wider social concern. This was not a concern Drummond intended to put in the play, but one the audience discovered for itself. I spoke to Drummond about it:

> When I did the show in New York, there was definitely a different atmosphere in the room. In Britain, a gun is almost seen as a cheeky, frivolous thrill. It's exciting rather than dangerous. But in New York, they took it a bit more seriously. It's dangerous to make sweeping generalizations because some people in New York were

very blasé about it, but if you could sum up the feeling, the gun meant something different, it read differently on stage.[3]

Drummond told me he had noticed another cultural difference. His American volunteers were far more likely to be confident handling a weapon than their counterparts in Britain. Where guns are more prevalent, people are more used to handling them:

In Brazil, they didn't have any problem handling the gun at all. It was like second nature, it seemed. But then you go to Australia, where they don't have a big gun culture, and again that gun was handled with immense fear. It changes the nature of each show. You can find yourself in *Bullet Catch* in a comedy or a very tense thriller, depending on what the audience are doing.

Speak to theatremakers and you'll find many examples of plays taking on different shades of meaning as they travel. In London, Lucy Prebble's 2009 play *Enron* was widely acclaimed for its timely response to the global financial crisis that had begun the year before, and to the biggest collapse in corporate history when the financial trading company Enron filed for bankruptcy in 2001. It broke box office records at the Noël Coward Theatre and raked in the awards. On its transfer to Broadway, however, the reception was tepid to hostile (Ben Brantley called it a 'flashy but labored economics lesson'[4]) and the show closed almost immediately. 'When we opened, it was the first hit of the credit crunch and nobody knew whether it meant the end of the world,' director Rupert Goold told me. 'When we were in New York, we were at the height of Obama pushing through new financial regulations, which Democratic New York couldn't bear, and it played in a very different political context.'[5]

From these reactions, we cannot infer that one group of critics was right and the other wrong. They were simply responding in different contexts. As a cultural relativist would say, truth itself is determined by your cultural environment. It is for reasons such as these that critics of the theatre need to be especially sensitive to context. In recorded artforms, such as cinema, literature, music and video games, we generally assume the work to be the same thing regardless of whether it is enjoyed alone or in company, whether it is experienced on state-of-the-art equipment or rudimentary technology and whether the audience is in Toronto, Adelaide or Dublin. In theatre, by contrast, it isn't just the difference between audiences from country to country, city to city and district to district, it is the difference on a daily basis from performance to performance. A show may be affected by time of day, the architecture of the auditorium, the state of the weather, events in the news, the price of the tickets, the mood of the actors and the temperament of the audience. Because of this, theatre critics are aiming at a moving target. To make matters even harder, they have to shoot from a moving position; the minute-by-minute variables in their own personality see to that.

Context manifests itself in five forms and the more aware you are of each of them, the more attuned you will be to the specifics of the theatrical event:

1 THE CRITIC'S CONTEXT. This is the context you bring with you, the complex pattern of prejudices, influences, moods, enthusiasms and expectations that make up your personality.

2 THE SOCIAL CONTEXT. This is to do with the audience in this particular performance space: their age range, their class, their noisiness, their tastes, their communal history and expectations.

3 THE MODERN-DAY CONTEXT. This is the context created by the conditions that affect us all, ranging from the weather to the state of the economy to the songs in the charts to the latest tabloid scandal.

4 THE THEATRE'S CONTEXT. This is to do with the production: the conditions under which it was made, the audience it was created for, what it was setting out to achieve.

5 THE PLAY'S CONTEXT. In the case of productions of adaptations, translations and old plays, this is the context in which the original script was created, the values, assumptions and politics of the era that are inextricably locked into the work.

Let's look at each of them in turn.

The critic's context

In 2011, Howard Sherman, a New York arts administrator and producer, wrote a blog post about being brought to tears in the theatre. Under the heading 'Streaming', he described seeing David Cromer's Obie-award winning production of Thornton Wilder's *Our Town*. Even though this was the second time Sherman had seen it, he found himself crying throughout the third act, something that hadn't happened the first time around:

> What had changed between my visits? I had lost a good friend, suddenly, and too soon, just a few weeks before the second viewing. Wilder's graveyard of the departed, talking about those still alive, had acquired a new inhabitant, who sat on that stage as surely as did any of the actors.[6]

Sherman watched exactly the same production, but because of an event in his life, he now had a more intense reaction. From his point of view, it was as if he were watching a different show. Neither Cromer nor his actors could have had any control over this. The meaning changed because Sherman changed. Something similar happened to Amy Taylor when, as a student critic, she was commissioned to review a touring production of *Carrie's War*. In 'Crying in the Theatre', a touching post on her Taylor Trash blog, she described the experience of weeping throughout the performance. Part of the reason for this, she thought, was the play's 'underlying sense of guilt', a theme that had a particular resonance for her. She knew, however, that what she was really crying about was her recent romantic break-up:

> I was sitting in the stalls and I was aware that the chair next to me, the chair my now ex-partner would have normally sat in, with his hand on my knee, was empty. In fact, the chair next to that chair was also empty, and so was the chair next to that one. In a theatre where everyone else was packed in like sardines, I nearly had half the row to myself.[7]

It was a vivid evocation of the loneliness she was feeling as she watched the performance. From her perspective, it was as if the auditorium itself was conspiring to make her feel bad. The combination of her existing emotional state, the theatre's seating arrangements and the trigger of *Carrie's War* was enough to set her off 'crying over all that I'd lost in the past year'. This is the personal context that she brought into the theatre. Everyone else in the audience would have brought their own contexts with them as well, perhaps not as emotionally extreme, but variously grumpy, happy, anxious, excited, tired, energetic and preoccupied, as the case may be. This is one reason there will be as many opinions about a show as there are people in the audience. However masterly the control of the theatremakers, each spectator will always hit the production from a slightly different angle. As Sherman's anecdote attests, even the same spectator can see a show in a different light on a different day.

Critics are not neutral. They may have the look of dispassionate scientists, notebook at the ready, gaze fixed and attentive, not even sullying their hands with money to pay for their tickets, but they can hardly be said to observe laboratory conditions. The theatre is a contaminated space. It does not happen in a vacuum. Like everyone in the audience, critics bring the outside world in with them; their own concerns, their own moods, their own preoccupations. Most likely, they will bring with them the impression of the show they saw the night before or, if it's a festival, the three productions they've already seen that day. All this will affect the meaning of the thing they are observing.

As well as bringing a set of cultural expectations about the status and nature of criticism itself, critics may carry with them prejudicial memories of previous performances and, in small theatre communities, have had professional or personal dealings with the artists. Professional critics will have strategies to compensate for this and will try to consider the new work as open-mindedly as possible, but they couldn't claim to be entirely neutral observers. For any critic who wants to be taken seriously, this presents a challenge. On the one hand, you can't deny you are a product of your time and place, an emotional being subject to public and private pressures, a creature with a distinct social, cultural and political history. On the other, you would like to write something that was more than a hermetic reflection of your subjective worldview with all its prejudices and quirks, being of no consequence to anyone else.

The solution lies in two areas. One is to recall our first question: 'What were the theatremakers trying to do?' By placing yourself in the world of the artist, you step outside your own subjective concerns. For some critics, this means consciously making an effort to clear their heads on entering the theatre, to cleanse the memory of previous shows and to think beyond their day-to-day moods and preoccupations. The personality of the critic will eventually and inevitably come into play, but in the first instance, the intention of the theatremakers is paramount.

The other area is for critics to develop a high degree of self-awareness. They must be prepared to interrogate themselves as well as the work they are observing. The question is not only, 'Why did the production have this particular effect?' but also, 'Why did I react to it in this particular way?' You will not cure yourself of your biases nor extract yourself from your historical environment, but you can get better at understanding how you are affected by those things and to account for them in your writing. The more you understand yourself, the better you will be able to explain what it is you have experienced and where you sit in relation to it.

EXERCISE

Next time you are about to set off for the theatre, make a note of how you are feeling: your mood, your level of tiredness, events in your private life and your feelings about the evening ahead. What kind of a show do you think you will see? Why do you have that opinion? How many assumptions have you already made?

The social context

Audiences arrive at the theatre with their own collective and individual agendas. Critics may not always make direct reference to this, but they will almost always make some account of the social nature of the theatrical event. The audience for a children's show brings with it a different set of expectations and a different way of behaving from the audience for a Broadway musical. A community show in a deprived inner-city area will attract a different crowd from a rural summer repertory theatre. Critics are part of that audience too and can have their expectations similarly moulded. The context shapes the intensity of their reaction. Without even thinking about it, they would assume a prestige show by a well-funded national theatre would have higher production values than a thriller put on in a village hall by an amateur dramatics company. That doesn't imply anything about the level of enjoyment – audiences and critics instinctively adjust to the setting and make allowances – but it does mean any production has to work on its own terms. In the village hall you may overlook a wobbly set, but not so with a national theatre.

As a theatre critic, you often feel like a social anthropologist. For much of the time, you will be going to theatres in towns where you do not live, sitting alongside people who do not match your demographic profile, writing about shows that were not created with someone like you in mind. Unless you have the freedom to go only to shows that appeal to your taste and visit only familiar venues where you feel at home, you will commonly find yourself like an outsider looking in.

Occasionally, this raises ethical dilemmas. Would a middle-class white female critic be qualified to comment on a production aimed at unemployed Asian men? Does being part of the majority culture mean you simply can't understand the experience of a minority culture? However well intentioned you are, will you inevitably miss the point? Will you be so steeped in one tradition, so enmeshed in its values and assumptions, that you do not even have the language to talk about the performance in its own terms? As a feminist critic, Jill Dolan argued that context was a legitimate area of consideration that could reveal a lot about the theatrical event: 'Space and place are political; they signal power and position, taste and cultural influence.'[8] This is an important part of answering our first question, 'What were the theatremakers trying to do?'

The actor–audience relationship is so fundamental that only the most esoteric of theatremakers take no account of who they are performing to. Such artists do exist, but far more common are those whose every choice is influenced by the audience they want to communicate to. The better the critic understands the social context in which a performance takes place, the more rooted their review will be in the event.

EXERCISE

Write a 250-word review that focuses on the audience, their number, age, class, gender, race, mood and volubility. Write about the production only to the extent it tells you something about them. How much have you absorbed about the event even before the actors have come on stage?

The modern-day context

On the death of former British prime minister Margaret Thatcher, several newspapers carried articles about the West End productions of *Billy Elliot: the Musical* and Peter Morgan's *The Audience*, both of which alluded to Thatcher's three terms at the head of government. In *Billy Elliot: the Musical*, which was set at the time of the miners' strike of 1984–85, there was a song looking forward to her death; in *The Audience*, Thatcher was portrayed by actor Haydn Gwynne in an imagined argument with the Queen about domestic and foreign policy. The newspapers reported that *Billy Elliot: the Musical* had gone ahead only after the audience had been polled about whether the song should be performed (all but three had said yes) and the performance of *The Audience* had been preceded by a speech from Morgan. The voting and the speech were unusual, but what had made the shows newsworthy was an external event: the death of a former prime minister. Without a word being changed, the performances in the immediate aftermath of 8 April 2013 had a different resonance from those before that date. Had you been a critic in either of the theatres that night, you would almost certainly have been compelled to describe what happened on stage in terms of what had just happened in the outside world.

Thatcher's death is a particularly vivid example of a phenomenon that happens every day of the year. The nature of live theatre means every performance is born afresh in front of the audience and its meaning changes, sometimes imperceptibly, sometimes dramatically, in relation to an always changing society. A similar thought struck Joyce McMillan in one of her earliest reviews. It was February 1981 and the announcement had just been made of the engagement of Prince Charles and Lady Diana Spencer. McMillan had been asked by *The Scotsman* to review an amateur production of *The Pirates of Penzance*, the Gilbert and Sullivan operetta, which includes the line: 'So this is the little lady who is so unexpectedly called upon to assume the functions of royalty! And a very nice little lady, too!' She told me:

There was a ripple of applause, an intake of breath and the level of attention to the stage just went soaring upwards. It was one of the moments in my early career when I thought this is really strange: *Pirates of Penzance* is a decorative piece of work and people go because they want to hear the music and see the costumes; you don't expect it to have any connection with life. And yet because of one phrase that reminds people of something that's happened outside that day, it's like the whole world can rush into the theatre and bring all these resonances with it.[9]

In an earlier chapter, we looked at a *Chicago Tribune*[10] review of *The Wheel* by Zinnie Harris in which Chris Jones framed the performance in terms of events in Kenya and elsewhere in Chicago. Those events cannot possibly have been in the minds of the artists putting on the show, yet quite rightly, the critic saw *The Wheel* in this context. He was able to use the common currency of these news events to explain to his readers where the production sat in the world and why it was socially important. I asked Harris how this felt from her perspective as a playwright. She said it was wonderful because it suggested there was something in the play that went beyond her own immediate experience:

Chris Jones's review really said he got the play and he was responding to it as a man that lives in Chicago. He was able to pull out all those resonances for the world he was in. Theatre has got to do that. Even if it was a version of *Hamlet*, you would have to answer the question, 'Why does this play need to be seen by this audience now?'[11]

These examples demonstrate how high-profile topical events can have a dramatic influence on the way theatre is received. The cultural mood, however, is in a permanent state of flux and, on a more subtle basis, plays drift in and out of favour all the time. In *Hamlet Versus Lear*,[12] R.A. Foakes outlined the production history of the two

Shakespeare tragedies and observed how different eras have singled out one or other as the playwright's highest achievement. In 1830, John Keble called *Hamlet* 'the noblest and greatest of all [Shakespeare's] tragedies', whereas in 1971, Emrys Jones was able to say that for many critics *King Lear* was 'self-evidently the greatest'. Foakes attributed the change in perception to a period of political change intensified by the development of the hydrogen bomb in 1952 and the possibility of planetary destruction from nuclear fallout. Where once critics had seen *King Lear* as a 'pilgrimage to redemption', now it had become 'Shakespeare's bleakest and most despairing vision of suffering'. Without a word of Shakespeare being altered, the meaning of the play had changed. The liveness of theatre coupled with the fluidity of culture ensures you're never reviewing the same thing twice, even with such well-known plays. It turns the critic into a cultural thermometer, taking the temperature of the times as well as of what's on stage.

EXERCISE

Think about the last production you saw. Imagine it being performed in different places and different eras. Would it have been understood in exactly the same way a week ago, a year ago, fifty years ago and 300 years ago? How much would you have to explain to someone from another country or even another town? For how long in the future would audiences still get something from it?

The theatre's context

In its 2013–14 season, the National Theatre in London shut the 400-seat Cottesloe Theatre for renovations (later to reopen it as the Dorfman Theatre) and replaced it with a building known as The Shed. The first show to open in this temporary space was *The Table* by Tanya Ronder. In her review in *The Observer*, Susanna Clapp praised the play for its warmth and intelligence, applauded director Rufus Norris, name-checked lighting designer Paule Constable and singled out the actors. It was the kind of write-up that would have delighted the company.

Of particular interest to us, however, is how Clapp allocated the space in her review. Nearly two-thirds of it was about the building. First she outlined the story behind the Cottesloe's closure, then she described what The Shed looked like and finally she congratulated Haworth Tompkins, the firm of architects, for its work. She talked about the National Theatre as well as the egg in Bath and the Royal Court, Young Vic and Battersea Arts Centre in London. 'They started reshaping the stage when site-specific work was beginning to boom, reminding audiences of the importance of the places in which we see plays',[13] she wrote. 'Their impact has been as great as that of an artistic director.'

As well as being a rare instance of a critic making use of her sense of smell ('Built of raw steel and plywood, it smells of timber'), the review was a recognition of the role played by space in the theatrical experience. Architecture is an aspect we take for granted, largely because the auditorium is the same from one production to the next, but on the occasion of an opening, when the whole audience enjoys the thrill of discovery, Clapp saw fit to focus on it. She recognized also the place of the production in the wider theatrical landscape, in this case in the form of other buildings Haworth Tompkins had worked on. She understood that neither building nor show existed in isolation and that her appreciation of what was on stage was related to her enjoyment of the building and her familiarity with similar buildings. Just as Amy Taylor was affected by sitting in an empty row when she saw *Carrie's War*, so Clapp was affected by seeing *The Table* in this particular space.

It wouldn't be appropriate to talk in such detail about the building in every review. In the vast majority of cases, there will be many more pressing aspects of a production that demand your attention first. But a critic should be aware there is meaning in the theatrical space. Compare a pub theatre with a Victorian proscenium arch theatre, a converted sports arena with a black-box studio, a church hall with a cabaret bar. Each has an influence not just on practical things like sight lines and set changes, but on the atmosphere of the production and the socio-political nature of the event. The prestigious boxes in a classical auditorium reinforce the class system where the egalitarian layout of a theatre-in-the-round seeks to do the opposite. Before the show has even begun, you will have absorbed a whole load of values, in the layout of the bricks and mortar, in the friendliness of the box-office staff, in the availability of an induction loop for the deaf and hearing-impaired, in the design of the posters. All are part of the theatregoing experience and all could come under your scrutiny in the right circumstances.

Two books that consider these ideas in greater detail are *Architecture, Actor and Audience*[14] by Iain Mackintosh, a theatre architect's view of the environments in which performances happen, and *A Good Night Out*[15] by John McGrath, a socialist call to arms that contends that a truly left-wing theatre would need to be radical in form, including the place it takes place, as well as in content. Both will change the way you think about theatre.

EXERCISE

Write a 250-word review that focuses on the building, its location, its architecture and its atmosphere, with details about the foyer, bar, auditorium and sightlines. Write about the production only to the extent it tells you something about the space. How different do you think the performance would have been in a different kind of theatre?

The play's context

So much for the building, what about the context in which the play came into being? Every theatremaker creates their work in a particular time and place, and even if they are not trying to make a point about it, their era always makes its presence felt in their work. It's easiest to see this in classic plays. To understand the tragedy of Willy Loman in Arthur

Miller's *Death of a Salesman*, you need to know what the American dream was all about. To understand Anton Chekhov's *Three Sisters*, you need to have a feel for the unbreachable distance between a provincial Russian town and turn-of-the-century Moscow. To understand Jimmy Porter's vitriol in John Osborne's *Look Back in Anger*, you have to have a grasp of the cultural inertia of post-war Britain (also the kind of plays the playwright was reacting against). In each case, specific cultural conditions underpin the dramatic life of the play – otherwise Loman would settle into a happy retirement, the three sisters would jump on a train and Porter would stop complaining and get a job in the City.

The reason we regard these plays as classics is that (so far) they have transcended the particulars of their time and continued to strike a chord with at least some audiences, often revealing new shades of meaning as they do so. Many plays, successful in their day, prove less durable; they resonate for a while, then the culture moves on. Other plays, although continuing to work in performance, carry elements that can strike us as odd or even offensive. Audiences sometimes struggle to reconcile their vision of Shakespeare, the great humanist, with the apparent misogyny of *The Taming of the Shrew* and the apparent anti-Semitism of *The Merchant of Venice*. Those debates are long and complex, and depend on how you interpret the plays, but the least we can say is that the values of Elizabethan England are not the values we hold today. The same applies to any historical stage representation that conflicts with our modern sensibilities.

Critics can't ignore those developments, can't stop themselves being shaped by the history that followed, but if they do not have an awareness of the world in which the playwrights were operating, they will find it harder to answer our first question: 'What were the theatremakers trying to do?' If they are insensitive to the cultural conditions under which each play came into being, they can very easily miss the point. Not only must the critic understand these contextual factors, but they must explain them to their readers: 'These are the conditions the theatremaker was operating under, this is the question that needed to be resolved and this is the solution they came up with.'

Given a contextual explanation like this, the reader can see the play from a perspective that may otherwise have been unavailable to them. That's not to suggest the critic should blindly accept work that had its origins in a different time and place; you can still argue about the modern meanings a play carries, but to understand the past is to see the play on its own terms.

For critics to fulfil this function requires them to have a level of contextual background knowledge in the first place. It makes the job not just a subjective expression of opinion – 'I liked it because it entertained me'/'I didn't like it because it didn't entertain me' – but a more reasoned act of elucidation. Your opinion still stands but it is anchored in the work itself, treating it not as a spontaneous self-generated moment of isolated artistic expression but as an event with a rich contextual history. Whether you're talking about Bertolt Brecht's *Mother Courage* or Walt Disney's *The Lion King*, theatre is a product of its society, of its time and of the theatremakers' tastes (which are in themselves culturally determined) and there is a deep well of meanings and values beneath the surface. If critics penetrate that surface, dive deep into those meanings and values, they can give the reader a sense of a production's place in the world, to say not just whether the acting was good or bad but what relevance the whole enterprise had to our lives. The critic is not separate from these contextual factors but enmeshed in them. Our complicity and subjectivity can leave us exposed, so in the next two chapters we'll consider firstly our emotions, arguably the main reason we go to the theatre in the first place, and then how to deal with our inevitable bias.

EXERCISE

Write a 400-word review of a production of a modern or ancient classic in which you explain why the play could only have been written by that particular playwright at that particular time.

Notes

1 Drummond, Rob (2013), *Quiz Show* and *Bullet Catch*, Bloomsbury Methuen Drama.

2 Isherwood, Charles (11 April 2013), 'Here's hoping understudies aren't needed', in *The New York Times*.

3 Drummond, Rob (2 July 2014), interview with Mark Fisher.

4 Brantley, Ben (28 April 2010), 'Titans of tangled finances kick up their heels again', in *The New York Times*.

5 Fisher, Mark (7 November 2010), 'Preview: *Enron*, King's Theatre, Edinburgh', in *Scotland on Sunday*.

6 Sherman, Howard (8 November 2008), 'Streaming', on Howard Sherman (www.hesherman.com/2011/11/08/streaming/).

7 Taylor, Amy (17 September 2013), 'Crying in the theatre', on The Taylor Trash (http://thetaylortrash.com/2013/09/17/crying-in-the-theatre).

8 Dolan, Jill (2013), *The Feminist Spectator in Action*, Palgrave Macmillan.

9 McMillan, Joyce (7 July 2014), interview with Mark Fisher.

10 Jones, Chris (22 September 2013), 'Joan Allen on a roll through the years', in the *Chicago Tribune*.

11 Harris, Zinnie (9 June 2014), interview with Mark Fisher.

12 Foakes, R.A. (1993), *Hamlet Versus Lear*, Cambridge University Press.

13 Clapp, Susanna (21 April 2013), '*Table; Children of the Sun*', in *The Observer*.

14 Mackintosh, Iain (1993), *Architecture, Actor and Audience*, Routledge.

15 McGrath, John (1981), *A Good Night Out*, Eyre Methuen.

17
HOW TO WRITE ABOUT EMOTIONS

The empire of the passions

One of the complaints of Aaron Hill, founder of *The Prompter*, the first theatre journal in London in the 1730s, was that too many actors repeated their parts rather than acting them in an emotionally engaged way. This was just a few years before David Garrick appeared on the scene and ushered in a new era of naturalistic acting. Hill's argument against the unfeeling actors he saw was that: 'the Stage is the Empire of the Passions; where nothing languid, unmark'd, or indifferent, ought to have Place: but Every Thing shou'd be animated, picturesque, and alarming.'[1] Even today, we'd be hard pressed to come up with a better phrase to describe the theatre than an 'Empire of the Passions'. Erin Hurley would concur: in *Theatre and Feeling*, she wrote that 'theatre is bound up with feeling in the most elemental way',[2] concluding that 'we attend the theatre to feel *more*, even if it doesn't make us feel better; we go to have our emotional life acknowledged and patterned, managed into coherent storylines, and exposed in all its tumult (or its banality)'.

But this gives us a dilemma. In his autobiographical reflection *The Summing Up*,[3] the novelist Somerset Maugham argued that the job of judging made critics the wrong people to comment on an artform that traded in feelings: 'He must hold aloof from the contagion that has captured the group and keep his self-possession. He must not allow his heart to carry him away; his head must remain well-screwed on his shoulders. He must not become part of the audience.' Similarly, in *The Critics,*[4] a survey of New York reviewers in the 1970s, Lehman Engel argued that by commenting on 'every single element of a new show', from the choreography to the lighting, the city's daily reviewers were prone to overlook its overall impact. By profession, Engel was a Broadway conductor and he believed that only by surrendering himself to the 'total experience' of a production could he see it as it was intended. His implication was that reviewers were too cerebral, too analytical, to appreciate the pull a show could have on their hearts.

I would argue that the challenge to critics is to do both things at once. They need to be emotionally immersed in the event and they also need to be intellectually conscious of the aspects that go towards creating the emotion. Just as a film critic can identify the different effects created by a long lens and a short lens, and just as a music critic can understand how different moods are built by major and minor keys, so the theatre critic should have an awareness not only of what was achieved but also of how. This is not an alternative to feeling, it's an addition. They must develop the ability to move in and out of the dream state created by theatre, to experience it as fully as anyone else in the audience and also to maintain a sense of the relative qualities of that dream. In broadest terms, critics do their emotional work during the performance and their intellectual work when they write the review. In practice, the distinction may be less clear-cut – during the performance critics continue to think analytically, just as in the writing of the review they re-experience the emotions – but it should be possible to do both.

First person or third?

When it comes to writing the review, the critic can choose, if they so desire, to stick to a tone of cool distance, to talk about 'the effect of the production' and not 'the effect the production had on me'. But theatre is an emotional place and emotions affect you intimately. There are times when sober analysis seems appropriate, but other times when it is more honest to talk directly about your feelings. In *The Smile Off Your Face, Internal* and *A Game of You*, the Belgian company Ontroerend Goed subjected the audience to one-to-one experiences, including a blind-folded sensory tour and a piece of theatrical speed-dating. These felt custom-built for each spectator and, with nothing to go on but your own subjective response, it was almost impossible to discuss them without placing yourself and your own reactions at the centre of the review.

There is a tradition of writing that imagines the critic looking in at the theatrical event from the outside. Scientists tell us only about the behaviour of their lab rats and not about how they felt about the behaviour; similarly, this kind of critic keeps an emotional distance from the performance. But what place can such a critic have in the 'Empire of the Passions'? When emotion is so central to the audience's experience, isn't the idea of a buttoned-up critic nonsensical? Sure, the theatre offers many technical and intellectual pleasures that call on the critic's analytical powers, but a critic who failed to acknowledge a production's subjective, emotional impact would be overlooking the main reason people go to the theatre in the first place. That would seem a pretty big omission.

It's telling that when critics move to the informal medium of Twitter, they often find themselves more emotionally free. 'I actually wept at Bolton Octagon last night when Blanche DuBois throws herself on the kindness of strangers', tweeted *The Guardian*'s Lyn Gardner after a production of *A Streetcar Named Desire*.[5] A week earlier, I had tweeted in a similar vein: 'Just out of *Sunshine on Leith* for a third time. In bits again.' The casual, colloquial and, above all, personal phrase 'in bits again' was not one I used in my published review of The Proclaimers musical in *The Guardian*.[6] Both Gardner and I wrote about our emotional reactions in our full-length reviews, but it was in a more sober and reflective way than the tweets. This wasn't necessarily because of newspaper tradition: we had good reason for sparing the readers our statements of private emotion. Who cares that Gardner wept and I was in bits? Our reactions could not be contested. You couldn't disagree that we'd felt that way. But neither could you make any sense of our feelings without further information. That is why it is incumbent on the critic not only to describe their reaction but to explain how the show provoked it. In this way, a review is an intellectual response to an emotional stimulus.

That's as it should be, but the explanatory function can also be a form of defence. The critic who writes with academic authority about Tennessee Williams or with pop-cultural erudition about The Proclaimers is in safe territory. They can hide behind their clever theories and flashy turns of phrase, confident that readers will be impressed and their status will be maintained. But the critic who admits to feeling frightened, sad or sexually aroused has no place to hide. As we grow up, we all adopt strategies about how to behave in the public sphere. We keep our clothes on, we hold our emotions in check and we appear as grown-up as we can. Only in private do we allow ourselves to be naked, emotional and childlike.

The paradox for the critic is that the act of writing is private but the finished article is public. You have the advantage of time to craft what you write and not to blurt out the wrong thing, but you also have the potential to reveal more than you'd say in other circumstances. It takes a certain bravery but, if you are willing, you may get further by admitting to being vulnerable, weak and naked, instead of maintaining the illusion of authority. The risk is of you being judged as silly and emotional, a less-than-serious critic, not one of the grown-ups. The potential pay-off is people's admiration for you being honest in a world where everyone is pretending to be in control.

One reason the former *Daily Telegraph* critic Charles Spencer was so widely quoted when he described Nicole Kidman as 'pure theatrical Viagra'[7] in *The Blue Room* is that he was emotionally unguarded. For an adult writer in a sensible broadsheet newspaper to describe Kidman in terms of her aphrodisiac appeal was to go public with a private emotion. He was using the sophisticated language of the brain's prefrontal cortex to express the impulsive desires of the primitive brain. In doing so, he was risking embarrassment and opprobrium. Spencer was almost certainly expressing what other people were thinking; the difference is that he had the nerve to say it. He had the perfect sound bite of a phrase, of course, but what mattered was his emotional honesty. He later claimed that translator David Hare had accused him of 'getting "carried away" in "what you might call an 'I-wouldn't-mind-giving-her-one' review" '.[8] To match such honesty in your own writing takes courage and resolve.

Can emotions be trusted?

It also takes emotional self-knowledge. Have you genuinely fallen in love with a production or have you, like the characters in *A Midsummer Night's Dream*, been overtaken by a temporary and inexplicable passion? The irrational side of your brain is saying you've just seen the best show ever; the rational side is wondering whether you shouldn't be calming down a little. Getting it into perspective with a deadline looming is a tough call. Sometimes it pays to exercise a little caution.

One judgement to make is how much your emotional reaction has been governed by your personal circumstances and how much those are relevant to the reader. Something in your life may make you react in a particularly intense way to a production. It would be entirely justified to talk about the intensity, but it is not necessarily of any interest to the reader to know the autobiographical reasons you felt that way. I remember, for example, finding myself crying as I wrote a review of Michel Tremblay's *If Only* . . . It's a play about the playwright's relationship with his late mother and, as my own mother had been recently diagnosed with cancer, it struck a raw personal note. Looking back at what I wrote, however, I see I made no reference to that fact. I knew there was nothing special about my perspective – people's parents get ill all the time – so however sad it was, there was no light my own experience would have shed on the show.

Amy Taylor faced the same dilemma when she came to write the review of *Carrie's War* that we looked at in the last chapter. This was the occasion when she found herself feeling bereft as she sat in a symbolically empty row in the theatre at a stressful time. It seemed to her, however, that the emotions she felt during the performance said more about her, and her recent split with a boyfriend, than they did about the show. She even wondered whether it was right to review the production at all, given her state of mind. After allowing herself a few days to cool down (the deadline for *The Journal*, a student publication, was not pressing), she decided it would be unprofessional not to file a review. A little embarrassed by her own reactions, she thought she should try, as she said, to be 'as logical and cold, if that's the best word, as possible'. She later told me in an email: 'I also felt it was inappropriate to discuss my emotional reaction to the play; I mean, who wants to read about how I was crying my heart out because of a boy, and not because of the play?'

If the play had had a more direct connection to her emotional state, perhaps she would have taken a different approach. As it was, she did her best to talk about the production in its own terms. She wrote about the story, the transition from novel to stage, other adaptations of the book, the tone of this version, the fluidity of the staging and the 'sense of camaraderie and community'[9]. She was fair, measured and warm, without giving a hint of what she'd really been feeling. All the same, the experience made a lasting impression. 'I'll never forget that night in the theatre', she told me. 'And maybe these are the kind of nights that every young critic needs to face.'

EXERCISE

Write a 350-word review focusing on your personal feelings and treating the theatre as an 'Empire of the Passions'. Consider the plot in terms of your hopes and fears for the characters. Write about the performances in terms of how you felt emotionally towards the actors. Think about set, lighting, music and sound in terms of what they made you feel. What is gained and what is lost by this approach?

Notes

1 Gray, Charles Harold (1931), *Theatrical Criticism in London to 1795*,
    Columbia University Press.

2 Hurley, Erin (2010), *Theatre & Feeling*, Palgrave Macmillan

3 Maugham, Somerset (1938), *The Summing Up*, Heinemann.

4 Engel, Lehman (1976), *The Critics*, Macmillan.

5 Gardner, Lyn (20 September 2010), '*A Streetcar Named Desire*', in *The
    Guardian*.

6 Fisher, Mark (16 September 2010), '*Sunshine on Leith*', in *The Guardian*.

7 Spencer, Charles (23 September 1998), 'The Blue Room', in *The Daily
    Telegraph*.

8 Spencer Charles (31 August 2002), 'Top five theatrical sex scenes', in
    The Daily Telegraph.

9 Taylor, Amy (14 October 2010), '*Carrie's War*', in *The Journal*.

18
HOW TO WRITE ABOUT YOUR BIAS

The moral majority?

The unnamed critic who reviewed the 1757 Covent Garden revival of Aphra Behn's *The Rover* for *The London Chronicle* made it sound a hoot. They described with a ribald wit the reaction of the audience to an actor removing his breeches, attributing smutty jokes to the women ('Is that all? . . . I never saw any Thing in the Shape of it') and expressing surprise that people in the upper gallery didn't shout out, 'Down with the Drawers'. But there was a curious tension in the review. Despite making clear how much fun it all was, the critic became sternly moral about the standards expected in the modern theatre, eighty years after Behn's play had first been staged: 'But to be a little serious, it should be remembered by all Managers that this Play was written in the dissolute Days of Charles the Second; and that Decency at least is, or ought to be, demanded at present.'[1]

To our eyes, the relish with which the critic described the audience is at odds with the review's prim insistence on 'Decency'. They seemed to enjoy the fun, but some other impulse told them 'to be a little serious'. Locked into the review were a whole load of values, independent of the production, about the necessity for art to be instructive, edifying and improving. Even a critic who so brilliantly captured a sense of the audience's enjoyment could not accept that such pleasure was a worthwhile end in itself. Never mind that the theatre was fulfilling its aim to entertain an audience, this writer seemed to be saying, what mattered was that decency 'ought to be' demanded.

When the job of the critic was to determine whether a play had adhered to a preordained set of rules, it is not surprising that many plays failed to find favour. The approach applied not only to questions of morality but also of aesthetic taste: an actor could fall foul of a critic's judgement simply for not looking the part. But we shouldn't imagine these views are some quaint characteristic of the olden days. You can draw a line from this review of *The Rover* to the prudish outrage over the plays of Ibsen at the end of the nineteenth century, the media storm around Howard Brenton's *The Romans in Britain* in 1980 and the tabloid titillation surrounding Daniel Radcliffe's naked appearance in *Equus* in 2007. Theatre critics have always had to the make the choice between swimming with or against the moral tide.

In theory, any critic who takes our first question seriously should be able to avoid the problem of bias. There's a world of difference between asking, 'What were the theatremakers trying to do?' and 'What *should* the theatremakers be doing?' That's the theory. In practice, none of us is free of bias, whether in our ethical values or in the aesthetic principles we formulate about 'good' theatre. The neo-classical method was a way of making sense of art and that's all any critic, ancient or modern, is trying to do. Even the best of us will be directed by some aesthetic compass, some criteria for discriminating one thing from another, some fast-track for sorting good from bad. Those criteria may not be as inflexible as the Aristotle-inspired rules, but they're likely to be rules of thumb, helpful approximations that make sure that, for the most part, we're in the right area. If modern critics have the advantage over their forebears, it's in their willingness to drop their preconceptions, rather than in the preconceptions themselves.

EXERCISE

In Shakespeare's *Titus Andronicus*, a woman is raped and mutilated. In Edward Bond's *Saved*, a baby is stoned. Discuss with your friends whether such material is acceptable on the stage. If you believe it isn't, what would you find acceptable? If you believe it is, what would you find unacceptable? Why?

How to move with the times

As a critic gets older, so the challenge of avoiding bias becomes greater. The wealth of knowledge accumulated over years of theatregoing is a valuable commodity, but the critic needs extra reserves of self-awareness not to turn the experiences of yesterday into the regulations of today. Theatre is a present-tense medium and the critic needs always to react in the moment and to maintain their capacity to be surprised. This takes work. If, like J.C. Trewin, you have clocked up a total of eighty-five productions of *Hamlet*,[2] how do you bring something fresh to the eighty-sixth? Only by staying alert to what it means today can you take advantage of your experience. The more you stick to the tried and tested, the more immune you will be to innovation and change.

To keep moving with the times can be hard, because artforms go in cycles. Watch for long enough and you'll see each new generation rediscovering the past and adapting it for its own purposes. At best, your insight will enrich your writing with contextual depth. At worse, it will make you contemptuous of the present. If the experienced critic wrote in a seen-it-all-before tone of superiority, it would be at the risk of missing what made each new event special for today. Such critics appear stuck in the past. Instead of using their knowledge to illuminate the present, they retreat to the security of a time they know better, complaining that things are not as good as they used to be (things, of course, are never as good as they used to be). A more reflexive critic recognizes the similarities but celebrates the differences. Fortunately, theatre, having the capacity to be alive to the moment, compels you to stay in tune with the culture and defies you to get old.

How to deal with personal taste and cultural bias

However open to new experiences we are, there are always some things we respond to more enthusiastically than others. All of us have our aesthetic predilections, the kind of theatre we like and the kind we could do without. When you follow critics over a period of time, you start to notice that one favours political theatre, another musicals; one well-made plays, another performance art; one classical narratives, another physical comedies. If a show engages in an urgent topical debate, the critic who likes politics will be drawn to the interplay of ideas and is likely to be more forgiving of production weaknesses. If a performance is all choreography and athleticism, the critic who likes physical theatre may choose to ignore its lack of original thought. Every critic ends up reviewing the whole range of genres, both favourably and unfavourably, but will always be more at home with one than another.

The more versatile the critic, the better they will cope, but all of us, whatever our tastes and backgrounds, will be confronted with theatre we would instinctively react against if we weren't doing the job. As a matter of taste or prejudice, we might find certain forms offensive, distasteful, banal, elitist or bewildering. Some people hate pantomime, others despise opera. The critic can't afford to do either. To avoid appearing indignant, ignorant or out-of-touch, you have to hold on to our first question, 'What were the theatremakers trying to do?' This is true even if the answer is, 'They were trying to upturn conventional critical ways of thinking, challenge rational thought and push me out of my comfort zone.'

We also have to be careful about the conclusions we draw from the evidence of history. Just because Sarah Kane's *Blasted* shocked London critics who later decided they had misjudged it, we cannot deduce that all shocking plays are good. The pressure not to miss the next big thing can make critics rush to embrace the ephemeral, the fashionable and the superficial. On one side we have the conservative fuddy-duddy, tediously muttering about how much better theatre was in the old days; on the other, we have the critic as fashionista, praising the fabulous new clothes and not noticing the emperor is naked. It's more fruitful to be generous to the new than to write as a hostile reactionary, but better still to welcome the innovative while recognizing the meretricious for what it is.

Even then, we are often unaware of our own biases because they are so deeply rooted in our culture. Despite the best of intentions, none of us is free of the values and assumptions of our age. Hard though it may be to comprehend, Beverley Baxter actually seemed to mean well when he began a review with the astonishingly racist generalization that 'Children, Jews and negroes are natural actors'.[3] Perhaps he even thought himself open minded as he went on to write approvingly about 'primitive' emotions and 'colourful' personalities. Had this kind of stuff been thought shocking in 1944, it would not have been published in a newspaper as mainstream as the *London Evening Standard*.

Take a more recent example. Writing in the Australian cultural journal *Meanjin*, Geoffrey Milne described the case of *God's Best Country*, a play about Aboriginal land rights. Written by the non-Aboriginal Gordon Francis, it concerned a confrontation between the new and traditional owners of a cattle station in the Northern Territory. It had been modestly received by non-Aboriginal critics in Perth in 1987, but it was 'trenchantly attacked'[4] in the *Sunday Territorian* by Galarrwuy Yunupingu, a leading indigenous Australian land-rights campaigner, on the grounds of its 'inherent prejudice and racism'. It would be surprising if either the critics or the playwright regarded themselves as prejudiced or racist, yet from his perspective, Yunupingu saw the play in exactly those terms. As one of the few Aboriginal voices in the Australian media, he raised awkward questions about who was setting the mainstream agenda. That's not to say Yunupingu didn't have his own received opinions (how could he not?), but his contribution to the debate exposed biases the critics of Perth would have been quite unconscious of.

The story was echoed on the other side of the world more than twenty years later, when London's Royal Court scored a critical hit with *Clybourne Park* by Bruce Norris after its US premiere at Playwrights Horizons in New York. A response to Lorraine Hansberry's *A Raisin in the Sun*, the play is set in a Chicago neighbourhood which, in 1959, is all white and facing a slump and, in 2009, all black and facing gentrification. When the black director, actor, playwright and critic Kwame Kwei-Armah saw it in London, he was enraged. As he saw it, the play unintentionally implied that 'whites build and blacks destroy'.[5] He told *The Observer*: 'And what was worse was that in all the reviews I read of the play – written almost exclusively by middle-class white men – not one of them even hinted that they had seen that message in the play.'

As Kwei-Armah then became artistic director of Baltimore's Center Stage, he had a rare opportunity to correct the balance. In 2013, he told the same story from a different perspective in his own play, *Beneatha's Place*, which he staged with mostly the same cast on alternate nights to a production of Norris's play. The conceit confronted audiences and critics with their own bias and ignited a debate about race relations, as Tim Smith noted in his review in *The Baltimore Sun*:

Audiences cannot help but get into the conversation, too, and my guess is that intermission chitchat is more animated and substantive than ever at Center Stage these days . . . There are many . . . moments . . . when Kwei-Armah gives a firm tug on the rug, causing characters (and, I suspect, audiences) to lose their bearings for a moment, suddenly unsure of where they stand.[6]

At least these debates were out in the open. Chicago critic Chris Jones in his anthology *Bigger, Brighter, Louder* noted that the *Tribune* 'virtually ignored'[7] the important African American company Skyloft Players in the 1940s. You can see the bias of editors and critics in what they decide not to cover as well as in what they actually write.

So how should you avoid becoming the kind of blinkered critic Yunupingu, Kwei-Armah and Jones identified? I introduced myself at the start of the book as a white, middle-class, middle-aged, able-bodied, heterosexual male. If someone saw that description of me, they may assume I was some kind of pillar of the establishment or one of those patronizing top-down critics of old. It doesn't feel that way to me – I'm not wealthy, posh or privately educated – but it's fair to say I have not been oppressed or discriminated against. I do not walk into the theatre as one of society's excluded. On the contrary, the very act of walking into the theatre suggests I'm an insider, someone who feels comfortable in what is so often a bourgeois meeting place. But if I can't deny my privileged position, I can be aware of it, conscious that there are other ways of looking at the stories being told, the manner of their telling, the perspective they take and the conditions under which they are presented.

Whatever your background as a critic, the corrective to your inevitable bias is to be as engaged in society as possible, keeping yourself alive to inequalities and questioning received assumptions. You need to analyse deeper meanings and not just accept surface details. As film and theatre critic Jill Dolan put it: 'While many critics write about story or narrative structure, and sometimes direct our attention to design choices, camera angles, shot composition and editing, a feminist critic also looks at the frame for what it tells us about gender and race.'[8]

The more you do this, the better a critic you will be, but it will never stop you being you. Because of their backgrounds and political passions, Yunupingu and Kwei-Armah were sensitive to representations involving race. That was their strength and why their contribution to the critical debate was valuable, perhaps even revolutionary. But that isn't to say another critic with a different background couldn't have disagreed with them. Or that another critic still could have agreed with their sentiments, but felt the production raised other concerns that were more worthy of discussion. A feminist critic could have been angered by the representation of women; a Marxist critic by the economic analysis; a right-wing critic by left-wing values . . . and so on. All of them would have added to the picture, even – or perhaps especially – if they contradicted each other. And none of them on their own could possibly have covered all bases and biases. So although a receptivity to ideas and a reflexivity of thought are essential attributes, the problem is bigger than any one critic could cope with. It would be more practically solved by giving voice to a wider range of critics, so Kwei-Armah's 'middle-class white men' would not be alone in leading the discussion. The onus is on those of us who are on the inside to encourage and support those voices whenever we get the chance.

It would also be an advantage if those 'middle-class white men' (or their equivalent in the seat of power) were honest with themselves and their readers about their inevitable biases. Dolan, who (as noted above) characterizes herself as a feminist theatre critic, believes it is important to 'debunk objectivity'.[9] Speaking at a two-day colloquium on criticism in 2014 at Brock University in Ontario, she said she was bemused by the way some critics took umbrage at the suggestion their work was 'tainted by ideology' and was 'by necessity political'. 'All critics should explore their ideological positions,' she said. Critics, such as Dolan, who describe themselves in terms of their perspective ('feminist', 'queer', 'African American', 'Marxist' or whatever) are easy to spot, but that is not to say that other critics are without bias. The more a critic is part of the mainstream, the more their bias becomes subsumed into the general mood of the times and the harder it is to identify it, but it is still there. The critics who insisted on sticking to the rules, who condemned the theatre for its immorality, who were affronted by its challenge to the social order were not the exceptions but the conventional voices of their day. Thanks to the passage of time, we can see their bias for what it is – just as in 200 years' time, our descendants will be bemused by many of the values we take for granted.

EXERCISE

Write a list to describe yourself in terms of sex, race, ability, age, nationality, class, politics and any other attitudes that are important to you. Go back to the last three reviews you have written and ask yourself how many of your opinions and critical approaches might have been different had you had a different profile.

Managing expectations

Some of the values that apply to mainstream thought also apply to the established dramatic canon. Every time we see a classic drama, we tend to assume it is a good play because history tells us it must be. We also inherit a set of opinions about what makes it good. But received wisdom could be wrong. Every classic was once a new play. If you delve into the archives, you may be surprised at the things critics said about work that is now part of the canon but was then just the latest show.

In a review of a new play in 1895, George Bernard Shaw said 'the humour is adulterated by stock mechanical fun to an extent that absolutely scandalizes one in a play with such an author's name to it'.[10] The play was *The Importance of Being Earnest* and the author was Oscar Wilde. In 1962, Kenneth Tynan said Samuel Beckett's *Happy Days* was 'much too long, too full of infertile pauses, and should really have been staged in one act'[11] (he also said you shouldn't miss it). In 1975, Roger Dettmer in the *Chicago Tribune* said local playwright David Mamet had not yet 'finished or polished' *American Buffalo* and that 'we come away with the feeling that Mamet writes dialog first, the characters to fit it, and lastly tries to relate them coherently and meaningfully'.[12]

I pick out these examples not to suggest the critics were wrong, but to point out they felt free to say what they genuinely thought. They weren't defying convention; they were just writing about another night in the theatre. This gives the modern-day critic a dilemma. On the one hand, a play achieves classic status because of general cultural agreement about its lasting quality. If theatremakers keep on wanting to stage it, if audiences keep on wanting to see it and if critics keep on praising its strengths, then it will acquire a status that is hard to challenge. On the other hand, no play is so perfect that it is beyond criticism. However endurable it has proved, it must have its strengths and weaknesses – as contemporary critics have frequently shown. Yet it would take a brave or foolhardy critic to fly in the face of received opinion and challenge the status of a classic. You may have your reasons for thinking *Macbeth* is a dud, but you will need an uncommonly persuasive argument to overturn 400 years of production history, academic study and audience enjoyment. If you succeed, you will earn a reputation as a brilliant iconoclast. If you fail, you will just look silly.

The subjective and the objective

Theatre critics have one bias in common: they are implicitly sympathetic to the theatre by dint of their chosen profession. It's hard to do the job if you don't like the artform. Despite their reputation for harshness, critics are more likely to be too generous than too begrudging. This is the bias you may find the hardest to keep in check.

On occasion, you may become aware of a bias that is particular to you. Reviewing a production of *Twelve Angry Men* directed by Harold Pinter in 1996, Benedict Nightingale admitted to having a very particular perspective. Reginald Rose's play is about the jurors on a murder case who are all set to come to a speedy verdict of guilty when one of their number, played by Henry Fonda in the famous film, starts questioning the reliability of the evidence. We watch as their prejudices unravel. In the second paragraph of Nightingale's review in *The Times*, he revealed how a personal experience had made him see the play in an unusual light:

> Can I be personal for a moment? I found myself questioning the *Angry Men* myth when I sat on a jury recently and found I was the only member convinced that the defendant was guilty of theft. It was deeply disconcerting to be the lion in a den of Fondas.[13]

His opening phrase ('Can I be personal for a moment?') has a lot hiding behind it. For one thing, it's a clever rhetorical question that creates the illusion of intimacy with the reader. As soon as we give the only possible answer ('Yes, Benedict, of course you can be personal'), it's as if we have been sucked in to a close conversation with him. That fuels our interest in what he has to say. It's a compelling narrative device: having had such an emotive real-life experience, we ask ourselves, how will this critic respond to a play that challenges it? We can only read on. As it happened, he liked the production, a judgement that seems all the more credible (and creditable) given his opening admission.

There is something else about Nightingale's request to be personal. That he asked the question in the first place suggests he felt he was violating some rule. Perhaps bringing his own life so blatantly into the review would be perceived as indulgent or irrelevant. Perhaps it would make him look less objective, less dispassionate, less likely, in the words of Matthew Arnold, 'to see the object as in itself it really is'.[14] But although this is a relatively rare example of a critic declaring his bias up front, it is a reminder that theatre reviewing is a subjective business. How could Nightingale be anything other than personal?

Such instances draw attention not only to the impossibility of writing a purely objective review but also in the value of declaring your bias. If you can't stop being the person you are, you can at least explain where you're coming from. After taking part in the National Critics Institute, 'a boot camp for theater writers' at the Eugene O'Neill Theater Centre in Connecticut, musical-theatre tutor Christopher Caggiano suggested the critic should not aspire to objectivity but 'informed subjectivity'.[15] Criticism that rests entirely on the whims and passing fancies of the critic is of no more use than a tweet declaring, 'I liked it'. But if the critic's inevitable subjectivity is backed by an informed perspective, one that takes into account what the theatremakers are attempting and what the production means in the greater scheme of things, then the review becomes more than just an expression of the critic's ego.

Friends in the wrong places

What, though, if the critic's bias threatens to undermine the credibility of the whole review? This is how Andrew Haydon began a review of *The Seagull*, translated by John Donnelly, on his Postcards from the Gods website:

> In the spirit of full disclosure: I've known John Donnelly since his *A Short Play About Sex and Death* at Leeds Uni was the reason I first went to the National Student Drama Festival in 1997. And we've been mates ever since. And since that NSDF is pretty much the single reason I'm where I am today (in a pub writing a review. Thanks a bunch). The first thing I ever directed was a short play by John Donnelly (starring Lucy Ellinson. Yes, *that* Lucy Ellinson). And, on the night I saw this *Seagull* in Watford, the actor John Hopkins (currently rehearsing with the RSC), who'd starred in *A Short Play About Sex and Death*, was also there (which in itself says something about the loyalty of university theatre friends). And we all went for a drink after and I was introduced to director Blanche McIntyre and half the sodding cast. So, yeah. This is about as compromised a review as it's possible to imagine.[16]

What he was describing is a longstanding problem, one that goes back pretty much as far as periodical theatre journalism itself. In the mid 1730s, Aaron Hill dedicated three issues of *The Prompter*, the first theatre journal in London, to *The Double Deceit, or a Cure for Jealousy* by William Popple. The playwright wasn't just a friend; along with Hill, he was one of the two principal writers of *The Prompter*. In the face of a cool reception by audiences, Hill rallied to the play's defence in a long essay that sang its praises.

How you deal with the question of friendships depends on your temperament and how you see your role as a critic. As a freelance writer covering a relatively small theatre community, I am frequently employed to interview the same theatremakers whose work I will end up, sooner or later, reviewing. In such instances, I move from collaborator, helping articulate the artist's intentions to the general public, to commentator, passing independent judgement on their work. 'Adversary' may be too strong a word for a critic, but 'colleague' doesn't seem quite right either. Even if I politely turn down the invitation to a first-night party, I'll be on friendly terms with many of the people who'll be attending. Sometimes I have to accept we may be on less friendly terms after my review is published. The blur between professional responsibility and social engagement is a tricky one to navigate. In a couple of instances, where my friendships with theatremakers have become closer, I have made the decision to stop reviewing their work. Even if I managed to stay true to myself and not to offend my friends, I would find it impossible to convince the outside world that I had acted ethically.

My approach is somewhere in between that of Ben Brantley, who avoided theatre people as much as possible, and that of John Lahr, who regarded his friendships as a way of getting behind-the-scenes insight. Both of these policies have the advantage of avoiding ambiguity. The same was true for Katharine Brisbane, who came from a small town where everyone was in each other's pocket. As a result, by the time she stared writing for *The Australian* in 1967, she 'had already learnt that if you can't know nobody then it's better to know everybody'.[17] She made it her business to develop relationships with the profession and took an interest in campaigns and causes that was reflected in her feature writing.

In the case of Haydon and his review of *The Seagull*, after declaring his friendship with the artists, he proceeded to engage in the production's ideas and to discuss other critical reactions to it, arguing it was more of a 'war between the sexes' than, as others had suggested, a 'battle of youth versus age'. In this way, he managed to be respectful to the artists without being fawning, while appearing to be true to his own opinions: 'What the production lacks in Marxist rigour, it makes up for in excellent jokes and painfully acute characterisations.' Haydon was under no obligation to write about the show at all. Had he felt truly compromised, it would have been easier to say nothing. By flagging up his relationships at the start, he freed himself to talk openly, without having to be circumspect. Should you find yourself in the same position, you'd have to ask yourself how honest you were prepared to be with your readers and your friends.

Notes

1 Gray, Charles Harold (1931), *Theatrical Criticism in London to 1795*, Columbia University Press.

2 Trewin, J.C. (1987), *Five & Eighty Hamlets*, Hutchinson.

3 Baxter, Beverley (1949), *First Nights and Noises Off*, Hutchinson & Co.

4 Milne, Geoffrey (Spring 1994), 'The other side of the story', in *Meanjin*.

5 Adams, Tim (2 February 2014), 'Kwame Kwei-Armah: "I was constantly moaning in London" ', in *The Observer*.

6 Smith, Tim (17 May 2013), 'Centre Stage premieres "*Beneatha's Place*", Kwei-Armah's answer to "*Clybourne Park*" ', in *The Baltimore Sun*.

7 Jones, Chris (2013), *Bigger, Brighter, Louder*, University of Chicago Press.

8 Dolan, Jill (2013), *The Feminist Spectator in Action*, Palgrave Macmillan.

9 Dolan, Jill (21–22 February 2014), 'The Changing Face of Theatre Criticism in the Digital Age: A Colloquium', at the Marilyn I. Walker School of Fine and Performing Arts at Brock University, St Catharines, Ontario.

10 Shaw, George Bernard (1932), *Our Theatre in the Nineties*, Constable.

11 Tynan, Kenneth (1975), *A View of the English Stage*, Davis-Poynter.

12 Jones, Chris (2013), *Bigger, Brighter, Louder*, University of Chicago Press.

13 Nightingale, Benedict (24 April, 1996), 'Making the heart grow Fonda', in *The Times*.

14 Arnold, Matthew (1993), *Arnold: Culture and Anarchy and Other Writings*, Cambridge University Press.

15 Caggiano, Christopher (20 July 2010), 'A theatre critic's manifesto', in *Everything I Know I Learned From Musicals*.

16 Haydon, Andrew (6 May 2013), '*The Seagull* – Headlong at Watford Palace Theatre', on Postcards from the Gods (http://postcardsgods. blogspot.co.uk/2013/05/the-seagull-headlong-at-watford-palace.html).

17 Brisbane, Katharine (2005), *Not Wrong – Just Different*, Currency Press.

19

HOW TO WRITE ABOUT CULTURE, SOCIETY AND POLITICS

Finding shared reference points

The West End opening of *Charlie and the Chocolate Factory* in 2013 was accompanied by much fanfare. Director Sam Mendes was fresh from the James Bond movie *Skyfall*. Round the corner at the Cambridge Theatre, another Roald Dahl adaptation, *Matilda*, was already a global success. In the leading role of Willy Wonka, Douglas Hodge was an Olivier Award winner and Broadway star. By the time *Charlie . . .* opened in June, it had already been seen in previews by 70,000 people. It was an unabashed attempt at scoring a mainstream hit and its ambitions were international. Consequently, it was reviewed by Ben Brantley, chief theatre critic on *The New York Times*,[1] and also occupied the most prominent slots in the London newspapers and blogs.

Writing in *The Guardian* in a substantial and largely enthusiastic over-night review,[2] Michael Billington discussed the show as the piece of popular entertainment it sought to be. He described it as a children's classic, made comparison's to Dahl's 1964 novel and appreciated the importance of the visual spectacle. This is what you'd expect. Some of his other allusions, however, were not so predictable. In the dark detail of Jon Driscoll's projections, for example, Billington was reminded of Giovanni Battista Piranesi, an eighteenth-century Venetian printmaker. In the succession of chambers in Wonka's factory, he felt the influence of the magical castle in Wagner's *Parsifal*. Elsewhere in the show, some of the creatures made him think of the dwarfs in the same composer's *Ring Cycle*.

In making such references, Billington was performing several tasks at once. The first was simply to express his subjective point of view. These were thoughts that had struck him personally. Whether or not the theatremakers had Piranesi and Wagner in mind is beside the point; Billington brought with him his own store of cultural knowledge and made the connections for himself. As far as I can tell, he was the only critic to have referred to either Piranesi or Wagner (perhaps others thought it and didn't write it down), but being a true reflection of what was going on in his mind, the observations are perfectly legitimate. As legitimate, in fact, as Brantley's references to Toys 'R' Us, Rube Goldberg, Walt Disney, Salvador Dalí, *The Jetsons* and *Shockheaded Peter* in his *New York Times* review. More than this, they were an attempt to give any reader who hadn't seen the performance an idea of what it was like.

One of the critic's jobs is to give an impression of an experience that is rich, fluid and complex; whatever they write will always be an approximation, so allusions are a handy shortcut. If readers know what one thing is like, they are half way down the road of understanding what something similar is like. The adage that a picture is worth a thousand words applies here: Billington was able to keep his word-count in check by capitalizing on the reader's cross-cultural knowledge and putting an existing image in their heads instead of explaining at impossible length exactly how the show looked. 'You know Piranesi?' he was saying, 'Well, this is a bit like him.'

That covers the readers who hadn't seen the show. What then of those who had? For these people, Billington's allusions had the potential to enrich their experience. If his references were apposite, he stood to make them think about the hidden forces at work in the production. Did Dahl and Wagner have similar artistic impulses? Is there a connection between the brooding visions of Piranesi and the darker fantasies of Dahl? Does Charlie Bucket go on the same kind of journey into the soul as the great archetypal heroes? Everyone will have a different answer; it's not a question of Billington being right or wrong, but it is the critic who makes the comparisons and opens up the debate.

Critics need not confine themselves only to what they see before them on stage. Billington discussed *Charlie and the Chocolate Factory* in terms of what was outside the theatre as well as inside. His review was not just about the strengths and weaknesses of the acting, songs and special effects, but also about the wider cultural context, be it Dahl's book, a Venetian illustrator or a German composer. The seriousness of this approach, coupled with the weightiness of the allusions, had the additional effect of lending gravitas to the show itself. To use a Stanislavskian phrase, the subtext of Billington's review was that *Charlie and the Chocolate Factory* was a production worthy of consideration alongside two of the great names of European art. He was not necessarily saying it was better or worse than Piranesi or Wagner, but he was saying it deserved to be given the same respect. This was a show that should be treated not merely as a piece of throwaway fluff but as an artistically well-intentioned enterprise. Without explicitly saying as much, the cross-cultural references gave credence to the production.

There are a number of risks here. I would say that talking about Wagner in the context of Dahl is an exciting provocation, demanding the reader take seriously a show that could easily be dismissed as an insubstantial family musical. But the more you choose to juxtapose such dissimilar artists, the more you risk inadvertent comedy. Take the idea too far and you'll sound like the Monty Python sketch *Mrs Premise and Mrs Conclusion Visit Jean-Paul Sartre* in which two women discuss the merits of the existentialist French philosopher while sitting in a laundrette. There's a fine line between making stimulating cross-cultural connections and sounding ridiculous. If your reference points don't strike a chord and fail to illuminate anything about the work in question, your review may simply seem pretentious. Before you make such a reference, whether highbrow or lowbrow, you should ask yourself if you are adding something to the reader's understanding or merely showing off your arcane knowledge. As we have seen, the subtext of a clever-sounding allusion could be to bathe a production in glory by association, but it could equally be to advertise the critic's erudition. Even an apposite reference could be the critic's self-indulgent attempt to persuade the reader of their authority and of the importance of their opinions. At worst, this is nothing to do with the show and everything to do with the ego of the critic. If a reference says more about you than it does about the show, you should consider cutting it.

References, however, are a valuable tool. It is the nature of theatre to be seen in confined spaces by small numbers of people and there is a high likelihood that the reader of your review will not have been among them. One way to give that reader a sense of what the show was like is to allude to some other shared experience. It's the same technique film trailers use all the time. 'From the director of *Bridesmaids*', goes the advert for *The Heat*. 'From Ridley Scott, director of *Gladiator*', goes the advert for *Robin Hood*. Audiences understand that '*Gladiator*' equates to 'historical action movie' and decide whether they want to see the new movie on that basis. Unlike the film critic, however, the twenty-first century theatre critic cannot assume the reader will have a theatre-centric field of reference. As a specialist, I happen to have seen 90 per cent of the plays of David Greig. I regard him as one of the most significant dramatists of the past twenty years, but I recognize that few of the people flocking to *Charlie and the Chocolate Factory*, which Greig adapted, will even have heard of him. That's why in the opening paragraph of this chapter, I name-checked James Bond and *Matilda*, not any of Greig's plays. There's a reasonable chance you'll know what I'm talking about if I mention *Skyfall*, the first film to take more than £100m at the UK box office; less of a chance if I talk about Greig's *Gobbo*, even though it is one of the best children's shows I've ever seen. This is not a matter of elitism – I loved *Skyfall* too – it's a question of using a shared language.

This has not always been such an issue. There was a time, not so long ago, when a theatre critic could make a lot of assumptions about the primacy of the artform and the nature of the audience. Going to the theatre, in the West End or on Broadway, was a mainstream activity enjoyed by a well-to-do middle class who had been through the same education system, the same historical changes and had a working knowledge of broadly the same cultural talismans. Today, by contrast, it is difficult to assume anything about the reader. Not only do we live in a less stratified society, but we have fewer experiences that are universally shared. Capitalism has created not one mass market but many, and rarely do they overlap. The modern celebrity may be on every teenager's bedroom wall, yet be unknown to their parents. The parents, meanwhile, will have a field of reference that means nothing to their children. With all our texting, tweeting and social networking, it feels like there's more communication going on than ever, yet we can't assume anyone is speaking the same language.

For the critic, this has two consequences. One is there's no reason to suppose theatregoing will be a routine part of the reader's life. Their leisure time could be spent in too many different ways. I'm writing these words in the bar of a hotel and I can overhear the receptionist phoning the local theatre. 'I'd like to book some tickets, please', she says. 'It's for *Lady Windermere's Whatever It Is*.' To me (and I think to you), it is funny she doesn't know the title of Oscar Wilde's most famous play. But from her point of view, it's just another event a guest has asked her to book. Why should she know it? Just because theatre is central to my life doesn't make it central to hers. All this means your writing has to convince the reader not only that it's worth discussing a particular show – be it *Lady Windermere's Fan* or the very latest multimedia experiment – but that the medium of theatre itself has any relevance to their lives. It's hard to make grand statements about a play's importance when your potential readers have so many other ideas about what's important.

The second consequence is your readers may be ignorant about cultural reference points you take for granted (and vice versa). It's no good comparing *Charlie and the Chocolate Factory* with *Matilda* if they've never heard of *Matilda*. If I made a joke about a handbag, would the hotel receptionist have any idea it was a famous quote from a famous play? Yet if you tried to take a truly all-inclusive approach, you could end up saying nothing at all. I can't say for certain that everyone reading this book will have heard of James Bond, I imagine some won't have heard of Roald Dahl and I'm certain many won't have seen *Skyfall*, but my hunch is that most will have at least a rough idea of what I'm going on about. But how far can I push it? At what point does my useful insight into the creative landscape of a production become a list of meaningless allusions?

If you are writing on the internet, you have the opportunity to use hyperlinks to give the reader as much background detail as they need. Even then, you have to work hard to keep them on side. To return to Billington's *Charlie and the Chocolate Factory* review, it's fair to say many readers will have had no knowledge of Piranesi (I didn't) and even if they had heard of Wagner, would have had a flimsy grasp of the plot of *Parsifal*. Billington knew this. The important thing is he structured his sentences in such a way that the reader could infer his meaning. If you were not familiar with Piranesi's prints, you could figure out that they had a 'dark intricacy'. If you'd never seen *Parsifal*, you would still understand that the opera had got something to do with 'sylvan seductiveness' and a 'magic castle'. Billington rewarded those readers who shared his field of reference without penalizing those who didn't.

This isn't always the case and there are many times when a straight description will serve you better than resorting to an 'if you like that, you'll also like this' formula. At the same time, making references to other artforms, topical events and popular talking points can draw the reader in and acknowledge what shared cultural landscape we have. Your readers live in a world of pop songs, soap operas, art exhibitions, Hollywood blockbusters, classical concerts, video games, airport novels, Facebook campaigns, super bowl tournaments, celebrity sex stories and political scandals. Your reviews are part of this tapestry and, unless you believe theatre should somehow be elevated above the hubbub of daily life, there is no reason you should ignore this. On the contrary, if you think theatre is worthy of people's attention, you have a responsibility to talk about it in terms they understand. To do otherwise is to risk alienating them from an artform that has already lost much of its mainstream status. This is not about dumbing down (you can still forward exactly the same arguments), but about being polite enough to find common ground with your readers and to represent theatre as a connected, engaged and relevant part of the culture.

Critic Neil Cooper has equal passions for music and theatre and often deliberately lets the two influence each other. 'When I started out, my maxim was that I wanted to make theatre reviews as exciting as music reviews and music reviews as serious as theatre reviews,'[3] he told me. As a teenage reader of the *NME*, he found himself being educated by music journalists such as Ian Penman and Paul Morley who were prone to referencing Friedrich Nietzsche and Samuel Beckett in reviews of post-punk bands such as the Pop Group. Likewise, Cooper is as likely to drop a reference to Polish avant-garde theatre director Tadeusz Kantor in a live review of Mark E. Smith and the Fall[4] (and to mention the band's name comes from a novel by Albert Camus) as he is to namedrop the Britpop era in a review of a Philip Ridley play:[5]

> On one level, it gives the reader a loose shorthand, something to grab hold of, but it's also to show there is an interconnectedness of things and how everything overlaps. Things don't exist in a vacuum. In the case of Mark E. Smith, there is something instinctively performative about him that makes me think of theatre directors of Kantor's ilk. I'm deadly serious about it – when I wrote it in a review, I wasn't being ironic. As soon as you start exploring something, once you have the frames of reference to decode it and put it in a historical context, you can go one of two ways: it either becomes less interesting, because you think you've heard it all before and

that it has nothing new to say, or it becomes more interesting, because you realize that the historical and contemporary connections and comparisons make it richer in a way that says something about now.

There's often an element of playfulness in this approach. When Ian Shuttleworth described an adaptation of *Emil and the Detectives* as 'an exhilarating cross between Fritz Lang's *M* and *The Famous Five*',[6] he was deliberately juxtaposing an art-house movie classic and an Enid Blyton adventure series to surprise and amuse the reader. He was also suggesting something of the distinctive quality of the occasion, as if to say to the reader, 'Imagine a show that could contain such extremes'. In the same review, incidentally, Shuttleworth alluded to expressionist cinema and J.M. Barrie's *Peter Pan*, as well as name-checking animator Oskar Fischinger and the Schöneberg district of Berlin. Just because a show is aimed at children doesn't mean it can't be rich in allusive detail.

If you choose your reference points well, they will have some resonance with the production. If you choose them badly, they may offer what James Elkins called a 'frisson of campy pleasure'[7] and Cooper called a 'postmodern pick and mix',[8] a cultural relativism that gives the impression everything is the same and nothing is to be taken seriously. There's certainly a danger that this kind of writing becomes laden with so much postmodern irony that everything, high art and low, is made to seem a bit of a laugh. To steer clear of this, you need to choose your references with respect.

EXERCISE

Write a 400-word review that makes as many cultural references as possible. Let your mind make all the associations it can. What effect do your allusions have? Do they help in conveying an impression of the event?

What the theatremakers are thinking

The allusions you choose are likely to say as much about you and the things you are interested in as they do about the show. But what about the references a production makes deliberately? The critic has no choice about these. To understand the theatremakers' associative world is also part of the job. Failing to do so can mean missing the point. Imagine a production of *Julius Caesar* in which the cast wore Nazi uniforms: if the critic were ignorant about the Second World War, they'd be unlikely to appreciate the significance of the design and the director's intention. If they had never seen a 1950s sci-fi B-movie, they would be lost in space when it came to *Return to the Forbidden Planet*. And if they had never heard of Abba, they'd be three steps behind the audience with *Mamma Mia!*.

This was the challenge laid down to Charles Isherwood when he reviewed *Disaster!* at the St Luke's Theater for *The New York Times*.[9] This parody of 1970s disaster movies relied on the audience sharing a very particular field of knowledge. Fortunately, Isherwood was up to the task. In his review of the show, he successfully demonstrated familiarity with films including *Earthquake, The Poseidon Adventure, The Swarm, Jaws, Airport 1975* and *Barracuda*; television shows including *Fantasy Island, Kojak, Room 222* and *Hawaii Five-O*; as well as at least a dozen songs including *Torn Between Two Lovers, The Hustle* and *Don't Bring Me Down*. As Isherwood said himself, it was the kind of show that would leave you bewildered if you didn't get these references. But think of the pressure on the critic. This is a show that traded on the decidedly trashy end of popular culture, and from four decades previously. Even though the references were mainstream, it would have been no surprise if a critic had been too young, too studious or too busy watching theatre to have had much awareness of them. Yet to do the job, to answer the 'what were the theatremakers trying to do?' question, the critic needed this knowledge. It was the kind of trivia no college course would teach you, but it would have been shared by nearly everyone who chose to buy a ticket. If Isherwood were ignorant of it, he might as well have been seeing the show in a foreign language for all the sense he would have made of it.

This, though, is the critic's lot. In the fortnight before seeing *Disaster!*, Isherwood had reviewed plays that required familiarity with Sean O'Casey, Bertolt Brecht, *Romeo and Juliet*, Jeff Buckley, *A Midsummer Night's Dream* and the Cotton Club. That's as well as the magic show he saw. Between the Electric Light Orchestra (who released *Don't Bring Me Down* in 1979) and *The Good Person of Szechwan* (written by Brecht in 1943) lie acres of cultural territory and Isherwood needed to provide a reliable road map for it all. I'm not making value judgements about high and low art here, just pointing out that the critic's cultural awareness must be much broader than average. The people who went to the magic show were unlikely to be the ones that saw *Juno and the Paycock*, but both audiences would expect the critic to treat their performance with as much seriousness and understanding as any other.

So far, I have concentrated on allusions to other plays, films, books, songs and TV shows, but the critic's vision extends further than that. For the regular attendee, the theatre is like a branch of the further-education system. If Michael Frayn chooses, as he did in *Copenhagen*, to write about the meeting in 1941 between Danish physicist Niels Bohr and his German protégé Werner Heisenberg, then it's the duty of the critic to write persuasively on splitting the atom and the politics of the Holocaust. If Gregory Burke decides to focus on the fate of one of Scotland's oldest regiments in Iraq in *Black Watch*, then the critic needs to be au fait with internal army politics and something of the history of conflict in the Middle East. None of these is a subject they teach at drama school, nor is the infinite range of topics that may be alluded to. The critic needs to be alive to the world just to keep up with it all.

EXERCISE

In my explanation of the danger of making incongruous references, I used the example of a Monty Python sketch. Ask yourself the following questions.

- Did you know what Monty Python was?
- Did you know who Jean-Paul Sartre was?
- If you hadn't known, would you have understood the point I was making?
- Was my subsequent description ('two women discuss the merits of the existentialist French philosopher while sitting in a laundrette') enough to make things clear to any reader?
- Would you have understood the point if I hadn't included that subsequent description?
- What did my allusion to Monty Python contribute to the chapter?
- Would it have been better without it?
- Can you think of another example of an incongruous juxtaposition that would make the same point?
- Ask yourself the same questions about my use of the word 'Stanislavskian' in the previous paragraph.

Notes

1 Brantley, Ben (26 June 2013), 'Bratty children, beware', in *The New York Times*.

2 Billington, Michael (26 June 2013), '*Charlie and the Chocolate Factory*', in *The Guardian*.

3 Cooper, Neil (1 July 2014), interview with Mark Fisher.

4 Cooper, Neil (26 April 2010), 'The Fall', in *The Herald*.

5 Cooper, Neil (8 May 2014), '*Mercury Fur*', in *The Herald*.

6 Shuttleworth, Ian (5 December 2013), '*Emil and the Detectives*', in the *Financial Times*.

7 Elkins, James (2011), *What Happened to Art Criticism?*, Prickly Paradigm Press.

8 Cooper, Neil (8 May 2014), '*Mercury Fur*', in *The Herald*.

9 Isherwood, Charles (6 November 2013), 'Just when you thought it was safe to relive the '70s', in *The New York Times*.

20
HOW TO PUT EVERYTHING TOGETHER

Criticism for theatre's sake

In any discussion about theatre and criticism, there's usually one wag who stands up and says: 'Those who can – do. Those who can't – criticize.' Everyone laughs because it seems the critics have been cut down to size. How humiliated they must be to be exposed as failed actors (or failed directors or failed playwrights, according to the accusation). Even the critics laugh for fear of appearing aloof. And to be fair, it is a viewpoint with a fine pedigree. Samuel Taylor Coleridge said critics are 'usually people who would have been poets, historians, biographers, if they could; they have tried their talents at one or the other and have failed; therefore they turn critics'.[1] Percy Bysshe Shelley said much the same thing: 'As a bankrupt thief turns thief-taker in despair, so an unsuccessful author turns critic.'[2] But the argument crumbles under scrutiny for these three reasons:

First, it's just an assertion. The remark has an aphoristic quality that makes it sound like an immutable truth. But it is no such thing. Switch the words around and it makes just as much sense: 'Those who can – criticize. Those who can't – act.' To take Coleridge's example, you can quite imagine someone failing as a critic and becoming a biographer instead. Of course some theatremakers have become critics, just as some critics have become theatremakers, but that doesn't make it a universal truth.

Second, it presupposes that criticism is in some way lesser, that it requires a diminished set of skills and that it is a last resort. But critics take up the job not out of desperation nor to wreak revenge on an industry that has let them down, but because they want to. That may be a difficult concept for a theatremaker to grasp, but all the unpaid bloggers who write reviews for the love of it demonstrate it to be the case.

Third, for the sake of argument, let's imagine it were true and all critics were failed artists. If that were a bad thing, wouldn't most theatre workers be in the same boat? 'Those who can – act. Those who can't – work in the box office.' Yes, theatre critics are reactive, but that is true of nearly everyone involved: accountants, publicists, technical crew, agents, administrators, producers . . . none of them can function without the theatremakers creating something first. Theatres are full of people in non-artistic jobs with drama degrees, many of whom once held dreams of acting, writing, designing or directing. Are all of them to be regarded as failures? Or isn't it quite normal for different people to find their metier doing different things? What's wrong with wanting to be a critic and aiming to be a good one?

Related to this is the contention that only those who have worked as a theatremaker should be allowed to criticize. The people who make this argument are invariably the artists themselves. In her autobiography *Nothing Like a Dame*, actor Elaine C. Smith admitted to having had 'glowing, hellish and not very good reviews'[3] and added that 'many have been pretty accurate and helpful too'. Nonetheless, she took issue with the critics because 'they don't respect the individual, as they are generally failed writers, failed actors or people who couldn't walk on stage and perform if you paid them a million quid'. We've just dealt with her first assertion, but what about the idea that critics would be no good as performers? In this, Smith is right. There's no reason to suppose they'd be up to much as directors, designers or stage managers either. That, however, is irrelevant. The critic's job is to assess the results, not to do better themselves. As Samuel Johnson said: 'You may abuse a tragedy, though you cannot write one. You may scold a carpenter who has made you a bad table, though you cannot make a table. It is not your trade to make tables.'[4] A master carpenter may know best about how to fix the bad table, but the critic can still observe it is wobbly

Expert knowledge is valuable, but artists do not necessarily make the best critics nor does their expertise always help. Writing about her twin roles as musician and critic, Roseanna East argued that less of her insider knowledge as a violinist was as convertible to her role as a music critic than you might think:

> I'm not saying that the critics can never really know – rather that audience and performers know different things. Performing and reviewing happen simultaneously, but in parallel worlds. It is this separation and difference between the two practices which, far from disqualifying one, can make criticism valuable. What matters most to the participants isn't always the most important thing to the wider world.[5]

Many of the liveliest conversations you can have about theatre are with actors, playwrights and directors as they comment indiscreetly on the work of their peers. They will be heated, opinionated, funny and full of insight, but they are nearly always too driven by their own artistic vision to be impartial. Their intense reaction to other people's art is one of the things that inspires them to make art of their own. That's as it should be, but their impulse to create can cloud their judgement. They could find it hard, as critics, to judge a work on its own terms or, at the opposite extreme, they could be too conscious of the labour involved to write honestly about a show's shortcomings. In both respects, the critic's distance from the profession is an asset. That's not to deny the benefits of a theatrical training nor to argue that many of the best critics, such as Harold Clurman and George Bernard Shaw, have not also been practitioners. It's simply to say that insider experience, on its own, does not guarantee anything. As Kenneth Tynan said, 'A critic is someone who knows the way, but can't drive the car.'[6]

So, it's time now to enter East's parallel world and Tynan's critical car and to take on the role of a theatre critic. Put all the previous chapters together and you have a paintbox of colours. And just as the artist feels no need to use every shade in their palate, you can afford to be selective about the tools you use. Rather than having a checklist and pedantically ticking off each theatrical element in turn – first acting, then writing, then lighting, then direction, then costumes and so on – you will use the approach that the performance itself most warrants. That could be anything from your journey to the theatre to the extraordinary curtain call; from the history of the company to the decor of the lobby; from a swansong performance of a theatrical legend to the stunning debut of a vital talent; from the playwright's vision to the director's interpretation.

There are no rules.

All you can do is get out there and paint.

Notes

1   Coleridge, Samuel Taylor (1823), *Specimens of the Table Talk*, Harper and Brothers.

2   Shelley, Percy Bysshe (1821), preface to *Adonais* (later removed).

3   Smith, Elaine C. (2009), *Nothing Like a Dame*, Mainstream Publishing.

4   Boswell, James (1791), *The Life of Samuel Johnson*, Penguin Classics.

5   East, Rosanna (20 July 2013), 'When the music critic is the performer too', in *The Herald*.

6   Tynan, Kenneth (2001), *The Diaries of Kenneth Tynan*, Bloomsbury.

INDEX